*Rev*

# Contract Law

Fourth edition edited by

**P A Read** LLB, DPA, Barrister

HLT Publications

HLT PUBLICATIONS
200 Greyhound Road, London W14 9RY

First Edition 1990
Reprinted 1991
Second Edition 1992
Reprinted 1992
Third Edition 1994
Fourth Edition 1995

ISBN 1 0 7510 0600 9

British Library Cataloguing-in-Publication.

A CIP Catalogue record for this book is available from the British Library.

Printed and bound in Great Britain by
Hartnolls Limited, Bodmin, Cornwall

# CONTENTS

# ACKNOWLEDGEMENT

Some questions used are taken or adapted from past University of London LLB (External) Degree examination papers and our thanks are extended to the University of London for their kind permission to use and publish the questions.

## Caveat

The answers given are not approved or sanctioned by the University of London and are entirely our responsibility.

They are not intended as 'Model Answers', but rather as Suggested Solutions.

The answers have two fundamental purposes, namely:

a) To provide a detailed example of a suggested solution to an examination question, and

b) To assist students with their research into the subject and to further their understanding and appreciation of the subject of Laws.

# INTRODUCTION

This Revision WorkBook has been designed specifically for those studying contract law to undergraduate level. Its coverage is not confined to any one syllabus, but embraces all the major contract topics to be found in university or college examinations.

However, since it is anticipated that many students will be intending to sit the University of London LLB external examinations, the questions used are primarily from past contract law papers from that course.

Each chapter contains in its first few pages, brief notes explaining the scope and overall content of the topic covered in that chapter. There follows, in each case, a list of key points which will assist the student in studying and memorising essential material with which the student should be familiar in order to fully understand the topic. Recent cases and statutes will be noted as necessary. However, on the assumption that the student will already possess a textbook/casebook, case law has been kept to the bare minimum for the sake of simplicity.

Additionally in each chapter there will be a question analysis which will list and compare past examination questions on similar topics in contract papers. Students are reminded that in order to derive maximum benefit from this WorkBook, they should possess a full set of past examination papers issued by University of London for this subject, for the years 1983–94 inclusive. The purpose of such a question analysis is to give an appreciation of the potential range of questions possible, and some idea of variations in wording, different formats in questions and alternative modes of combining different issues in one question.

Each chapter will end with up to six (depending on how popular the topic has proved) typical examination questions, together with skeleton answers and suggested solutions. Wherever possible, the questions are drawn from University of London external contract law papers 1983–94. However it is inevitable that, in compiling a list of questions by topic order rather than chronologically, not only do the same questions crop up over and over again in different guises, but there are gaps where questions have never been set at all. Where a topic has never been covered in an examination question, a specimen question will have been written as an example, together with skeleton answer and suggested solution.

Undoubtedly, the main feature of this Revision WorkBook is the inclusion of as many past examination questions as possible. While the use of past questions as a revision aid is certainly not new, it is hoped that the combination of actual past questions from the University of London LLB external course and specially written questions, where there are gaps in examination coverage, will be of assistance to students in achieving a thorough and systematic revision of the subject.

Careful use of the Revision WorkBook should enhance the student's understanding of contract law and, hopefully, enable him to deal with as wide a range of subject matter as anyone might find in a contract law examination, while at the same time allowing him to practise examination techniques while working through the book.

INTRODUCTION

In this revised 1995 edition the final chapter contains the complete June 1994 University of London LLB (External) Elements of the Law of Contract question paper, followed by suggested solutions to each question. Thus the student will have the opportunity to review a recent examination paper in its entirety, and can, if desired, use this chapter as a mock examination – referring to the suggested solutions only after first having attempted the questions.

# HOW TO STUDY CONTRACT LAW

The general body of contract law is immense and this fact creates one of the student's greatest problems. The sheer volume of information facing a student revising a contract course at degree level, may seem to make it a daunting if not downright impossible task. However, if from the beginning the student's grasp of the underlying rules is a sound one, the topic can be more readily appreciated.

The general principles of contract law are still, to a large extent, of a judge-made origin. That is to say, these rules were formulated by the courts over a period of time in the course of litigation on contractual matters. Some of these cases are very old, sometimes several centuries old, but a great number date from the time of the industrial revolution. It is still true that if the student is familiar with moral, economic and social history, of the nineteenth century in particular, such background knowledge will serve him in good stead in understanding the rationale behind the courts' decisions in many of these major cases.

This is not to say, however, that English contract law is still rooted in the past century. Since the late nineteenth century, though, it has been more common for developing rules and principles of contractual law to become incorporated into statutes. Most of these statutes are quite detailed and cover a particular type of transaction, though one or two are of a more general nature.

For example, the greater part of commercial law is now governed by legislation concerning sale of goods, partnership agreements, carriage of goods, provision of credit facilities, and so on. A similar process has seen the development, by means of Acts, like the Fair Trading Act of 1973 and the Trade Descriptions Act of 1968, of competition law and the decline of the influence of judge-made law in this field. As regards contracts of employment, a great mass of statutes linked with voluntary codes has virtually removed the influence of ordinary principles of contract from the sphere of labour law.

In order to understand English contract law as it developed during the nineteenth century the student must appreciate that the cornerstone of the law at that time was the doctrine of freedom of contract. The courts were not concerned to control the terms of a contract, nor were they concerned if one party was treated harshly or unfairly by the other; they assumed, in accordance with the doctrine, that the parties were of equal status and completely free in their ability to negotiate contracts. The courts of the day saw their role as, primarily, the upholder of a contract, wherever possible, rather than analysts of its terms.

Over the last century or so, probably the greatest single factor to influence contractual law has been the decline and fall of the concept of freedom of contract. It became increasingly apparent that the theory of equality of bargaining power, presumed to exist between parties, was a myth. English law responded to the growing awareness of this fact in two main ways. In the first instance, as has already been noted, there has been an ever increasing body of statutes to regulate certain specific areas of contractual law. Secondly, the approach of the courts themselves has changed very considerably. They are now very much more concerned with the reality and genuineness of consent in 'agreements' reached between parties of disparate bargaining strengths. For example, nowadays it is increasingly the practice of large-scale suppliers of goods and services to use standard-form contracts when dealing with consumers. This 'take it or leave it' approach leaves the weaker party, the individual consumer with little choice but to agree, but his apparently voluntary consent is obviously obtained under pressure. In such cases, the courts have tried, wherever possible, to redress the balance of power between the two parties.

Similarly the courts will, if need be, turn to the possibility of implying terms into a contract, in order to give it greater effectiveness and determine more closely exactly what the respective obligations of the parties are. That is not to say that the courts will import terms into the contract and impose them willy-nilly on the parties against their wishes! To that extent, the doctrine of freedom of contract is still sacrosanct. But, increasingly, it is clear that the courts will try, wherever possible, to ascertain the exact intentions of both parties and give effect to them, even though the parties may not have set these intentions down as express terms.

In the final analysis, therefore, the student must think of the general principles of contract law as a set of ground rules, theoretical rules, for governing any transaction in business or commerce. The degree of importance attached to these, from an abstract point of view, is to say that ALL contracts, regardless of subject matter, or parties or money involved, are governed by general contractual law. In reality, in some areas (like employment law) it will be clear that ordinary common law rules of contract have little or no application, having been superseded entirely by legislation; in others (like commercial law), although general rules of contract have considerable relevance they need to be read in conjunction with certain statutes. These statutes will add specific legal regulations to the existing general contract law for certain types of transaction only. By and large the general rules of contract law are not in any way inconsistent with legislation, such as exists in the field of commercial law. The legislation simply adds detail to the broad framework of the common law.

# REVISION AND EXAMINATION TECHNIQUE

Whole books have been written on how to study and this brief note makes no pretence at being an infallible guide. In any case, skill in revision and examination techniques is an art best acquired by actual practice.

The more you study, the more you devise your own short cuts for efficient preparation for exams. Unfortunately, it is only when you actually sit the examination that you can see whether your particular method of revision is successful. If it is not, it is an expensive and frustrating way to find out.

While it is true that examination techniques are best learned actually sitting examinations, it is not necessary to wait until the real thing. 'Mock' examinations, tackled under realistic conditions, can be very helpful. Revision aids like this WorkBook, not only give some idea of potential questions and possible solutions, but can be used most efficiently by the student as a form of examination rehearsal. For example, select a question and, without looking at the skeleton answer, write out your own. Compare it with the skeleton answer in the WorkBook and if you appear to be working along the right lines, then proceed to write a full solution – preferably under simulated examination conditions. Once you have completed your own solution you can see how it tallies with that given in the WorkBook.

Or, if you have time, tackle a full quota of four or five questions at once – as a mock examination.

Remember, none of the solutions given is represented as the 'only' solution, nor need the exact sequence be the same – the main aim is to give you guidance as to a possible way of tackling the question and as to presentation of your answer. Also, it should be noted that sometimes the answers are a little longer than would be possible in an actual examination; the opportunity having been taken to cover alternative answers. At this level there is almost certainly no one correct answer, but several equally viable alternatives. The opportunity has been taken where appropriate, to develop themes, suggest alternatives and set out alternative material to an extent not possible in an examination.

The short list of do's and don'ts below attempts to set out some suggestions which it is hoped most students will find of practical use in planning their revision and tackling examinations.

## Do's

*Before the examination*

i)   Do plan ahead and make your plans increasingly detailed as you approach the examination date.

Allocate enough time for each topic to be studied, bearing in mind the time actually available to you before the exams.

ii)  Do exercise constant self-discipline, especially if studying at home.

iii) Do, during your course of study, especially once revision starts, constantly test yourself orally and in writing.

iv) Do keep up-to-date. While examiners do not require familiarity with changes in the law during the three months prior to the examination, it obviously creates a good impression to show you are acquainted with any recent changes. Sources that you might look at in order to be up to date include: leading journals such as Modern Law Review, Law Quarterly Review and New Law Journal; cumulative indices to law reports such as the All England Law Reports, and such sources as the Law Society's 'Gazette' and the Legal Executive 'Journal'.

v) Do familiarise yourself with past examination papers, and try at least one 'mock examination' well before the date of the real thing.

*In the examination room*

vi) Do read the instructions on the examination paper carefully. While any last minute changes are unlikely – such as the introduction of a compulsory question – it has been known to happen.

vii) Do read the questions carefully. Analyse problem questions – work out what the examiner wants. PLAN YOUR ANSWER before you start to write.

viii) Do note mark allocations (if any) on the question paper. It is pointless to spend an excessive amount of time in producing a perfect answer to a part of a problem that carries only a tiny percentage of the marks.

ix) Do allow enough time to re-read your answers. A misplaced word (a 'not' in the wrong place, for example) may turn a good answer into gibberish.

## Don'ts

i) Don't finish the syllabus too early – constant revision of the same topic leads to stagnation – but DON'T leave revision so late that you have to 'cram'.

If you are the sort of person who works better to a deadline – make it a realistic one!

ii) Don't try to learn by rote. In particular, don't try to reproduce model answers by heart. Learn to express the basic concepts in your own words.

iii) Don't answer the question you expect to see! By all means 'problem-spot' before examinations by going over old exam papers but make sure that what the examiner is asking for really does match what you are preparing to write about.

and above all –

iv) DON'T PANIC!

Finally, it may be useful at this juncture to say a few words about the structure of your answers in the examination. Amost all examination problems raise more than one legal issue that you are required to deal with. Your answer should:

i) *Identify the issues raised by the question*

This is of crucial importance and gives shape to the whole answer. It indicates to the examiner that you appreciate what he is asking you about. This is at least as important as actually answering the questions of law raised by that issue. The issues should be identified in the first paragraph of the answer.

ii) *Deal with those issues one by one as they arise in the course of the problem*

This, of course, is the substance of the answer and where study and revision pays off.

iii) *If the answer to an issue turns on a provision of a statute, CITE that provision briefly, but do not quote it in detail from any statute you may be permitted to bring into the examination hall*

Having cited the provision, show how it is relevant to the question.

iv) *If there is no statute, or the meaning of the statute has been interpreted by the courts, CITE the relevant cases*

'Citing cases' does not mean writing down the name of every case that happens to deal with the general topic with which you are concerned and then detailing all the facts you can think of.

You should cite only the most relevant cases – there may perhaps only be one. No more facts should be stated than are absolutely essential to establish the relevance of the case. If there is a relevant case, but you cannot remember its name, it is sufficient to refer to it as 'one decided case'.

v) *Whenever a statute or case is cited, the title of the statute or the name of the case should be underlined*

This makes the examiner's job much easier because he can see at a glance whether the relevant material has been dealt with, and it will make him more disposed in your favour.

vi) *Having dealt with the relevant issues, summarise your conclusions in such a way that you answer the question*

A question will often say at the end simply 'Advise A', or B, or C, etc. The advice will usually turn on the individual answers to a number of issues. The point made here is that the final paragraph should pull those individual answers together and actually give the advice required. For example, it may begin something like: 'The effect of the answer to the issues raised by this question is that one's advice to A is that ...'

Make sure that you have answered the question completely. If the question says 'Advise A, B, C and D', don't leave D out. Don't get diverted into discussing advice to parties whom you are not required to advise.

# TABLE OF CASES

# TABLE OF STATUTES

# READING LIST

This list is not meant in any way to be an exhaustive one, simply a reminder to students of books with which they will (hopefully!) already be familiar. Browsers in a law library or bookshop will already be aware that there are numerous texts on the subject of contract law.

| | |
|---|---|
| ANSON (Ed: Guest) | *Anson's Law of Contract*, Oxford |
| ATIYAH | *Introduction to the Law of Contract*, Oxford |
| BEALE, BISHOP & FURMSTON | *Contract Cases & Materials*, Butterworths |
| CHESHIRE, FIFOOT & FURMSTON | *Cheshire & Fifoot's Law of Contract*, Butterworths |
| CRACKNELL | *Contract – Cracknell's Law Students' Companion*, Old Bailey Press |
| DAVIES | *Contract*, Sweet & Maxwell |
| GOFF & JONES | *The Law of Restitution*, Sweet & Maxwell |
| LEWISON | *The Interpretation of Contracts*, Sweet & Maxwell |
| SMITH | *The Law of Contract*, Sweet & Maxwell |
| TREITEL | *An Outline of the Law of Contract*, Butterworths |

# 1 OFFER AND ACCEPTANCE

1.1 Introduction

1.2 Key points

1.3 Analysis of questions

1.4 Questions

## 1.1 Introduction

The method traditionally adopted by the courts to ascertain whether the parties have, in fact, reached agreement is to analyse the dealings between the parties in the context of offer and acceptance. The test is an objective one. The question the courts ask is whether one party has made a definite offer and the other responded with an unqualified acceptance of that offer.

In the complex commercial transactions found nowadays it may be difficult to pinpoint the exact stages of offer and acceptance. See, for example *New Zealand Shipping Co Ltd* v *AM Satterthwaite & Co Ltd* (1975).

Opinions seem divided among the judiciary as to whether the old traditional approach of analysing 'stages' of offer and acceptance is still a viable method, or whether it is an unduly constrictive approach in the modern commercial world, which produces false and unrealistic results. On balance, it seems to be Lord Diplock's view, that only 'exceptional' cases cannot be analysed in the orthodox way, that holds sway. Certainly, other more flexible approaches have been suggested eg Lord Denning's test in *Butler Machine Tool* v *Ex-cell-o Corp (England) Ltd* (1979), but these have, so far, not found favour.

## 1.2 Key points

It is important that the student understand the following:

a) *The offer*

An offer might be defined as an expression of willingness to contract made with the intention that it shall become binding on the offeror, immediately, when accepted by the offeree. Offers may be in writing, verbal or implicit in conduct. They may be made to one person, a group or the world at large. They may be unilateral or bilateral.

One of the first and most important tasks for a potential offeree is to sort out whether what has been addressed to him is really an offer, or some other form of preliminary proceeding. Offers alone are capable of acceptance and therefore need to be carefully distinguished from such 'look alikes' as invitations to treat. The distinction between offers and invitations to treat is often blurred, depending to a large extent on the parties' intentions. For convenience the courts have, over the years, developed a series of presumptions whereby certain types of activity (such as shop window displays, advertisements, invitations to submit tenders and so on) are regarded as invitations to treat. Like all presumptions these are capable of rebuttal, if it can be established that there are special circumstances. The student should consult a textbook for a more detailed account especially as to case law on the subject.

b) *Duration and termination of offer*

Once made, an offer will continue in existence until it is brought to an end. While it continues to exist it is capable of acceptance. There are a number of possible ways an offer may be brought to an end.

i) Revocation

Until such time as it is accepted, the offer can be revoked at any time by the offeror.

There are complex rules, particularly as to communication of revocation, and the student should refer to a textbook for further details.

ii) Rejection

Once rejected, an offer dies and cannot subsequently be resurrected. True rejection should however be distinguished from mere requests for further information. See (c) Acceptance and counter offers, below.

iii) Lapse of time

An offer will remain open for a fixed span of time, and then automatically lapse, if such a time is specified in the offer. If no such time is specified the offer will end after a reasonable time.

iv) Conditional offers

Some offers are made, conditionally, dependent on some event happening or not happening. Should the condition be such, that if applicable the offer will cease, then on the occurrence of the conditional event (or non-occurrence of some qualifying event) the offer will be no longer capable of acceptance.

v) Death

Death of the offeror may not always terminate the offer. It depends on the nature of the offer – whether, for example, it was for personal services. Similarly there are no formal rules as to the effect of death of the offeree. It is most probable that if the offer was made to one person alone and that person dies this effectively becomes a form of rejection.

vi) Insanity, incapacity, insolvency or impossibility

c) *Acceptance and counter offers*

Acceptance might be defined as a final and unqualified agreement to all the terms of the offer. If there are any reservations or conditions this is not final and there is no true acceptance.

Once acceptance has been made, there is (all other circumstances being favourable) a valid binding contract in existence.

Methods of acceptance vary. The mode of acceptance may be dictated by the offeror, in which case not to comply precisely may mean that this is not true acceptance. Otherwise it is usually assumed that the acceptance will be in the same form: written, verbal or implicit in conduct, as the original offer.

It should be noted that sometimes, in purporting to accept, the offeree raises new issues or requests further information. The student should make himself familiar with the whole issue of counter offers and related topics. Sometimes in the preliminary negotiations of a particularly complex contract there may be a whole series of responses to the original offer. These may be simply requests for clarification, which advance the parties no further. Or if the offeree introduces new terms or conditions it may be a counter offer. Not until the response of one party matches exactly the latest offer of the other will there be a true acceptance.

It is usually said that acceptance should be made, in the full knowledge of the offer and with definite intention to accept. The student will see, on referring to other authorities in more detail, that there have been cases where a person has 'accidentally', so to speak, accepted an offer he is unaware of, or had no intention of accepting. It seems that unless the necessary intention to create legal relations, referred to previously, is present any apparent acceptance will not be valid.

d) *Communication of acceptance*

The general rule is that acceptance must be communicated to the offeror. Silence will never normally be acceptance. There are however a number of very important exceptions to this rule, so that there are cases where a contract may be formed without acceptance ever having been communicated to the offeror.

One such group of exceptions is cases where the offeror expressly or impliedly waives his right to have acceptance communicated to him. This is a common occurrence, for example, in cases where the acceptance is to take the form of some sort of conduct, perhaps over some period of time, by the offeree. While silence alone will never be acceptance, such activity might very well be and the offeror might not realistically anticipate being informed as to the offeree's progress in accepting. Acceptance will be automatic when the requisite conduct is completed by the offeree.

Another area where the normal rules as to communication do not apply is in offer and acceptance by post. For convenience, a series of (at times somewhat arbitrary) rules, have been evolved by the courts to cover cases where postal offers, revocations and acceptances have gone astray, been delayed or crossed in the post. For full details the student should consult a textbook.

## 1.3 Analysis of questions

As might be expected the subject of offer and acceptance has always been a favourite of examiners. Over twelve years of University of London External Contract papers, there has never been a year when this topic has not cropped up in some form. It does not necessarily follow that all the question will centre on offer and acceptance. For example, Question 6 from the 1993 paper combines a multiplicity of issues including not only offer and acceptance, but also breach and damages for breach.

Each of the questions quoted below is fairly typical. All problems (the essay type question is rare); they do to some extent overlap, that is inevitable. However it will be seen, comparing them, that each needs an answer applied to the particular problem. An overall 'blanket' approach would be inappropriate.

## 1.4 Questions

QUESTION ONE

Alban manufactures office equipment. Earlier this year he developed a revolutionary stapler. On 18 May he telexed Bruno and David, both wholesalers whom he had dealt with previously, asking each of them whether he would be interested in becoming sole distributor of the staplers. On 20 May Bruno and David each telexed Alban independently stating that he was interested in becoming sole distributor for the stapler and would like further information.

On 22 May Alban telexed Bruno: 'I offer you the post of sole distributor of the stapler at a basic 10 per cent commission. If I hear nothing from you by 31 May, I will assume that this is acceptable to you.'

Bruno immediately posted a first class letter to Alban in which he accepted Alban's offer. The letter did not arrive until 2 June.

Meanwhile on 31 May, David, having heard nothing from Alban since the telex of 18 May, posted a letter to Alban in which David offered to become Alban's sole distributor for a 5 per cent commission.

Alban received David's letter on 1 June. Alban immediately telephoned Bruno and told him that the post of sole distributor was no longer available. Bruno insists that there is a binding contract to appoint him.

Advise Alban, who wishes to appoint David as sole distributor.

University of London LLB Examination
(for External Students) Elements of the Law of Contract June 1988 Q1

*Skeleton Solution*

- Is there a contract between Alban and Bruno?
- Telex – postal rules?
- Who makes offer? A's telex to Bruno on 22nd?
- Silence as acceptance. Estoppel
- Letters of acceptance, letters of revocation.

*Suggested Solution*

The question here is whether there is a concluded contract between Alban and Bruno or whether Alban is free to conclude a contract with David.

To answer this question it is necessary to conduct the traditional analysis of offer and acceptance. Lord Denning MR has suggested in *Butler Machine Tool Co Ltd v Ex-cell-o Corporation (England) Ltd* (1979) and in *Gibson v The Manchester City Council* (1979) that in many cases the traditional analysis of offer, acceptance and so forth is out of date. In the latter case, however, in the House of Lords, Lord Diplock

4

stated that although there may be certain types of contract which do not fit into the normal analysis of a contract as being constituted by offer and acceptance these were exceptional and a contract made by an exchange of correspondence between the parties was not one of these. It is submitted, therefore, that the traditional approach is required in this case.

It is clear that the initial telex from Alban and the replies of Bruno and David to that telex communication are merely preliminary negotiations and can in no way be considered contractual offers or acceptances. This does not require further elaboration.

Alban's telex to Bruno of 22 May is, it is submitted, an offer. Treitel defines an offer as 'an expression of willingness to contract on certain terms made with the intention that it shall become binding as soon as it is accepted by the person to whom it is addressed'. Clearly Alban's telex of 22 May accords with this definition. The question is: has Bruno accepted the offer?

An acceptance is a final and unequivocal assent to the terms of an offer. There appears to have been an act of acceptance on Bruno's part. When he posts the letter to Alban he clearly indicates by his conduct that he wishes to accept Alban's offer. The question is: has there been communication of the acceptance?

Alban appears to be saying that silence shall be deemed to be acceptance of his offer. *Felthouse* v *Bindley* (1862) is authority for the proposition that silence cannot be imposed on the offeree. But this rule has been established for the protection of the offeree who should not be put to the trouble or possible expense of rejecting an offer. But whilst silence cannot be imposed on the offeree, this is not an argument for protecting an offeror who waives communication of acceptance. It could be argued here that Bruno, by his conduct, had accepted the offer and, alternatively, that Alban by virtue of the terms of the offer and Bruno's reliance on the offer was estopped from denying that his offer had been accepted. If this estoppel does operate in Bruno's favour it could, therefore, be argued that by merely posting the letter Bruno has accepted David's offer and that a contract has therefore been concluded between them. It could be objected that estoppel does not create a cause of action but Chitty does not regard this as a serious objection.

If the estoppel argument does not hold up, it remains to consider whether the posting of the letter by Bruno constitutes a communication of the acceptance. This requires discussion of the rule relating to acceptances through the post. The rule established in *Adams* v *Lindsell* (1818) is that where there has been communication through the post the acceptance is complete as soon as the letter has been posted. If the postal rule applies the contract is concluded even though the letter of acceptance never reaches the offeror: *Household Fire and Carriage Accident Insurance Co Ltd* v *Grant* (1879). It should also be considered as to whether this is an occasion where postal rules apply; or whether the communications by telex ('instantaneous') take priority. Compare *Brinkibon Ltd* v *Stahag Stahl* (1983) with *Yates Building Co* v *Pulleyn* (1975). The postal rule only applies if it was, in the circumstances, reasonable to use the post: *Henthorn* v *Fraser* (1892). There is authority for the view that it would not normally be reasonable to attempt to accept a telegraphic offer by posting a letter: *Quenerduaine* v *Cole* (1883). It might therefore be suggested that it would be equally unreasonable to reply to a telex by posting a letter. It is submitted however that this argument cannot be sustained in view of the fact that Alban waived communication of acceptance. Moreover Alban appears to have given Bruno nine days in which to consider whether or not he wishes to reject the offer.

It is trite law that an offer can be revoked at any time before acceptance. But the revocation must be communicated before communication of the acceptance: *Byrne* v *Van Tienhoven* (1880). Alban purports to revoke the offer on 1 June. However it has been submitted that as Alban has waived communication of acceptance and as Bruno has relied on that waiver, Alban is estopped from denying the validity of Bruno's acceptance. Moreover, if the postal rule applied, acceptance is deemed to be communicated when the letter is posted, not when it is received. The postal rule can be excluded by the terms of the offer: *Holwell Securities Ltd* v *Hughes* (1974). In contrast to that case, however, so far from requiring actual communication of the acceptance, Alban has waived such communication.

Accordingly it is submitted that Alban has a binding contract with Bruno and is, consequently, not free to be able to make an offer to David.

QUESTION TWO

Bob owns a stamp shop in Muncaster High Street. On Monday he places an item in the advertisement column of the Muncaster Evening Gazette. 'Utopian Penny Red Stamp, one only, £750 or nearest offer.'

Later that day, Alan, a stamp collector, telephones Bob and says, 'The Utopian Red for sale, I'll take it for £700.' Bob replies, 'I cannot accept less than £725 but I will not sell it to anyone else before Saturday. Let me have a reply by Friday if you want it.' Alan says, 'That is kind of you. Remind me to buy you a drink when I see you.'

On Wednesday Alan telephones Bob and leaves a message on his answering machine stating 'I accept your offer'. Unfortunately Bob's infant son later presses a button on the machine which erases the message before Bob listens to the recording. Later that day Bob sells the stamp to Cedric for £750.

On Thursday Alan meets Cedric's aged mother who tells him that she has seen Cedric's nine year old son who told her that his father was very excited at having acquired a Utopian Penny Red from a High Street dealer.

Alan rushes home and posts a letter to Bob confirming the message which he had left on the machine. On the same day Bob writes to Alan withdrawing his offer.

On Friday morning Alan receives Bob's letter and at lunchtime Bob receives Alan's letter.

Advise Alan.

University of London LLB Examination
(for External Students) Elements of the Law of Contract June 1987 Q1

*Skeleton Solution*

- Advertisements – invitation to treat.
- Alan's reply – offer.
- Bob's response: rejection/counter offer?

- Promise to keep offer open – effect if any.
- Communication of acceptance.
- Postal rules on offer, acceptance, revocation. Do postal rules apply here?

## Suggested Solution

In advising Alan, one must carefully analyse the various actions of and communications passing between the parties in order to determine whether at any stage he entered into a contract with Bob to buy the stamp in question.

The first material event was Bob's placing of an advertisement in the Gazette. Although there is no reason in principle why an advertisement should not constitute a contractual offer, this will normally only be so in the case of unilateral contracts (eg *Carlill* v *Carbolic Smoke Ball Co* (1893)). Since the envisaged contract here is bilateral, a court would construe Bob's advertisement as being an invitation to treat only: *Partridge* v *Crittenden* (1968).

Alan's telephone reply, although couched in terms of an acceptance, can only be offer as there has been no prior offer capable of being accepted. A statement can be an offer although expressed as an acceptance: *Bigg* v *Boyd Gibbins Ltd* (1971).

Alan's offer is not accepted by Bob. The latter's reply, however, gives rise to a problem of construction: it could be regarded as a rejection and counter offer (*Hyde* v *Wrench* (1840) and *Butler Machine Tool* v *Ex-cell-o Corporation* (1979)) or a rejection together with a statement as to price (similar to *Harvey* v *Facey* (1893)). It is submitted that the last part of Bob's reply, giving Alan until Friday to respond, indicates that the first construction is correct.

Bob has promised to keep his counter offer open until Friday. It is to be noted that he is under no obligation so to do so. A gratuitous promise to keep an offer open for a fixed period time is not binding on the offeror, *Routledge* v *Grant* (1828), and he can revoke the offer at any time. The only way an offer may be irrevocable for a fixed time is if the offeree furnishes consideration for the offeror's promise not to revoke, but Alan has not done so. Alan's promise to buy Bob a drink is a consequence of Bob's promise to keep the offer open, it was not requested by him nor was it given in return for Bob's promise in the contractual sense: *Combe* v *Combe* (1951).

Next Alan dictates a message of acceptance on Bob's answering machine on Wednesday. The general rule is that an acceptance is ineffective unless and until communicated to the offeror: *Holwell Securities Ltd* v *Hughes* (1974). Although different principles apply to acceptance by letter or telegram (to be dealt with below), in *Entores* v *Miles Far East Corporation* (1955), approved in *Brinkibon* v *Stahag Stahl* (1983), the Court of Appeal held that an acceptance by telephone or telex is only effective when received.

This principle was formulated on the proposition that telephones and telexes are instantaneous means of communication. That is obviously not the case where an acceptance is left on an answering machine. It is submitted, though, that there is no warrant for extending the postal acceptance rule to messages left on answering machines and that Alan's acceptance would only be effective when heard by Bob.

Due to the activities of Bob's son, he never heard it. Although one might refer to dicta in *Entores* (1955), and also *The Brimnes* (1975), as indicating that where one party's failure to receive communication is due to his own default, he is to be treated as having received it, it is doubtful whether the infant's activities can be placed in this class.

Thus when Bob sells the stamps to Cedric, and also when Alan hears news of Cedric's excitement, Alan has not accepted Bob's offer. Equally, though Bob has not revoked it, since revocation of an offer must be communicated: *Byrne* v *Van Tienhoven* (1880).

In *Dickinson* v *Dodds* (1876) it appears to have been held either that sale of the subject matter of the offer, or at any rate communication of the fact of the sale by a third party to the offeree operates to revoke the offer. Whatever the true ratio of that case, which has been much criticised, it is very unlikely that a court would hold that the information given to Alan by Cedric's mother acquired from Cedric's son constituted revocation of Bob's offer. Although Alan may have suspected it was the same stamp, he could not have known it was, nor even that the information was strictly correct.

Bob's offer is thus still capable of acceptance when Alan posts his letter. The key issue now is whether the postal acceptance rule applies. If it does, a contract was concluded when Alan posted his letter: *Adams* v *Lindsell* (1818); *Household Insurance* v *Grant* (1879) and *Henthorn* v *Fraser* (1892). Conversely it is settled law that Bob's letter of revocation is effective only when received by Alan: *Byrne* v *Van Tienhoven* (1880).

The postal acceptance rule does not invariably apply. It is a rule of convenience which may (inter alia) be ousted by contrary stipulation: *Holwell* v *Hughes* (1974). Although the language used by Bob was not totally clear, the words 'Let me have a reply by Friday' suggested that to be effective the acceptance must be received by him. On this interpretation, as Alan's letter of acceptance arrived after Bob's letter of revocation, it is submitted that no contract was concluded.

One's advice to Alan is, therefore, that he has no claim.

QUESTION THREE

On May 11 A wrote to B offering 300 bags of cement at £10 per bag. On May 13 B posted a reply in which he accepted A's offer but added that if he did not hear to the contrary he would assume that the price included delivery to his (B's) yard. The following morning, before B's letter arrived at A's office, A heard a rumour that the price of cement was about to fall and he immediately sent a fax to B stating 'our price of £10 includes delivery'.

On receiving A's fax at 10am on May 14 B wrote and posted a letter to A confirming his acceptance of A's terms. At lunch, however, B also heard the rumour that cement prices were about to fall and at 2pm B sent a fax to A stating 'Decline your offer of cement'.

The price of cement fell to £8 per bag and B refuses to accept any cement from A.

Advise A.

University of London LLB Examination
(for External Students) Elements of the Law of Contract June 1990 Q4

## Skeleton Solution

- Is there a contract?
- Traditional analysis of offer/acceptance/counter offer/revocation.
- Postal rules.
- Fax and other 'instantaneous' methods of communication.
- Alternative analysis of what constitutes agreement.

## Suggested Solution

This is a question which requires discussion of some of the common problems of offer and acceptance. As with most questions in this area it is necessary to analyse each stage of the transaction chronologically.

The letter from A to B of May 11 is clearly an offer. What has first to be considered is whether B's reply of May 13 is an acceptance or a counter-offer. Treitel defines an acceptance as 'a final and unqualified expression of assent to the terms of an offer'. If a new term is introduced in the reply it is not an acceptance, but a counter-offer. But if B does not intend to introduce a new term in his reply the statement with regard to delivery does not prevent it being an acceptance: *Butler Machine Tool Co Ltd v Ex-cell-o Corporation (England) Ltd* (1979). It is at least possible that delivery to B's yard is not a new term, but one that the law would imply, if that was the custom in the particular trade. In that event, as A made the offer through the post the postal rule would apply and there would have been an acceptance of A's offer when B posted his letter: *Adams v Lindsell* (1818); *Henthorn v Fraser* (1892). However this is unlikely as B contemplates a reply to the contrary.

Having ruled out the possibility that B's letter is an acceptance, it follows that it is a counter-offer. It has been long-established that a counter-offer destroys the original offer and constitutes a fresh offer which the original offeror, now the offeree, is free to accept or reject: *Hyde v Wrench* (1840). B is now the offeror in his letter of May 13 and he states that he assumes that the price includes delivery unless he hears to the contrary. An offeror cannot impose silence on the offeree: *Felthouse v Bindley* (1862). But, as Treitel suggests, this rule is arguably for the protection of the offeree, the offeror can waive communication of acceptance and be contractually bound by the offeree's silence. Thus the further possibility must be considered that, there being no reply to the contrary, a contract is concluded on the terms of B's letter. However this proposition is not free from doubt, and it is necessary to proceed to the next stage of negotiations.

If no contract has as yet been concluded at this stage A's fax stating that 'our price of £10 includes delivery' constitutes a fresh offer. When he sends this fax A has not received B's letter, and there is authority for the view that cross offers are not an acceptance of each other: *Tinn v Hoffman & Co* (1873). It is assumed, therefore that, at this stage, a contract has still not been concluded.

If that assumption is correct then A's fax is a further fresh offer. B writes to the effect that he accepts that offer. The next question is – has that acceptance been effectively communicated?

As stated above, the normal postal rule is that acceptance is deemed to be communicated when the letter of acceptance is posted. However it is questionable whether the postal rule applies to an offer made through the medium of a fax. It is, of course, clear that an offeree must comply with the offeror's stipulated mode of acceptance but he may adopt a mode as or more expeditious than the one prescribed: *Manchester Diocesan Council for Education* v *Commercial and General Investments Ltd* (1970). However the transmission of the offer by fax implies that A requires instantaneous communication, and that a posted acceptance would be ineffective. In *Quenerduaine* v *Cole* (1883) it was held that it would not normally be reasonable to attempt to accept a telegraphic offer by posting a letter. *A fortiori* it would not be reasonable to answer a fax message by letter. A strict application of this principle would lead to the conclusion that as B's letter of acceptance is invalid no contract has been concluded.

This conclusion, however, would violate common sense. B has elected to use the post and should not be allowed to avail himself of the argument that the method he has himself chosen is ineffective. In *Holwell Securities Ltd* v *Hughes* (1974) Lawton LJ said that the postal rule probably does not operate 'where its application would produce manifest inconvenience and absurdity'. It is submitted that his Lordship's approach should be adapted, and that here *not* to apply the postal rule would lead similarly to 'inconvenience and absurdity'. It must be concluded, therefore, that the offer made by A through the medium of the fax has been effectively accepted by B.

B, however, purports to revoke his acceptance by the fax which he in turn transmits. There is no clear authority in English law as to whether an offeree, who has posted a letter of acceptance, can revoke his acceptance by a speedier method of communication. A strict application of the postal rule would deny that this is possible. This view derives support from the New Zealand decision in *Wenkheim* v *Arndt* (1873) and that of a South African court in *A-Z Bazaars (Pty) Ltd* v *Minister of Agriculture* (1974). There is a US decision to the contrary: *Dick* v *US* (1949).

In the absence of binding authority it is submitted that, as a matter of policy, B should not be permitted to withdraw his acceptance, especially in view of B's clear prior indication that he wished to accept A's offer provided that the price included delivery. A should therefore be advised that B is contractually bound to accept delivery of the 300 bags of cement.

This conclusion has been arrived at by applying the traditional analysis of offer and acceptance. An alternative approach should be considered. In *Butler Machine Tool Co* (above) Lord Denning MR had the view that in many cases 'our traditional analysis of offer, counter-offer, rejection, acceptance and so forth is out-of-date'. Lord Denning said that this had been observed by Lord Wilberforce in *New Zealand Shipping Co Ltd* v *A M Satterthwaite & Co Ltd, The Eurymedon* (1975). He went on to say that 'The better way is to look at all the documents passing between the parties and glean from them, or from the conduct of the parties, whether they have reached agreement on all material points ...'. Lord Denning also rejected the conventional analysis in favour of this approach in *Gibson* v *Manchester City Council* (1979). But this did find favour in the House of Lords where Lord Diplock said that by departing from the conventional approach the majority of the Court of Appeal had been led into error. In the course of his speech Lord Diplock said:

'... there may be certain types of contract, though I think they are exceptional, which do not fit easily into the normal analysis of a contract as being constituted by offer and acceptance; but a contract alleged to have been made by an exchange of correspondence between the parties in which the successive communications other than the first are in reply to one another is not one of these.'

In the present question the application of Lord Denning's approach would also lead to the conclusion that a binding contract existed between the parties; they had, it is submitted, clearly 'come to an agreement on everything that was material'.

In view of Lord Diplock's strictures, however, a court might well be chary of adopting such an approach. Nor would it be necessary to do so: the conventional approach leads to the same result.

QUESTION FOUR

David advertised his car for sale in Monday's newspaper for '£550 for quick sale – best offer secures'. Eric came to see the car on Tuesday and said that he would give David £500 for it: he told David to let him know by Friday. On Wednesday Frank examined the car: after returning home he posted a letter to David in which he said, 'I agree to buy the car for £550 asked by you' but before David received this letter Frank telephoned and told him that he did not want the car after all.

On Thursday David posted a letter to Eric agreeing to sell the car for £500, but Eric did not receive this letter until Saturday. Eric then went to David's house and produced £250 in cash saying, 'that's the best I can do', but David refused.

Advise David.

University of London LLB Examination
(for External Students) Elements of the Law of Contract June 1991 Q1

*Skeleton Solution*

• David and Eric:
  – invitation to treat;
  – offer;
  – postal rules;
  – offer not in the form anticipated.

• David and Frank:
  – invitation to treat;
  – frank's response – offer or acceptance?;
  – revocation;
  – postal rules.

*Suggested Solution*

David is involved in negotiations with Eric and Frank. It is convenient to examine these two sets of negotiations in turn.

David's advertisement in the newspaper is, it is submitted, an invitation to treat, not an offer: *Partridge* v *Crittenden* (1968). It might be argued that the addition of the words 'best offer secures' converts what would be otherwise be an invitation to treat

11

into an offer, binding the offeror to accept as best the highest price he in turn is offered, by analogy with *Harvela Investments Ltd* v *Royal Trust Company of Canada* (1985). But the facts of that case were very different. There the invitation to submit tenders had been addressed to two parties with the unequivocal undertaking to accept the highest offer. The decision in *Harvela* cannot be extended to embrace an advertisement in a newspaper addressed to the public at large.

It follows, therefore, that when Eric offers £500 for the car it is he (Eric) who is making an offer in the legal sense. What has to be determined is whether this offer has been accepted.

David posts a letter accepting Eric's offer on the Thursday. Where the postal rule applies communication of the acceptance is deemed to have taken place when the letter of acceptance is posted. This rule was established in *Adams* v *Lindsell* (1818) and has been frequently applied. However the rule is not an inflexible one. Two aspects have to be considered: firstly whether communication through the post was envisaged by the parties – *Henthorn* v *Fraser* (1892); secondly whether the terms of the offer preclude the operation of the rule: *Holwell Securities Ltd* v *Hughes* (1974).

Eric's offer was an oral one, and it is at least arguable that the parties envisaged an oral reply and not a reply by post. In this event the postal rule would not apply. Even if communication through the post was, or should have been, anticipated, Eric requires David 'to let him know by Friday'. This implies that Eric stipulates for actual notice, thus precluding the operation of the postal rule – see *Holwell Securities Ltd* v *Hughes* (above). In this event communication of the acceptance only occurred when Eric actually received David's letter. But Eric also stipulated that such acceptance must be notified by the Friday. When the letter was received on Saturday the offer had lapsed. It is trite law that, if an offer requires acceptance within a specified time, it will lapse if it has not been accepted within that time. There is, therefore, no concluded contract between David and Eric at this stage. Eric's fresh offer to purchase the car for £250 is refused and David is, of course, entitled to refuse it.

David is accordingly advised that there is no contractual relationship between Eric and himself.

Consideration must now be given to the situation in relation to Frank.

It has already been argued that, notwithstanding its wording, David's advertisement in the newspaper is an invitation to treat. In this case the letter from Frank on Wednesday appears to be an offer to purchase the car for £550. It is also trite law that an offer can be revoked at any time before acceptance: Frank has telephoned to revoke his offer. This would mean that no contract has been concluded between these parties either.

However the wording of Frank's letter is 'I agree to buy the car for £550 asked by you'. This suggests that, at least in Frank's view, the letter is one of acceptance. Indeed the objective appearance of the letter leads to the conclusion that it is an acceptance and the law pays due regard to objective appearance: see *Smith* v *Hughes* (1871). But the objective principle is not the sole factor. In order to find that the letter is an acceptance it must be found that it was so regarded by David: *The Hannah Blumenthal* (1983). As to this there is no clear indication in the problem. But the possibility of Frank's letter being construed as an acceptance must be considered.

If Frank's letter is an acceptance, the question arises as to its communication as it was sent by post. If the postal rule applies, as previously set out, the contract between David and Frank is concluded when the letter is posted. It is not open to Frank to assert the inapplicability of the postal rule, as he elected to use the post.

It remains to consider the effectiveness of Frank's purported revocation of his acceptance. There is a dearth of English authority on whether a posted acceptance may be withdrawn before the letter has reached the offeror. In a South African case it was held that such revocation was not effective, the offeree remained bound by his posted letter of acceptance: *A-Z Bazaars (Pty) Ltd v Minister of Agriculture* (1974). The New Zealand case of *Wenkheim v Arndt* (1873) is also quoted as authority for this proposition, but the decision in this case did not turn on that point. The position in English law is therefore not without doubt. Professor Hudson ((1966) 82 LQR 169) has argued that the postal rule is merely one of convenience, and should not be inflexibly applied. In similar vein Lawton LJ in *Holwell Securities Ltd v Hughes* (above) suggested that the postal rule should not be applied where it would lead to 'manifest absurdity and inconvenience'.

It is submitted that this more flexible approach is preferable and that in the present situation Frank's withdrawal of the acceptance is effective. Consequently no contract has been concluded between David and Frank either.

QUESTION FIVE

On Monday, A telephoned B offering to sell A's Greenacre field to B for £18,000. B said, 'I'll think about it and let you know.' A replied, 'Don't leave it too long.' On Tuesday, B decided not to buy the field and posted a letter to A telling him that he was not interested. B later changed his mind and telephoned A, leaving a message on A's answer-phone stating, 'I would like to buy it.' Because of the failure of A's answering machine it never played back the message. On Friday, the value of Greenacre field doubled. B telephoned A and said, 'When will I be hearing from your solicitor?' A believed that B was referring to another matter between them and said, 'It is all right – no need for concern.'

Advise the parties.

University of London LLB Examination
(for External Students) Elements of the Law of Contract June 1992 Q3

*Skeleton Solution*

• Was there an offer?
• Has there been a rejection of the offer and was it communicated?
• Was the acceptance communicated?
• Does any form of estoppel apply?
• Section 2 Law of Property (Miscellaneous Provisions) Act 1989.

*Suggested Solution*

It must be assumed that A's telephone call to B constitutes a firm offer to sell Greenacre field, although *Clifton v Palumbo* (1944) suggests that the court may consider that A did not intend to be bound to a transaction concerning real property in such an informal way.

B requires time to consider the offer, and it appears that A requires a reasonably swift response.

When B sends the letter on Tuesday he is rejecting A's offer. It is clear that the rejection of an offer terminates the offer: *Tinn* v *Hoffman & Co* (1873). But the rejection of an offer has no effect until it is communicated to the offeror. Unlike acceptances through the post there is no rule of convenience requiring the rejection to be deemed to be communicated when the letter of rejection is posted. If B accepts the offer, and this acceptance is communicated before the letter of rejection reaches A, a contract will have been concluded.

Later on the Tuesday B purports to accept the offer; the question is, however, whether that acceptance has been communicated. There is no clear authority regarding the leaving of a message on an answering machine. In discussing instantaneous communications in *Entores Ltd* v *Miles Far East Corporation* (1955) Denning LJ said:

'But if there should be a case where the offeror without any fault on his part does not receive the message of acceptance – yet the sender of it believes it has got home when it has not – then I think there is no contract.'

B apparently believes that his message has got home. Can it be assumed that A is at fault because of the failure of his answering machine? A's demand for a swift response to his offer suggests that he does, or should, expect a telephone call from B. If the failure of the machine is due to the fault of A it might be possible to argue that the message of acceptance was deemed to be communicated when A should have heard it. Perhaps some slender support for this suggestion could be gleaned from *The Brimnes* (1975) though that case concerned the termination of a contract, not its formation, and dealt with the communication of a telex message during normal office hours. That case is, therefore, not authority for the view that, even if A were at fault, he could be deemed to have received B's message. Moreover there is nothing to suggest that A was at fault.

At this stage, therefore, the offer has not been effectively rejected, nor has it been accepted.

On the Friday, when B enquires as to when he will be hearing from A's solicitor it is clear that he believes that his message of acceptance has been received. We are not told whether or not A has received the letter rejecting his offer. If he had, then the rejection would have been communicated before the acceptance, and the offer would have been terminated and could not be revived by subsequent acceptance: *Hyde* v *Wrench* (1840).

But the possibility must be considered that when this telephone call was made A was still unaware of the letter of rejection. In this event it becomes necessary to examine the import of Friday's telephone conversation. Clearly the parties had a different understanding of it. For B to succeed in a contention that a contract had been concluded he would have to convince a court that, in the light of the circumstances, A should have known that he (B) was referring to the purchase of Greenacre field and must be deemed to have known that his offer had been accepted.

B would then argue that A's conduct had led him to believe that a contract had been concluded and that he had relied on this. The basis of B's contention would be that A was estopped from denying that a contract had been concluded. Whatever the limits of promissory estoppel, it is submitted that the doctrine cannot be stretched this far. *Combe* v *Combe* (1951) is still authority for the rule that promissory estoppel does not create a cause of action where none existed before, and the decision in the contrasting Australian case of *Walton Stores (Interstate) Ltd* v *Maher* (1988) could not be applied here. There is, furthermore, nothing to indicate that B has acted to his detriment so as to found a proprietary estoppel.

It is submitted, therefore, that no contract has been concluded between the parties, nor has B any other basis for a cause of action.

It remains to note the effect of the **Law of Property (Miscellaneous Provisions) Act 1989.** Under s2 of that Act the contract for the sale of Greenacre field would have to be in writing and all the terms agreed would have to be in a document signed by or on behalf of both parties. Clearly none of these requirements have been met.

QUESTION SIX

K advertised in a local newspaper that he offered a reward of £2,000 for the return of his lost cat of which K was inordinately fond. K had lost the cat when he had moved house. L realised that the cat may have tried to return to its former home and took a train ticket costing £76 return to K's former home. Eventually, when L had spent five days at a local hotel, the cat arrived. Two days earlier K had put a notice in a local shop window withdrawing his offer of reward because he had been given a new kitten by his girlfriend. L paid his hotel bill of £45 a day and after a return trip by train he took the cat to K's address. K refused to pay L and L refused to let him have the cat. L fed the cat for 10 days (costing £4 a day) before K snatched the cat from L's garden.

Advise L.

University of London LLB Examination
(for External Students) Elements of the Law of Contract June 1993 Q4

*Skeleton Solution*

• The advertisement; offer or invitation to treat.
• Revocation of the offer, whether effective.
• K's refusal to pay; breach of contract.
• L's remedies.
• The effect of K having 'snatched the cat from L's garden'.

*Suggested Solution*

The first point for decision is whether K's advertisement constitutes an offer. It appears beyond doubt that an offer of a reward (unlike offers to buy or sell articles) is an offer in the legal sense, and that it can be made to the world at large: *Carlill* v *Carbolic Smoke Ball Co* (1893). This problem is an example of a 'unilateral' contract; an offer which matures into a contract after performance; see also *New Zealand Shipping Co Ltd* v *Satterthwaite & Co Ltd, The Eurymedon* (1975).

In such unilateral contracts acceptance and performance may coincide. It is clear here that the return of the cat would constitute acceptance of K's offer. It is trite law that an offer may be revoked at any time before acceptance. But the revocation must be actually communicated to the offeree before the acceptance: *Byrne & Co v Van Tienhoven & Co* (1880). Has K effectively revoked the offer before acceptance by L?

K's offer is contained in a newspaper advertisement. In order for that offer to be effectively revoked the revocation must be communicated to L, and communicated before L has accepted the offer, or be deemed to have done so.

There is no clear authority in our law as to what would constitute an effective revocation of an offer contained in a newspaper advertisement. As the offeror cannot ensure that the revocation comes to notice of the offeree, it seems that it would be sufficient if he takes all reasonable steps to do so. In *Shuey* v *US* (1875) an American court decided that the revocation, published in the same newspaper as the preceding offer, was deemed to be effective. It is doubtful, however, whether the placing of a notice in the shop window would be regarded as having taken all reasonable steps to communicate revocation of the offer. Even it it were, it appears that L might be regarded as having commenced performance of the contract before publication of the revocation.

There is authority for the view that, in a unilateral contract, the offeror cannot withdraw the offer once the offeree has commenced performance: *Errington* v *Errington and Woods* (1952). The position appears to be that the condition for L being able to claim the reward is the return of the cat, and short of that K is not bound; subject, however, to the qualification that there is an implied obligation on K not to prevent the condition being satisfied, and this obligation arises as soon as L starts to perform: see the judgment of Goff LJ in *Daulia Ltd* v *Four Millbank Nominees* (1978).

The question is: do L's actions in travelling to K's home and staying at the local hotel constitute the start of performance, or are they mere preparations for performance? It is submitted that the steps L has taken, being solely directed to the recovery of the cat, constitute clear commencement of performance.

I would conclude, on the question of revocation, that the placing of the notice in the shop window is not sufficient communication of the withdrawal of the offer and, if I am wrong on this, that L having commenced performance, K was debarred from withdrawing the offer. The purported revocation is therefore ineffective.

L, in taking the cat to K's address, has tendered performance of the contract. And K, in refusing payment of the promised reward, is in breach of contract. What must now be considered is the remedies available to L.

It is necessary, firstly, to deal with the situation before K removed the cat from L's garden.

If L had left the cat with K there is no doubt that he could then have claimed the reward of £2,000. However, he has not done so. He could have re-tendered delivery of the cat against payment of the reward, but it does not appear that he did this. The condition on which L could claim payment was the actual return of the cat, and this has not occurred. L cannot, in consequence, claim the reward. (This might be altered by K's subsequent conduct.)

However, K being in breach of contract, L is entitled to damages for that breach, based on reliance loss; the wasted expenditure he incurred in the performance of the contract. See for example: *McRae v Commonwealth Disposals Commission* (1951); *Hayes v James & Charles Dodd* (1990). This is subject to the rule that the loss is not too remote.

This rule limits the loss recoverable to that which was 'reasonably foreseeable': *Victoria Laundry (Windsor) Ltd v Newman Industries Ltd* (1949). The House of Lords in *The Heron II* (1967) preferred the expression 'within the reasonable contemplation of the parties', this denoting a higher degree of probability.

Adopting the latter expression, was it within the reasonable contemplation of K that an offeree would be 'likely to' or 'liable to' (terms used by their Lordships in *The Heron II* (1967)) incur expenses in the performance of the contract? This is not beyond doubt, but it can be concluded that the incurring of some expenditure was, or should have been, within K's reasonable contemplation. Furthermore if K could have been expected to contemplate the *type* of loss that would be incurred, it is no answer for him to say that he could not have contemplated the *extent* of that loss: *H Parsons (Livestock) Ltd v Uttley, Ingham & Co Ltd* (1978).

Applying these principles to the present facts it appears that K should have contemplated that an offeree would incur travelling expenses in recovering the cat. He might not have contemplated the extent of L's expenses – a return ticket costing £76 – but this does not avail him. In consequence L is entitled to recover for this expenditure.

L would have difficulty, however, in recovering the amount of his hotel bill. This appears to be too remote. It could not have been within the reasonable contemplation of K that an offeree would stay at a hotel. Moreover, by staying at the hotel for five days, L has unnecessarily increased his loss, contrary to the rule of the common law requiring him to mitigate such loss.

The remaining point to consider is the action of K in snatching the cat from L's garden, and the costs L incurred in feeding the cat.

By removing the cat K has effected the return of the cat, albeit by improper means, a return which was made possible by L having found it. This can be construed as acceptance of the return by L. In this event the condition for the payment of the reward has been fulfilled and L is entitled to payment of the £2,000. He would not then, of course be entitled to the expenses previously allowed. A plaintiff is entitled to reliance loss or expectation loss, but not both. But in wrongfully refusing payment when L took the cat to his address K was in breach of contract, and it would appear that the costs incurred in feeding the cat were a necessary expenditure, for which L is entitled to be compensated.

# 2 CONSIDERATION

2.1 Introduction

2.2 Key points

2.3 Analysis of questions

2.4 Questions

## 2.1 Introduction

Although the authorities speak of a doctrine of consideration, this is perhaps something of a misdescription. There is no one, cohesive, theory, indeed there are certain conflicting ideas underlying the doctrine. Safer to say, perhaps, that the courts have evolved a series of rules to attempt to define the concept of consideration.

Definitions abound, the one most commonly quoted in *Currie* v *Misa* (1875) in which valuable consideration is defined as: 'some right, interest, profit or benefit accruing to the one party or some forbearance, detriment, loss or responsibility, given suffered or undertaken by the other' seems to be the one most students remember.

Despite criticisms, the reciprocality of consideration, the benefit/detriment aspect is well worth stressing. In almost every straightforward commercial transaction this will exist. What *should* be remembered is that in one or two cases the benefit/detriment factor will exist, but, in the eyes of the law there will be no legal consideration.

There are a number of different forms of consideration capable of existing, the two most common legitimate forms being executed consideration (which is some act or forbearance completed in return for a promise) and executory consideration (which is a promise as to some act or forbearance to be performed in the future).

It is a general principle of English law that an informal gratuitous promise is not enforceable in the courts. This is not the same thing as saying such a promise has no legal effect at all. Either the promise must be formalised by incorporating it is a deed under seal, or it must be supported by consideration.

In the key points that follow, the student is reminded, briefly, of what constitutes sufficient consideration.

## 2.2 Key points

It is important that the student understand the following:

a) *The principles governing nature and sufficiency of consideration*

There are, essentially, four basic principles governing the rules as to consideration. Each of them is so qualified by exceptions that it would be difficult to say that the principles form a consistent set of rules on their own. Additionally, especially with regard to the fourth principle, equity has to a large extent softened the harshness of the old common law rules. The four principles are:

i) Consideration must move from the promisee

There is considerable overlap between this and the doctrine of privity of contract (see Chapter 10). Bearing in mind any promise sought to be enforced in court must be supported by consideration, this rule is a logical one. Obviously the person seeking to enforce the promise must establish that he has furnished consideration.

ii) Consideration need not move to the promisor

In cases where sustaining some detriment is part of the bargain struck, the promisor will obviously suffer no direct benefit from the consideration.

iii) Past consideration is not good consideration

There are two basic problems here. The first, fairly simply dealt with, is that there is a tendency to confuse past consideration with executed consideration. If it is always remembered that executed consideration will have been given in contemplation or furtherance of a *contract already negotiated* then the confusion should be eradicated. Past consideration, however, presents another problem, that of seeming exceptions to the rule in the *Lampleigh* v *Braithwaite* type of case.

The Privy Council (in *Pao On* v *Lau Yiu Long* (1980)) made it clear that an act, performed at the promisor's behest, where both parties clearly understood that this act was to be paid for (in cash or some other way) might be considered valid consideration for any promise made subsequently. The act, the promisor's request, and his subsequently promise could all be considered part of the same implicit agreement.

iv) Consideration must be sufficient but need not be adequate

The word 'sufficient' is incapable of precise definition. The courts have, on the whole, never been much concerned with the relative values of consideration of the parties. Adequacy or otherwise is not considered important. However, the consideration had to have some value, however small, and be legally valid – hence the sufficiency requirement. The student should read, in more detail, the rules relating to sufficiency of consideration and in particular any exceptions to the standard rules as there is no space to deal with them here.

If applied literally, this principle could have harsh effects, so the old common law rules are to some extent ameliorated by equity. This is of particular importance in the case of promissory estoppel (see key point (b) below).

b) *Promissory estoppel*

The question of whether a promise to perform, or performance of, an existing duty can constitute sufficient consideration is one with which, as has been noted above, there is insufficient space to deal here. With regard to part payment of a debt in particular, in common law, the rule in *Pinnel's Case* (1602) applies: that is, part payment of a debt does not discharge the whole. So, according to common law if a creditor says he will accept £80 'in full settlement' of a £100 debt; there is nothing legally to stop him suing to recover the remaining £20 outstanding should the debtor's circumstances improve.

The doctrine of promissory estoppel has provided a means of avoiding the harsh effects of the rule in *Pinnel's Case*. It should be noted that the doctrine is essentially defensive, it does not provide a cause of action in itself.

The doctrine has its principal source in *Central London Property Trust* v *High Trees House Ltd* [1947] 1 KB 130; though in tracing its development one can see that it has its origins in certain cases from as far back as the last century. Estoppel as a concept is one familiar both to common law and equity, it is a rule whereby a person is prevented from denying the existence of facts which he himself has previously asserted. Promissory estoppel is a further development, the most basic feature of which is that, having made promises as to future conduct, the promisor will be estopped from denying the existence of such promises and will not be allowed to act inconsistently with any such assertions he may have made as to his future conduct.

There are three main requirements which must be satisfied, in order for the doctrine to apply:

i)   there should be a clear and unambiguous promise that existing legal rights will not be enforced in the future;

ii)  the debtor should have relied on that promise, altering his legal position in some way so that;

iii) it would be inequitable for the promisor to go back on his promise.

The doctrine of promissory estoppel as first explored in the *High Trees* case has been since considered in a number of recent cases. However, it should be remembered that it has been suggested that promissory estoppel is not true estoppel at all; some authorities would argue that the doctrine is more akin to the concept of waiver or forbearance. It has yet to be decisively argued whether promissory estoppel is suspensive or extinctive. The whole doctrine needs to be exhaustively examined by the House of Lords in a major case. Pending such a decision, the student should familiarise himself with the existing case law, whilst bearing in mind that the scope and validity of the doctrine of promissory estoppel remain, to some extent, uncertain.

## 2.3 Analysis of questions

A question on consideration has appeared in each one of the London University past papers considered; except, surprisingly, 1991, and in 1993 when the topic formed only a minimal part of Q5.

There is sometimes some degree of overlap, for example as between consideration and intention to create legal relations or between consideration and privity of contract, so the doctrine of consideration should not be studied in complete isolation but related to other topics in the syllabus. The questions quoted below make it clear that there is a wide range of potential subject matter for questions. Although superficially very similar and covering some common ground, there are nevertheless very diverse topics considered in each, which do not coincide. The student should make sure he answers the exact question asked, rather then simply listing all the facts he knows on consideration.

## 2.4 Questions

QUESTION ONE

Colin made the following promises:

i)  to give his daughter, Diana, £500 if she will abandon her career as a photograhic model and become a social worker;

ii) to pay his secretary, Enid £250 for having been willing to give up her lunch hour when necessary during the previous three months;

iii) to pay Fred, who has a contract with the local newsagent to deliver the newspapers in that area, £10 if he delivers the newspaper by 8 am every day for a month and puts it through a letterbox without tearing it;

iv) to give his old lawnmower to George, a neighbour, if George collects it from the garden shed.

Advise Colin to what extent, if at all, the above promises are legally binding on him.

University of London LLB Examination
(for External Students) Elements of the Law of Contract June 1985 Q2

*Skeleton Solution*

- Prima facie there is consideration on both sides but, NB intention to create legal relations.

- Past consideration; exceptions to the rule.

- Sufficient consideration; promises to perform already existing contractual duties/varying or adding to such duties.

- Conditional gift; George's collection will not necessarily be consideration.

*Suggested Solution*

i)  If Diana does become a social worker, then prima facie Colin is bound by his promise: he has made an offer to her, and by abandoning her career as a model she both accepts the offer and furnishes consideration. However, Colin may be able to avoid liability if he can persuade the court that there was no intention to create legal relations.

The traditional approach of the courts to 'family' agreements of this nature is that there is rebuttable presumption that the parties did not intend to create legal relations: *Balfour* v *Balfour* (1919). It is perfectly possible for a parent and child to enter into a binding contract, but there must be clear evidence that they intended legal consequences to flow from their agreement. Thus in *Jones* v *Padavatton* (1969) the majority of the Court of Appeal held that a mother's promise to her daughter to pay her a monthly allowance if she moved from the United States to England and read for the Bar was held to be unenforceable. At first sight, *Jones* would appear to be close to the present case. However, one point of distinction is that in *Jones* the court was heavily influenced by the vagueness of the agreement; here, by contrast, the agreement is precise and specific.

Although this distinction of fact does exist, ultimately it would be likely that the court would hold on these facts, in the context of a parent-child relationship the presumption had not been rebutted and that Colin was under no liability to Diana.

ii) Colin's promise to Enid is in return for her having given up her lunch hour in the previous three months: this immediately raises the problem of past consideration.

Because consideration is given in return for the promisor's promise and, once furnished, the promise becomes binding and irrevocable, acts done prior to the making of the promise cannot constitute good consideration. Past consideration, so it is said, is no consideration: *Roscorla* v *Thomas* (1842) and *Re McArdle* (1951). A simple application of this rule would mean that Enid had no claim against Colin.

The rule is, however, subject to a number of exceptions. The relevant one here derives from the decisions in *Lampleigh* v *Braithwaite* (1615), *Kennedy* v *Brown* (1863) and *Re Casey's Patents* (1892), and was recently affirmed and restated in *Pao On* v *Lau Yiu Long* (1980). The exception provides that an antecedent act can be good consideration for a subsequent promise where: (a) it was done at the promisor's request; (b) it was understood that the act was to be remunerated by payment or the conferment of some other benefit; and (c) the payment or benefit, if promised in advance, would have been legally enforceable.

Accordingly, if Enid can satisfy these three conditions, Colin will be liable on his promise. If she cannot, and merely gave up her lunch hour in the hope, rather than the legal expectation, of payment, Colin is not liable. On the limited facts given it is impossible to reach a conclusion one way or the other.

iii) Fred is already bound by his contract with the newsagent to deliver newspapers: the issue raised is whether by delivering the paper by 8am and not tearing it, he furnishes consideration for Colin's promise. It is submitted that Fred does furnish consideration in one of two ways. First, unless his contract with the newsagent obliges him to deliver Colin's paper by 8am, in doing so he is doing over and above his existing contractual duty: *Hartley* v *Ponsonby* (1857). The same cannot be said about not tearing the paper since this must clearly be an implied if not an express term of his contract with the newsagent.

Secondly, and more simply, as the law stands it matters not whether Fred is doing more than he is bound to do by his contract with the newsagent, or whether he is merely performing his existing contractual obligation. A succession of cases in the nineteenth century, namely *Shadwell* v *Shadwell* (1860), *Scotson* v *Pegg* (1861) and *Chichester* v *Cobb* (1866), affirmed and followed recently in *New Zealand Shipping Co Ltd* v *A M Satterthwaite and Co Ltd* (1975) and *Pao On* v *Lau Yiu Long* established that the performance of an existing contractual duty owed to a third party (as opposed to the promisor) is good consideration. It therefore follows that Fred does furnish consideration for Colin's promise and the latter is bound to honour it.

iv) It is submitted that this instance illustrates the distinction between consideration and a condition. No contract exists between Colin and George because no consideration moves from the latter to support the former's promise. The true legal analysis is that Colin is promising to make a gift of the lawnmower to George providing the latter collects it, it is a conditional gift: *Wyatt* v *Kreglinger* (1933). At any time before George collects, Colin is at liberty to revoke his promise; once George has collected, the conditional gift becomes unconditional and complete and property in the lawnmower will pass to George.

QUESTION TWO

Giles engaged Illtyd, a landscape gardener, to construct a patio and fish pond in his garden for a fixed price of £3,000. The contract provided that the work was to be completed by 30 April 1988 and that payment was to be made in stages as the work proceeded.

In order to pay Illtyd, Giles borrowed £3,000 from Peter, agreeing to repay this sum, together with interest of £720, in twenty-four equal monthly instalments.

In March, while Illtyd was excavating the ground for the pond, he uncovered an ancient cannon which he could only remove by using special lifting equipment and he informed Giles that he could only continue with the work if Giles agreed to pay an additional £500. Giles objected but agreed to pay.

Soon after this Giles was made redundant. Peter then agreed that Giles need pay only the interest of the loan until he found a new job. Although Giles is still out of work he recently received a letter from Peter demanding immediate payment of the outstanding arrears of capital and the immediate resumption of payments of instalments at the agreed rate. Illtyd is also pressing for payment of the additional £500.

Advise Giles.

University of London LLB Examination
(for External Students) Elements of the Law of Contract June 1988 Q7

*Skeleton Solution*

• Performance of an existing contractual duty is no consideration. To perform some additional duty will be sufficient consideration to support a fresh promise.
• Economic duress?
• Part payment of a debt – rule in *Pinnel's Case*.
• Promissory estoppel – operation of the equitable doctrine – relevant case law.

*Suggested Solution*

This question involves discussion of a number of issues: the rule relating to sufficiency of consideration; duress; and promissory estoppel. There are two contracts in question, one between Giles and Illtyd, the other between Giles and Peter. These two contracts will be discussed in turn.

The contract between Giles and Illtyd:

The contract between Giles and Illtyd is for the latter to perform the construction work for the fixed price of £3,000. Illtyd then discovers that certain additional work is necessary and Giles has agreed to pay an additional £500. Two matters arise:

whether there was any consideration for the promise to make the additional payment and; whether the promise to pay was exacted by duress.

The question here is whether, in continuing the work, Illtyd was performing more more than an existing contractual duty, or whether he was now performing something over and above his original contractual obligations. It may well be that Illtyd undertook, in constructing the patio and fish pond, to do whatever was necessary to complete that task, and that if the removal of the cannon was necessary, it was part of his original obligation. If Illtyd is performing no more than his existing contractual duty, there is authority for the view that this is not sufficient consideration: *Stilk* v *Myrick* (1809); *North Ocean Shipping Co* v *Hyundai Construction Co, The Atlantic Baron* (1979). The recent case of *Williams* v *Roffey Bros & Nicholls (Contractors) Ltd* (1989) makes it clear, however, that if a party to an existing contract later agrees to pay an extra bonus to ensure the contract is completed the agreement will be binding and enforceable if the promisor is obtaining some new benefit or avoiding a disadvantage.

It is also possible that Illtyd is performing some extra task, in which case there has been fresh consideration for the promise to pay the £500: *Hartley* v *Ponsonby* (1857). I shall proceed on that assumption.

If there has been fresh consideration, the further question remains as to whether the promise to pay the additional amount was obtained by duress. Illtyd threatens to break his contract with Giles unless Giles pays the additional amount. There is now substantial authority for the proposition that a threat to break a contract constitutes economic duress: *Occidental Worldwide Investment Corp* v *Skibs A/S Avanti, The Sibeon and The Sibotre* (1976); *North Ocean Shipping Co* v *Hyundai Construction Co, The Atlantic Baron* (1979); *B & S Contracts* v *Victor Green Publications Ltd* (1984). In *Pao On* v *Lau Yiu Long* (1980), Lord Scarman stated that four criteria would have to be considered in order to decide whether or not there had been economic duress. These criteria were: (i) whether the victim had protested; (ii) whether the victim had an alternative legal remedy; (iii) whether the victim had had independent legal advice; and (iv) whether he took steps to avoid the transaction, after the duress had ceased.

The effect of economic duress is that the victim can have the contract set aside and may be entitled to claim damages in tort.

It is not clear, on the facts presented, whether or not Giles could establish that he had been induced to make the promise to pay the additional amount by virtue of economic duress, having regard to the criteria set out above. However, the courts have shown increasing readiness to recognise the concept of economic duress, and if Giles can establish, in particular, that he had no choice but to submit to Illtyd's demand, then he may well succeed in establishing economic duress. See the recent case of *Atlas Express Ltd* v *Kafco (Importers and Distributors) Ltd* (1989).

The contract between Giles and Peter:

In agreeing that Giles need only pay the interest on the loan and not the instalments, Peter has promised to suspend his contractual rights. At common law Peter's promise to suspend his contractual rights is unenforceable because there has been no consideration for that promise. This common law principle laid down in *Pinnel's Case* (1602) was affirmed by the House of Lords in *Foakes* v *Beer* (1884).

The common law rule has, however, been modified by the equitable doctrine of promissory estoppel. This doctrine derives from the decision of the House of Lords in *Hughes* v *Metropolitan Railway Co* (1877). It was developed further by Denning J (as he then was) in obiter dicta in *Central London Property Trust Ltd* v *High Trees House Ltd* (1947). Although the doctrine of promissory estoppel has been criticised as being inconsistent with *Foakes* v *Beer* (above) and with *Jorden* v *Money* (1854), it has become established. It has been recognised by the House of Lords in *Tool Metal Manufacturing Co Ltd* v *Tungsten Electric Co Ltd* (1955) and by the Privy Council in *F A Ajayi* v *R T Briscoe (Nigeria) Ltd* (1964). The essence of the doctrine is that when one party to a contract promises, in the absence of fresh consideration, not to enforce his rights, an equity will be raised in favour of the other party, which will estop the party who made the promise from going back on it.

In order to determine whether the equity operates in Giles' favour certain aspects have to be considered.

a) In order for the doctrine to operate Peter must have made an unequivocal promise: *Woodhouse AC Israel Cocoa SA* v *Nigerian Produce Marketing Co* (1972). He appears to have done so.

b) The further requirement is that Giles has acted on Peter's promise. It has to be shown that there has been reliance on the promise. The balance of authority suggests that it is not necessary to show that Giles has acted to his detriment: *W J Alan & Co Ltd* v *El Nasr Export & Import Co* (1972); *Société Italo-Belge* v *Palm and Vegetable Oils, The Post Chaser* (1981). (There is a suggestion to the contrary in the obiter dicta of Nourse LJ in *Goldsworthy* v *Brickell* (1987).) It is, however, necessary for Giles to show that as a result of Peter's promise he was led to act differently from the way he would otherwise have done. It is not clear, from the present facts, whether this is so.

c) It does not appear that Peter's promise was exacted by any form of pressure as in *D & C Builders Ltd* v *Rees* (1966). It could not be suggested, therefore, that it would not be inequitable to allow Peter to resile from his promise.

d) The further aspect that has to be examined is whether Peter's promise is extinctive or merely suspensive of his rights. In *F A Ajayi* v *R T Briscoe (Nigeria) Ltd* (1964) Lord Hodson stated that the promisor can resile from his promise on giving the promisee a reasonable opportunity of resuming his position. It is only when the promisee cannot resume his former position that the promise becomes irrevocable. This suggests that when Giles finds a new job Peter can demand the resumption of the payments of the agreed instalments, on giving Giles reasonable notice to do so. There is no direct authority as to whether or not Peter would be entitled to demand immediate payment of the outstanding arrears of capital. Lord Denning has stated extra judicially that the rights to the arrear payments in *High Trees* had been extinguished. This does not mean that Peter has abandoned any portion of the capital sum due to him, but that he has promised to extend the period of repayment. He might not be able to resile from this promise.

The difficulty for Giles is to establish that he relied on Peter's promise. If he cannot do so the doctrine of promisory estoppel cannot operate in his favour. If Giles can establish reliance, he is advised that Peter cannot resile from his promise until he

(Giles) has found a new job. When Giles obtains a new job Peter can demand resumption of payment of the agreed instalments until the full capital sum has been paid off. Peter would not be able to claim immediate payment of the outstanding arrears of capital.

## QUESTION THREE

Alban's house was badly damaged by a storm in March. He engaged Bruno, a builder, to repair the damage. Bruno told Alban that the work would cost £4,000 and it would be finished by 1 May. Alban wanted to put the house up for sale in May and accepted Bruno's terms.

Bruno started work in early April, but his progress was hampered by bad weather. Two weeks later he informed Alban that he could only continue with the work if Alban agreed to raise the contract price to £5,000 to cover overtime costs. Reluctantly Alban promised to pay the new price.

Bruno then completed the repairs before the end of April and sent Alban his bill for £5,000, but Alban said that he was now in financial difficulties and could only afford to pay £3,000. Fearing that he would otherwise receive no payment at all, Bruno accepted £3,000 in full settlement.

Bruno recently learned that Alban had plans to go to Africa on safari for two months later in the year.

Advise Bruno whether he can recover the rest of the money.

University of London LLB Examination
(for External Students) Elements of the Law of Contract June 1990 Q1

*Skeleton Solution*

- Sufficiency of consideration.
- Additional payments.
- Economic duress.
- Part payment of a debt – rule in *Pinnel's Case* (1602).
- Promissory estoppel.

*Suggested Solution*

This question involves discussion of two aspects of the doctrine of consideration: *firstly*, whether there was sufficient consideration for Alban's promise to pay the new price; *secondly*, whether the doctrine of promissory estoppel would operate to prevent Bruno recovering the rest of the money.

*The sufficiency of consideration*

The original contract between Alban and Bruno provided for the repair work to be done for the sum of £4,000. Subsequently Alban agreed to the increased price of £5,000 because, it appears, that Bruno would not continue with the work unless he did so. This raises two related issues: was there sufficient consideration for the promise to pay the additional amount? and was that promise exacted by duress?

It is not clear whether the bad weather required Bruno to perform additional work over and above his original contractual obligation. If the completion of the work involved merely the performance of Bruno's existing contractual duty there is authority for the view that this does not constitute sufficient consideration: *Stilk* v *Myrick* (1809). This case was declared to be good law in *North Ocean Shipping Co Ltd* v *Hyundai Construction Co, The Altantic Baron* (1979). However, the Court of Appeal has purported to refine and limit the principle in *Stilk* v *Myrick* in the recent case of *Williams* v *Roffey Bros & Nicholls (Contractors) Ltd* (1990) in which Glidewell LJ expressed the state of the law to be as follows:

'(i) if A has entered into a contract with B to do work for, or to supply goods or services to, B in return for payment by B and (ii) at some stage before A has completely performed his obligations under the contract B has reason to doubt whether A will, or will be able to, complete his side of the bargain and (iii) B thereupon promises A an additional payment in return for A's promise to perform his contractual obligations on time and (iv) as a result of giving his promise B obtains in practice a benefit, or obviates a disbenefit, and (v) B's promise is not given as a result of economic duress or fraud on the part of A, then (vi) the benefit to B is capable of being consideration for B's promise, so that the promise will be legally binding.'

It appears from the facts presented that there is the possibility that Alban's promise to pay the additional sum might have been given as a result of economic duress on Bruno's part. There is now considerable authority to the effect that a threat to break a contract can constitute economic duress: recent case examples are: *Atlas Express Ltd* v *Kafco (Importers and Distributors) Ltd* (1989) and *Vantage Navigation Corporation* v *Suhail & Saud Bahwan Building Materials, The Alev* (1989). In *Pao On* v *Lau Yiu Long* (1980) Lord Scarman stated that the relevant factors to be considered in deciding whether a promise had been exacted by duress were: (i) whether the victim had protested; (ii) whether he had an alternative (adequate) legal remedy; (iii) whether he had acted on independent advice; and (iv) whether he had taken timeous steps to avoid the transaction.

Whilst it is not possible to completely rule out the possibility of duress, the mere fact that Alban reluctantly promised to pay the new price does not in itself indicate that there was 'coercion of his will' or that he had 'no real choice' – expressions used in many of the cases to indicate the requisite degree of compulsion. Moreover Alban does not appear to have taken steps to avoid the transaction. It is submitted, therefore, that Alban would not successfully be able to contend that he was acting under duress in promising to pay the new price. Following the decision in *Williams* v *Roffey Bros* (above) it would seem that Alban's promise is legally binding even if Bruno was performing no more than his existing contractual duty. If, by virtue of the delay, Bruno was performing work over and above his previous contractual obligation, he furnished fresh consideration, and Alban would be bound by his promise: *Hartley* v *Ponsonby* (1857).

## The doctrine of promissory estoppel

It has been argued that Alban is contractually bound to pay the price of £5,000. Even if he is successful in maintaining that the promise to pay the additional amount was exacted by duress, he is clearly obliged to pay the amount of £4,000, as Bruno has performed his obligations under the contract. It appears that Bruno has accepted the lesser sum of £3,000 'in full settlement'. At common law the payment of a lesser sum does not discharge the debtor from payment of the balance unless he has furnished some consideration for the creditor's forebearance. This principle – the rule in *Pinnel's Case* (1602) – was affirmed by the House of Lords in *Foakes* v *Beer* (1884).

This common law principle has, however, been modified by the development of the doctrine of promissory estoppel. This derives from the decision of the House of Lords in *Hughes* v *Metropolitan Railway Co* (1877) as developed by Lord Denning MR, notably in *Central London Property Trust Ltd* v *High Trees House Ltd* (1947). In delivering the judgment of the Judicial Committee of the Privy Council in *F A Ajayi* v *R T Briscoe (Nigeria) Ltd* (1964) Lord Hodson defined the doctrine as follows:

'... when one party to a contract in the absence of fresh consideration agrees not to enforce his rights an equity will be raised in favour of the other party. This equity is, however, subject to the qualifications (1) that the other party has altered his position, (2) that the promisor can resile from his promise on giving reasonable notice, which need not be a formal notice, giving the promisee reasonable opportunity of resuming his position, (3) the promise only becomes final and irrevocable if the promisee cannot resume his position.'

The doctrine of promissory estoppel has been criticised as conflicting with the decisions in *Foakes* v *Beer* (above) and *Jorden* v *Money* (1854). However, it appears to be firmly established that it can prevail as a defence, though not as a cause of action: *Combe* v *Combe* (1951).

The definition of the doctrine can be divided into four elements. (i) There must be a firm and unequivocal promise: *Woodhouse AC Israel Cocoa SA* v *Nigerian Produce Marketing Co* (1972). This requirement appears to be satisfied. (ii) The promisee must have relied on the promise. The balance of authority is to the effect that it is sufficient if the promisee has altered his position; it is not necessary for him to have done so to his detriment: see per Lord Denning MR in *W J Alan & Co Ltd* v *El Nasr Export and Import Co* (1972) and per Robert Goff J in *The Post Chaser* (1982). It is not clear to what extent Alban has relied on Bruno's promise, though Lord Denning would hold that merely paying the lesser sum constitutes sufficient reliance: see his judgment in *D & C Builders Ltd* v *Rees* (1966). (iii) It must be inequitable for the promisee to go back on his promise. Thus in *D & C Builders* Lord Denning held that the promisor could resile from a promise that had been exacted by intimidation. It may well be, on the given facts, that Alban has dishonestly represented his financial position, and that this would entitle the court to find that it would *not* be inequitable for Bruno to go back on his promise. (iv) The final element is the effect of promissory estoppel; does it extinguish or merely suspend the promisor's rights? In *Tool Metal Manufacturing Co Ltd* v *Tungsten Electric Co Ltd* (1955) the Court of Appeal found that as regards existing obligations the effect is extinctive, as regards future obligations it is suspensory. This view has also been expressed extra-judicially by Lord Denning. This would suggest that, if the doctrine operates in Alban's favour, Bruno's rights to the balance have been extinguished.

Lord Hailsham LC stated in *Woodhouse* that the cases based on promissory estoppel 'may need to be reviewed and reduced to a coherent body of doctrine by the courts'. In his Lordship's view 'they do raise problems of coherent exposition which have never been systematically explored'. In view of the uncertainty still prevailing with regard to the doctrine, it would be unwise to give Bruno any positive assurance. On the assumption, however, that Alban has been less than honest regarding his financial position, it is submitted that Bruno can recover the rest of the money.

QUESTION FOUR

The doctrine of consideration causes nothing but difficulties. It should be replaced by a doctrine of intention. What is intended should be given legal effect.

Discuss.

University of London LLB Examination
(for External Students) Elements of the Law of Contract June 1992 Q2

*Skeleton Solution*

• Definition of consideration.
• 'Invented' consideration.
• Performance of an existing duty.
• A promise to forego rights.
• Abolition of the doctrine.

*Suggested Solution*

The definition of consideration commonly referred to is that of Lush J in *Currie* v *Misa* (1875):

'A valuable consideration, in the sense of the law, may consist in some right, interest, profit or benefit accruing to one party or some forebearance, detriment, loss or responsibility, given, suffered, or undertaken by the other.'

This definition may be said to be incomplete, and perhaps a more helpful definition is:

'An act or forebearance of the one party, or the promise thereof, is the price for which the promise of the other is bought, and the promise thus given for value is enforceable.'

This is the definition given by Pollock (*Principles of Contract*, p133) and approved by Lord Dunedin in *Dunlop Pneumatic Tyre Co Ltd* v *Selfridge & Co Ltd* (1915).

It appears from the latter definition that the element of bargain is essential to the enforceability of a promise; it might be said that English law enforces bargains, not gratuitous promises unless they are made by deed. Beale, Bishop and Furmston (*Contract Cases and Materials*, 2nd ed, p119) state that the reasons for this fall into two categories, the substantive and the formal.

The main substantive reason is that a gratuitous non-reciprocal promise is not part of the economic process by which resources are moved and exchanged. The main formal reason is that consideration provides evidence of the existence and purpose of a contract (see the articles referred to by Beale, etc). Not all promises are enforceable and the doctrine of consideration provides the basis for determining which promises should carry legal sanctions for their breach. It is difficult to deny, however, that the doctrine does cause some difficulties. These include the willingness of the courts – it is suggested – to 'invent' consideration; the problems caused in connection with the performance of an existing duty; and the question of the enforceability of a promise, in the absence of consideration, to forego or suspend legal rights.

## 'Invented' consideration

Treitel (*The Law of Contract*, 8th ed, p67) observes that the element of bargain is not always present in contracts which the courts are prepared to enforce:

'[They] often regard an act or forebearance as the consideration for a promise even though it may not have been the object of the promisor to secure it. They may also regard the possibility of some prejudice to the promisee as a detriment without regard to the question whether it has in fact been suffered.'

These practices, he says, may be called 'inventing consideration'.

It is a principle of the doctrine that consideration need not be adequate. The courts are not equipped to determine the adequacy of the consideration, and the principle is a sound one. However, it is a consequence of that principle that the courts have found that a grossly disproportionate payment for a property has provided sufficient consideration: *Midland Bank & Trust Co Ltd* v *Green* (1981), and that chocolate wrappers formed part of the purchase consideration: *Chappell & Co Ltd* v *Nestle Co Ltd* (1960). It is not suggested that, in these cases, the courts invented consideration, but to regard the consideration as sufficient does appear somewhat artificial.

## Performance of an existing duty

In this context the courts have not always appeared consistent. Performance of an existing public duty has been held not to be sufficient consideration for a promise: *Collins* v *Godefroy* (1831), although Denning LJ took a different view in *Ward* v *Byham* (1956). The performance of an existing contractual duty to a third party has, however, been found to be good consideration: *New Zealand Shipping Company Ltd* v *A M Satterthwaite & Co Ltd, The Eurymedon* (1975); *Pao On* v *Lau Yiu Long* (1980).

In *Stilk* v *Myrick* (1809) the principle was established that the performance of, or the promise to perform, an existing contractual duty to the promisor did not constitute good consideration. In what appear to be the interests of commercial practice, and perhaps common sense, the Court of Appeal has modified this principle in *Williams* v *Roffey* & *Nicholls (Contractors)* Ltd (1990). The court recognised that where the promisor obtains a benefit or avoids a disbenefit by the promisee's performance of his contractual duty that could constitute good consideration for the promise.

## A promise to forego rights made in the absence of consideration

The difficulty in this area, which, it is submitted, is not completely resolved, is to reconcile the decision in *Foakes* v *Beer* (1884) with the equitable principle of promissory estoppel based on the cases beginning with *Central London Property Trust Ltd* v *High Trees House Ltd* (1947). The common law principle is clear that a promise to forego legal rights is unenforceable where no consideration has been furnished for that promise. The desirability for certainty in the law demands adherence to that principle. But it seems less than just that a promisor can resile from a promise deliberately made where the promisee has relied on that promise. The reconciliation of these principles remains to receive systematic treatment.

But despite the difficulties attending the doctrine of consideration it is embedded in English law and serves the essential function of determining what promises should be enforced. Atiyah (*Essays on Contract* p240 et seq) argues that to talk of the abolition of the doctrine of consideration is nonsensical. Consideration means the reason for the enforcement of a promise. It cannot be suggested that all promises should be enforceable and to abolish consideration would require the courts to find new reasons for enforcement.

The suggestion that 'What is intended should be given legal effect' means that the consideration should be replaced by the formula of intention to create legal relations. But, as Atiyah states, it is questionable whether this formula would in the long run work any better than the rules of consideration.

QUESTION FIVE

The concept of so-called promissory estoppel has a dubious pedigree ... moreover, it is in practice almost totally unnecessary.'

Discuss.

University of London LLB Examination
(for External Students) Elements of the Law of Contract June 1993 Q7

*Skeleton Solution*

- The common law rule as to part payment.
- The origin of the doctrine – *Hughes* v *Metropolitan Railway Co* (1877).
- The development in *High Trees* (1947).
- Subsequent developments – the operation of the doctrine.
- Alternative legal concepts.

*Suggested Solution*

The common law rule is that payment of a lesser sum is no discharge of a greater sum: *Pinnel's Case* (1605); *Foakes* v *Beer* (1884). The reason behind this rule is that a promise to accept the lesser sum is unenforceable unless it is supported by fresh consideration. But, it was the view of Lord Denning MR in *D & C Builders Ltd* v *Rees* (1966) that:

'The harshness of the common law has been relieved. Equity has stretched out a merciful hand to help the debtor.'

Lord Denning was referring to the mitigation of the common law rule by the equitable doctrine of promissory estoppel.

The doctrine derives from the statement of the equitable principle by Lord Cairns LC in the House of Lords in *Hughes* v *Metropolitan Railway Co* (1877) that where the parties have entered into a course of negotiations, which has the effect of leading one of the parties to believe that the strict rights arising under the contract will not be enforced, or will be suspended, the person who might otherwise have enforced those rights will not be allowed to enforce them where it would be inequitable to allow him to do so. Lord Cairns did not cite any authority in support of this principle.

*Hughes* v *Metropolitan Ry* was decided in the context of a landlord and tenant relationship in connection with the forfeiture of a lease. The principle there enunciated was extended beyond this context in *Birmingham and District Land Co* v *London & NW Railway* (1888). In both these cases the effect of this principle of equitable estoppel was held to be merely suspensive of rights, and no mention was made of promissory estoppel. The decision in *Jorden* v *Money* (1854), below, was not quoted.

The principle was developed by Denning J (as he then was) in *Central London Property Trust Ltd* v *High Trees House Ltd* (1947) into the modern doctrine of promissory estoppel. The effect of this development was to establish the principle that if a creditor promised to accept a lesser sum in satisfaction of a larger sum, this promise would suspend, or even extinguish, the creditor's rights to claim the balance.

This principle appeared to be in conflict with *Foakes* v *Beer* (above) and with the earlier House of Lords' decision in *Jorden* v *Money*. In the latter case Mrs Jorden had promised not to enforce a claim against Money. This promise was not supported by consideration, but it was argued that, having made this representation, she could not, in equity, resile from it. Lord Cranworth LC held that the equitable principle applied to representations of existing fact, and not to representations of future conduct.

Denning J in *High Trees* overcame these authorities by finding that the House of Lords in *Foakes* v *Beer* had not considered the equitable principle and that Mrs Jorden had not clearly promised not to enforce the claim.

Despite this perhaps 'dubious pedigree' the doctrine of promissory estoppel has received a measure of recognition by the courts, though with limited effect and with remaining areas of uncertainty.

The effect of the doctrine was limited in *Combe* v *Combe* (1951) where the Court of Appeal, which included Denning LJ, held that the principle of promissory estoppel did not create new causes of action where none existed before: it only served to prevent a party from enforcing his legal rights where it would be inequitable to allow him to do so. What is implicit in this decision is that for the doctrine to operate there must be a pre-existing legal relationship between the parties: this view has been challenged by the High Court of Australia in *Walton Stores (Interstate) Ltd* v *Maher* (1988).

At the risk of repetition, it is useful at this point to formulate the principle in precise terms. In the words of Lord Hodson in *F A Ajayi* v *R T Briscoe (Nigeria) Ltd* (1964):

'The principle, which has been described as quasi estoppel and perhaps more aptly as promissory estoppel, is that when one party to a contract in the absence of fresh consideration agrees not to enforce his rights, an equity will be raised in favour of the other party. This equity is, however, subject to the qualification (a) that the other party has altered his position, (b) that the promisor can resile from his promise on giving reasonable notice, which need not be formal notice, giving the promisee a reasonable opportunity of resuming his position, and (c) the promise only becomes final and irrevocable if the promisee cannot resume his position.'

The first qualification is that 'the other party has altered his position'. It is not beyond doubt what this entails. There are obiter statements to the effect that all that is required is that the promisee acts on the promise, in the sense that he does something he would not otherwise have done; it is not necessary for him to have acted to his detriment: Lord Denning in *W J Alan & Co Ltd* v *El Nasr Export and Import Co* (1972); Robert Goff J in *Société Italo-Belge etc* v *Palm and Vegetable Oils etc, The Post Chaser*, (1982). In *Goldsworthy* v *Brickell* (1987), however, Nourse LJ expressed the view, also obiter, that for promissory estoppel to operate the promisee must be shown to have acted to his detriment.

This, then, is one area of uncertainty. Another relates to the effect of promissory estoppel having in mind the further qualifications in Lord Hodson's formulation: does the promise merely suspend the promisor's rights or can it extinguish them?

It seems clear from *Hughes* v *Metropolitan Ry* that the effect of the estoppel there being considered was merely to suspend the landlord's rights. There is no decisive authority in our law that the effect can be extinctive. It was held to be so by a New Zealand court in *P* v *P* (1957). Lord Denning held that the landlord's rights to the arrear rentals had been permanently extinguished in *High Trees*, but this finding was not necessary for the actual decision in that case. Lord Denning has also expressed the view that the estoppel could be final and permanent in *D & C Builders Ltd* v *Rees* and *Alan* v *El Nasr*, but these findings were again obiter.

Whilst the doctrine of promissory estoppel has been recognised in a number of cases there is no clear case in which it has been unequivocally applied. In the Court of Appeal in *Tool Metal Manufacturing Co Ltd* v *Tungsten Electric Co Ltd* (1955) it was applied only to the extent of holding that the promisor could resile from the particular promise on giving reasonable notice. The decision in the House of Lords subsequently was confined to the question of whether the delivery of a counter-claim constituted reasonable notice. Their Lordships did not consider the correctness of the Court of Appeal's decision.

In the other cases previously mentioned in this answer the doctrine has been held either not to apply, or where Lord Denning has applied it, the other members of the Court of Appeal have based their decision on different grounds.

The view that the concept of promissory estoppel 'is in practice almost totally unnecessary' is further supported by a consideration of the judgments in the Court of Appeal in *Brikom Investments Ltd* v *Carr* (1979). The landlords in that case had made oral representations to the tenants that they would repair the roofs at their own expense. The leases which were subsequently signed provided that the tenants would contribute to these costs. All three members of the Court of Appeal held that the landlords' representations amounted to a collateral contract. But the main ground on which Lord Denning based his judgment was that the tenants could rely on promissory estoppel. Roskill LJ, with whom Cumming-Bruce LJ agreed, refused to decide the case on promissory estoppel. He held that in addition to the collateral contract the tenants were protected by 'a plain waiver by the landlords of their right to claim the cost of these repairs from these tenants.'

It can be argued therefore that, not only is the concept of promissory estoppel questionable as to its origin, but that it is uncertain in its operation and the desired result can be attained by the application of other, less controversial, legal concepts.

# 3 CERTAINTY AND FORM OF THE CONTRACT

3.1 Introduction

3.2 Key points

3.3 Analysis of questions

3.4 Question

## 3.1 Introduction

It has already been noted in Chapter 1, that if some condition and/or reservation is made by one of the parties, or if there is an essential term yet to be agreed, there will be no binding contract. One of the first rules of contract is that incompleteness will negate agreement. But if the parties' agreement is complete and full, the mere fact that the contract has not been set down fully in writing is not necessarily a bar to its validity.

If a contract is so vague that little or no sense can be made of it, the contract will be considered invalid for lack of certainty. However, it should be remembered that sometimes the parties will not bother to spell out every term, because the trade or profession to which they both belong traditionally implies certain terms into every contract. When the normal trade usages are taken into account the contract may make perfect sense. See for example, the recent Scottish case of *Neilson* v *Stewart* (1991).

Merely because some part of the contract appears meaningless does not necessarily invalidate the whole. It may be possible still to enforce the contract, as envisaged by the parties, while ignoring the ambiguity.

In some cases statutes will imply automatically, certain terms into a contract. In the case of some legislation the parties will have the option of excluding the term(s) implied; in others the legislation will impose strict liability. Finally, it should be borne in mind that no court will write the contract for the parties and impose terms on them regardless. They will imply only such terms as seem essential in order to give effect to the parties' obvious intentions.

With regard to form of the contract, the basic rule is that a contract can be made in any form whatever; bearing in mind, of course, that a purely verbal contract may be much more difficult to enforce than a written one; because of the purely practical problem of proof.

Exceptions: cases in which the contract must be in some particular form are listed below in the key points. Almost without exception, these exceptions to the common law rules are imposed by statute.

## 3.2 Key points

It is important that the student understand the following:

a) *Specific contracts required to be in writing*

A motley assortment of contracts are required by particular Acts to be in written form. They include:

i) bills of exchange and promissory notes (Bills of Exchange Act 1882);

ii) regulated consumer credit agreements, including hire purchase (Consumer Credit Act 1974);

iii) contracts of marine insurance must be written in the form of a policy (Marine Insurance Act 1906); and

iv) bills of sale must be in writing, in statutory form (Bills of Sale Act (1878) Amendment Act 1882).

b) *Contracts of guarantee*

The original definition in the Statute of Frauds 1677 was: 'a special promise to answer for the debt, default or miscarriage of another person'.

i) there must be three parties:

A – creditor

B – debtor

C – guarantor;

ii) there must be pre-existing liability between A and B which will usually be contractual but may be tortious; and

iii) there must be a promise made by C to A that C will assume B's liability if, *and only if*, B's debts are dishonoured.

Such contracts are not legally enforceable unless evidenced in writing. That is, there must be some written note or memorandum proving the contract's existence and its terms.

The statute has been construed consistently in a very stringent way, and, in particular, certain types of agreement very similar to contracts of guarantee have been held to fall outside the application of the Statute. These include, especially, contracts of indemnity and contracts where the guarantee is merely an incidental part of a much larger transaction. In the case of these, other similar agreements, the Statute will not apply and there is therefore no need for such agreements to be evidenced in writing. The student should familiarise himself with the relevant case law on this topic as lack of space precludes dealing with it here.

c) *Contracts for the sale of land*

All contracts for the sale or other disposition of land, or interests in land, should theoretically be in writing. For some considerable time the effect of s40 LPA 1925 was to lessen the effect of this strict rule by providing that if the contract was merely evidenced in writing it would be enforceable at law.

As from 27 September 1989 the Law of Property (Miscellaneous Provisions) Act 1989 repealed s40 of the 1925 Act. As a result a memorandum or note will again, as it was before 1925, be insufficient to found an action. The effect of this new legislation will again be that a contract for sale of land must be in writing, signed by both parties, and the written contract must be a full one, containing all the terms agreed on.

By the same token the doctrine of part performance will no longer be relevant in this context. For the record, as it were, it is worth noting that the phrase 'note or memorandum' has been over the past 60 years or so, the subject of exhaustive exploration by the courts. There is a wealth of case law on the subject with which the student should be familiar, because they may still have a bearing on existing contracts for some considerable time to come.

## 3.3 Analysis of questions

Questions on certainty and form of contract have not been the subject of many examination questions, either separately or together. Obviously there is a considerable amount of overlap with other areas here, where the topic might be combined with others.

Certainty for example, or lack of it, might occur in a question as to intention to create legal relationships, essence of agreement, or indeed contractual terms, whether express or implied. Formalities of a contract might be usefully combined with almost any other topic on formation of contract. (See for example Q3 of the 1992 paper, quoted in Chapter 1.)

## 3.4 Question

a) Discuss the ways in which the Law of Property (Miscellaneous Provisions) Act 1989 has changed the law with regard to sales or other dispositions of land.

(18 marks)

b) To what other contracts do special rules apply?

(7 marks)

Written by Editor

*Skeleton Solution*

a) • Old law under s40 LPA 1925.

    • Sufficient note or memorandum.

    • Doctrine of part performance.

    • Requirements of ss1–3 LP(MP)A 1989.

    • Changes.

    • Constructive trusts/proprietory estoppel.

b) • Statutes that require special form of contract.

    • Contracts of guarantee.

    • Statute of Frauds.

*Suggested Solution*

a) In general the law only requires a particular form of contract, when it is considered that the contract is of such importance that the parties need special proteciton.

The Law of Property Act (LPA) 1925, for example, made a number of provisions: ss52 and 54 require that any conveyance of a legal estate in land be in the form of a deed. Similarly a deed is required to create a lease of more than three years.

Originally, s40 LPA 1925 required that *all* contracts for the sale or other dispositon of land (with certain exceptions) had to be evidenced in writing. This might mean that the contract was written and signed in its entirety; but also it might simply mean that written evidence should exist, sufficient to prove to a court's satisfaction, both the existence and the terms of the contract.

This note or 'memorandum' was not defined by the Act. It was required purely for evidential reasons and the actual form it took was relatively unimportant. It might therefore consist of one document or several, provided that if there was more than one document there was sufficient cross referencing to establish that the documents belonged together as a group. Furthermore the documents need not have been deliberately prepared for the purpose of providing a note or memorandum (see *Law* v *Jones* (1974) and *Tiverton Estates* v *Wearwell* (1975)) provided the documents provided adequate identification of the parties, the property in question, the nature of the consideration provided and reference to any other terms deemed material by the parties. Section 40 required that the note or memorandum be signed by the party to be charged, and the burden of proof in establishing the existence and sufficiency of the memorandum is of course on the person seeking to rely on it. Probably *Timmins* v *Moreland Street Property* (1958) best sets out the criteria to be fulfilled in establishing that an adequate memorandum exists which would fulfil the requirements of s40 LPA.

Despite the flexibility of s40 requirements, there were still many instances when because of the lack of a written contract or written evidence of a contract, a party would be left remediless. To alleviate the harshness of the rule the doctrine of part performance was introduced by equity. The concept of part performance is based on a situation where one party in reliance of an oral contract, partly or wholly performed his side of the contract. In such circumstances it would be inequitable to allow the other party to escape from his obligations; it would be a fraud to allow the defaulting party to rely on s40. When it was first introduced, the doctrine was applied strictly, as in *Maddison* v *Alderson* (1883) but of recent years the approach of the courts has been more relaxed (see, for example, *Wakeham* v *McKenzie* (1968) and *Steadman* v *Steadman* (1976)).

The 'note or memorandum rule' and the doctrine of part performance will cease to have any relevance after the changes brought about by the 1989 Act. Part performance, it should be noted, has not been specifically abolished, but it will presumably simply cease to serve any useful purpose after a time. It should be remembered that, for a time, there is still a possibility that disputes concerning contracts made pre-1989 may come before the courts; in which case they will, of course, be assessed under the old law.

Section 2(1) of the Law of Property (Miscellaneous Provisions) Act 1989 provides that as from September 1989 a contract for sale or disposition of an interest in land must be in writing, contain all the terms as agreed by the parties and be signed by both of them. Section 2(2) does however allow some or all of the terms to be incorporated into another document, provided it is specifically referred to in the main signed contract.

There are certain exceptions, the main one being leases of less than three years, but the overall effect of the Act will be to require a full, written signed contract, incorporating all terms.

So far it is not yet known what will happen if the formalities are not complied with – cases have yet to come before the courts. It has been suggested that a doctrine of proprietory estoppel, or possibly some form of constructive trust, may replace part performance; or even that part performance (in some new form) may return.

Section 1 LP(MP)A 1989 came into force on 31 July 1990 and abolishes previous rules as to the making of deeds. Section 1 abolishes the requirement of sealing, for individuals, substituting instead a requirement for signature and attestation. Also, s1 introduces a new criterion that it should be clear on the face of it that the document is intended to be a deed. The old rule that deeds must be on paper or parchment is abolished by s1.

b) Special rules apply to certain contracts that are required statutorily to take some particular form. For example, the following contracts must be in writing: bills of exchange and promissory notes (Bills of Exchange Act 1882); bills of sale (Bills of Sale Act (1878) Amendment Act 1882); contracts of marine insurance (Marine Insurance Act 1906); hire purchase and other regulated sales (Consumer Credit Act 1974).

Additionally, it should be remembered that the 1677 Statute of Frauds requires that contracts of guarantee must be 'evidenced' in writing, that is, even though the contract is not itself in writing, there must be some 'note or memorandum' establishing the existence of and exact terms of the guarantee. It is not proposed in this brief answer to enter into a discussion of what constitutes a guarantee contract (as opposed, say, to a contract of indemnity: *Birkmyr* v *Darnell* (1704)) but obviously without such written evidence a contract of guarantee will not be enforceable in the courts.

# 4   CONTENTS OF THE CONTRACT

4.1   Introduction

4.2   Key points

4.3   Analysis of questions

4.4   Questions

## 4.1 Introduction

To define the nature and scope of the parties' obligations under a contract, several issues need to be covered. The first question is whether any statement made during the course of negotiations, whether oral or in writing, forms part of the agreement and constitutes a term of the contract. Having determined the terms of the contract the next step is to assess the relative importance of those terms. That is: will a breach of a particular term constitute a fundamental breach of contract? This factor is obviously of crucial importance in the context of remedies available to the injured party. Finally it should be remembered, that as mentioned briefly earlier on, terms may be implied into a contract, either by statute or by virtue of trade usage or customs. In such a case it may be that the parties never mention such implied terms in the course of their negotiations at all.

In the key points that follow, the major classifications of terms will be explored a little further.

## 4.2 Key points

It is important that the student understand the following:

a) *The distinction between terms and mere representations*

It has already been noted that, in the course of negotiating a contract each party may make a number of statements, that may be either verbal or written. The exact status of these statements is crucial, because it is this that determines the remedies available should the statement prove false or a promise implied in a statement subsequently be broken.

Leaving aside wild advertising claims and similar 'trade puffs', such statements will in the end usually fit into one of three categories:

i)   a term of the contract which if broken will allow a remedy for breach;

ii)  a mere representation, which if false will not give rise to an action for breach of contract, but may allow a remedy for misrepresentation; or

iii) a collateral contract.

In ascertaining the parties' intentions the courts will take into account a variety of factors including:

i)   the importance of the statement, especially to the injured party;

ii) whether the party making the statement had some special skill or knowledge compared to the other; the relative capability of one party to know the truth of the statement;

iii) was the contract written up after the statement was made and was the statement incorporated into the written version?

iv) the interval between making the statement and concluding the contract. While this is not absolutely decisive, the earlier in the process of negotiation a statement is made the more likely it is that the courts will treat it as a mere representation.

(For further details on representations, see Chapter 5 on misrepresentation, following.)

b) *Collateral contracts*

Even if a promise is not a term of the main contract, it may still be possible to enforce it separately as a collateral contract.

c) *Conditions and warranties*

Once a statement is defined as a term of the contract, it is possible to progress further and enquire whether the term is a condition or a warranty. Of recent years, in addition to the classic division between conditions and warranties, a third category has appeared on the scene: the intermediate or innominate term.

The most important distinction is between those terms which impose obligations, breach of which would entitle the injured party to claim redress for total failure of the contract and to repudiate the contract (conditions), and those which impose obligations which if broken merely entitle the injured party to claim damages (warranties).

In addition to the classic division between conditions and warranties, there is a possible third category called an intermediate or innominate term (the names are interchangeable). The main difference between this and the other two is usually thought to be the fact that it is not necessarily certain at the outset of the contract whether breach of an innominate term will entitle the injured party to repudiate the contract. Generally a term is most likely to be innominate when it is capable of being breached in both a very minor or very serious way. Thus since classification requires examination of consequences of breach, it is impossible to assess the severity of the breach until it actually happens.

d) *Express and implied terms*

It has already been noted in Chapter 3, that while some contracts are fully detailed, spelling out every detail expressly, others are very vague relying largely on terms implied by virtue of statute, custom or trade usage, for full effectiveness.

Even where the parties incorporate terms expressly, ambiguities may still arise and the courts may be called on to decide exactly what the terms of the contract are. As explained earlier, no court will write the contract for the parties, simply imposing new terms out of the blue. Rather they will seek to give effect to the parties' intentions as expressed in the dealings between them. To this end a complex series of rules have evolved which may loosely be summed up as the 'parol evidence rules'. Very briefly this means that evidence of the parties' intentions must be sought in the document (if there is one) and not from any extraneous source. There are, however, numerous exceptions and the student should make himself familiar, not only with the basic rules of law as to interpretation of contracts, but the parol evidence rule specifically (and its exceptions).

As to implicit terms some doubt has arisen as to whether implication of terms into a contract is a question of fact or law. The major authorities now take the view that where a contract is silent as to a particular matter and the courts imply such terms as they feel necessary to give effective working to the parties' intentions, this is a question of fact. In cases where the parties' dealing places them in a particular relationship, where legislation or trade customs apply, then implication of such statutory or customary terms will be a question of law.

## 4.3 Analysis of questions

Inevitably, the initial problem, that of classifying contractual obligations into terms of the contract or mere representations, overlaps with the topic of misrepresentation on which there are a large assortment of questions (see Chapter 5). Therefore, it is not uncommon in tackling a question which is predominantly on misrepresentation to have to spend an initial paragraph explaining how a mere representation may be distinguished from a term.

Three fairly typical questions appear below. While the central issue of categorising terms and identifying conditions, warranties or innominate terms is common to all, a rather different approach is required in each. The student must beware of simply repeating all the information available on the topic, without bothering to ascertain just what it is the examiner requires in the answer.

## 4.4 Questions

QUESTION ONE

J made a contract with K, a builder, for K to build an extension to J's house for a price of £8,000 to be paid on completion. The contract stated: 'It is a condition of this contract that all work will be performed with proper skill and care and that the house will remain habitable throughout the period of the works.'

The work was estimated to take six weeks to complete. Two weeks after work started J learned that other local builders would have done the same job for £6,000. A week after that L, a labourer employed by K, carelessly fractured a water pipe: the house was flooded and J and his family were forced to leave it for three days.

J hereupon informed K that he regarded the contract as cancelled, but K wishes to complete the job.

Advise K.

University of London LLB Examination
(for External Students) Elements of the Law of Contract June 1986 Q3

*Skeleton Solution*

- Express term(s).
- Orthodox classification into conditions and warranties.
- Parties' intentions; terminology used not conclusive.
- Innominate/intermediate terms.
- Implied term(s).
- Repudiation of contract; other remedies.

*Suggested Solution*

It is clear in this problem that the action of K's employee constitutes a breach by K of an express term of his contract with J. The question for determination is the importance of that term, that is whether the breach entitles J to treat the contract as repudiated, or whether it merely entitles J to a claim for damages.

It is therefore necessary to analyse the relative importance of contractual terms. Traditionally terms were classified as conditions and warranties, a condition being a term of such importance that any breach of it, no matter how trivial, entitled the innocent party to accept the breach and treat the contract as terminated; a warranty being a term collateral to the main purposes of the contract, the breach of which entitles the innocent party to a claim for damages but not to treat the contract as repudiated. Comparatively recently a third category of terms has been recognised by the courts – innominate or intermediate terms. In the *Hongkong Fir Shipping* case (1962) the Court of Appeal, particularly in the judgment of Diplock LJ, characterised certain contractual undertakings as being of a complex nature, which did not fit into the conventional categories of conditions and warranties. All that could be predicated of such contractual undertakings was that some breaches would and others would not deprive the innocent party of the substantial benefit of the contract. In these circumstances, in the absence of express provision in the contract, the legal consequences of the breach had to be examined in the light of the event to which the breach gave rise. The notion of the innominate term was accepted by a later Court of Appeal in *Cehave* v *Bremer* (1976) and by the House of Lords in *Reardon Smith Line* v *Hansen-Tangen* (1976).

What is paramount is the intention of the parties. If the parties clearly intend to classify the term as a condition the court will give effect to that intention. What has to be examined is the contract in the light of the surrounding circumstances: *Bentsen* v *Taylor, Sons & Co* (1893), and the intention is to be ascertained at the time the parties entered into the agreement: *The Mihalis Angelos* (1971).

Reverting to the present problem we are told that the contract describes the relevant term as a 'condition'. The use of this word is, however, not necessarily conclusive. The court will have to be satisfied that the parties intended to use the term 'condition' in the technical sense of the word; if not the court may disregard the label and examine the substance of the clause in order to determine its true nature. In *Schuler* v *Wickman Machine Tool Sales Ltd* (1974) one clause of the agreement was described as a 'condition' and was the only clause bearing this description. By a 4:1 majority the House of Lords held, that in the context of the agreement as a whole the clause could not be construed as a condition. The contract as a whole between J and K is not before us so it cannot be stated categorically that the parties intended to use the word 'condition' in its technical sense. It is arguable that they did not, as the clause in question is capable of breach in a minor or trivial manner which the parties could not have envisaged as entitling J to treat the contract as repudiated.

In *Bunge Corporation* v *Tradax* (1981) Lord Wilberforce made it clear that the time for determining whether a particular term was to be treated as a condition was at the time of contracting. His Lordship also recognised that the courts should not be too ready to interpret contractual clauses as conditions, but should not be reluctant to do so if the intentions of the parties, as shown by the contract, so indicated.

It is submitted that there are two provisions contained in the clause under discussion. The first is the obligation on K to perform the work with proper skill and care and the second is the obligation to ensure that the house remains habitable throughout the period of the works. It may be difficult to attribute the force of a condition to the first obligation in view of the possibility of breaches of this obligation being of a trivial nature. It should be observed that even if the obligation to perform with proper skill and care were not expressly provided for in the contract such a term would be implied. This implied term in contracts for the supply of services was recognised by the common law, see for example *Samuels* v *Davis* (1943); *Greaves & Co (Contractors) Ltd* v *Baynham Meikle and Partners* (1975). This common law implied term has been enshrined in statute in the Supply of Goods and Services Act 1982 (s13). It is to be noted that this statute does not specify whether this implied term is a condition or a warranty.

Whilst, for the reasons given, the court may be reluctant to construe the first obligation as a condition, it can be argued with some confidence that the requirement to maintain the house in a habitable state throughout the works was intended to be a condition, and that this intention was made manifest at the time the contract was concluded. In my view, therefore, J's later discovery that the work could have been done cheaper whilst possibly a motivating factor in his seeking to rely on the clause, is not relevant to the question of intention.

K should therefore be advised that J is entitled to accept his (K's) breach as a repudiation of the contract which J is accordingly entitled to terminate.

QUESTION TWO

'The nineteenth century distinction between "conditions" and "warranties" has given way to a more flexible text.'

(Anson's Law of Contract.)

Consider in the light of the existing case law.

University of London LLB Examination
(for External Students) Elements of the Law of Contract June 1987 Q3

*Skeleton Solution*

• Classification into conditions/warranties was the orthodox division. Apparently nineteenth century lawyers recognised no other.

• Appearance of innominate term: *Hongkong Fir* case (1962).

- Earlier case law reflects development leading up to *Hongkong Fir* shows concept of something like innominate term had appeared a lot earlier.
- Classifications possible now – definitions.
- Is there more flexibility – is Anson correct?

*Suggested Solution*

First it is necessary to define the subject matter of this answer. The distinction referred to between conditions and warranties is the apparent approach of nineteenth century contract lawyers to the classification of contractual terms. They appear generally (the reason for their qualification is given later in this answer) to have regarded the categories of conditions and warranties as being exhaustive: a contractual term had to be either one or the other. It is clear now, however, that English law recognises not two but three different types of terms: conditions, warranties and innominate terms (sometimes called intermediate stipulations).

A condition may be defined as a term, any breach of which entitles the innocent party not only to recover damages but also to terminate the contract if he so chooses, irrespective of the consequences of the breach. The right to terminate, which is an option not an obligation, arises because of the nature of the term broken, not because of the consequences which flow from the breach: *Hongkong Fir Shipping* v *Kawasaki Kisen Kaisha* (1962); *Bunge* v *Tradax* (1981); and *Lombard North Central* v *Butterworth* (1987).

An innominate term is a term, a breach of which entitles the innocent party to recover damages and may, in addition, entitle him to terminate the contract. The right to terminate is not always available, as with a condition, but only where the actual and prospective consequences of the breach are such as to deprive the innocent party of substantially the whole of the benefit of the consideration he bargained to receive under the contract (in short, where the breach goes to the root of the contract): *Hongkong Fir Shipping* v *Kawasaki Kisen Kaisha* (1962). Thus in the case of an innominate term, the existence of the right to terminate depends upon the severity of the consequences of the breach.

A warranty is a term, any breach of which is remediable in damages only: *Bettini* v *Gye* (1876). It would appear that no matter how serious the breach or its consequences, if the term broken is only a warranty then there is never a right to terminate the contract. Although this may seem harsh at first sight, to hold otherwise would so blur the distinction between innominate terms and warranties as to render it unworkable.

The reason for the qualifying remarks at the beginning of this answer can now be stated. Although this threefold classification of contractual terms has been accepted and applied in practice since *Hongkong Fir Shipping* v *Kawasaki Kisen Kaisha* (1962) in 1962, it has been suggested in some of the cases that innominate terms were recognised in earlier decisions in the twentieth century and in the nineteenth century too. The Court of Appeal made this point very forcibly in *Cehave* v *Bremer* (1976) and in *Bunge* v *Tradax* (1981) the House of Lords expressed similar views. For example Lord Scarman spoke of innominate terms being 'rediscovered' in *Hongkong Fir Shipping* v *Kawasaki Kisen Kaisha* (1962) but of always having been part of English law.

If these views be accepted, then Anson is wrong to suggest that a twofold classification only existed in the last century. However it is fair to say that even if innominate terms were known to English law before 1962, they were largely (though perhaps not entirely) overlooked by both judges and academics alike.

The threefold classification is in any event now established. Taken out of context, though, Anson's proposition could be read as meaning that the classification of terms (albeit into three rather than two categories) is no longer important. It is respectfully submitted that this is not so, nor did the editor of Anson intend so to suggest.

The classification of terms is important. For the parties to know their legal rights and liabilities, the nature of the term is crucial, particularly as regards the availability or otherwise of the rights of termination. Further, the character of all terms is ascertainable at the moment the contract is concluded. Nothing that happens after its formation can alter the status of a term, although in the case of an innominate term it will determine the availability of the right of termination. To hold otherwise would lead to unacceptable uncertainty: a contract term cannot have a status capable of changing from one day to the next.

The flexibility to which Anson refers is introduced into the law by the innominate term. Instead of saying that the innocent can, in the case of a condition, always terminate, or in the case of warranty, never terminate is manifestly inflexible. Innominate terms allow the courts to permit termination where the circumstances justify it and the consequences are sufficiently serious. It is for this reason that innominate terms were regarded with obvious favour in cases such as *Hongkong Fir Shipping* v *Kawasaki Kisen Kaisha* (1962); *Cehave* v *Bremer* (1976); *Schuler* v *Wickman Machine Tool* (1974) and *Reardon Smith* v *Hansen-Tangen* (1976).

Nevertheless innominate terms are only one of the three categories and the other two cannot be ignored. It may be, for example, that the term in question is expressly designated a condition as a warranty by statute, such as the Sale of Goods Act 1979, or has already been judicially classified, as was the case in *The Mihalis Angelos* (1970). Further, it is open to the parties themselves expressly to classify the term, in which case providing their intention is clear the courts will give effect to it: *The Chikuma* (1981) and *Lombard North Central* v *Butterworth* (1987). Lastly the courts may be of the view that the parties must have intended the term to be a condition, even though they did not bother so to call it. The most obvious examples here are stipulations as to time in mercantile contracts: *United Scientific Holdings* v *Burnley BC* (1978) and *Bunge* v *Tradax* (1981). In all these cases, there is no flexibility. The right to terminate for breach (or not, in the case of warranty) follows on from the classification of the term.

In conclusion, whilst Anson is right to suggest that there is now greater flexibility in this area of the law, the distinction between the different types of contractual terms remains of considerable importance.

QUESTION THREE

Xavier manufactures photocopying machines designed for customers with special requirements. It is his practice not to sell the machines, but to lease them to customers. His standard leasing contract contains the following provisions:

1) Punctual payment of the agreed monthly rent is deemed to be of the essence of the contract.

2) It is a condition of the contract that the lessee will disconnect the power supply to the machine at the close of business each day.

3) The lessee will notify Xavier immediately of any fault in the machine and will not permit repairs to be carried out by another person other than Xavier's authorised representative.

In March 1989, Linus leased a photocopier from Xavier for three years on the above terms at a monthly rental of £200. Xavier has recently discovered that Linus sometimes allows the power supply to remain connected overnight and has repaired minor faults himself on a few occasions. Linus was also two days late in paying last month's rent.

Advise Xavier, who could now charge £300 a month rent, if the same photocopier were leased to a new customer.

University of London LLB Examination
(for External Students) Elements of the Law of Contract June 1990 Q2

*Skeleton Solution*

- Terms of contract.
- Conditions or warranties.
- Innominate terms.
- Breach of contract, consequences.

*Suggested Solution*

The issue raised by this question is the relative importance of contractual terms. Traditionally the terms of a contract were classified as conditions or warranties. A condition has been defined as an 'essential term' of the contract; or one where 'performance of the stipulation (went) to the very root ... of the contract': *Bentsen* v *Taylor* (1893). A breach of condition can be regarded by the injured party as a repudiation of the contract and entitles him to terminate it and thereby discharge himself from further obligations. A warranty is a less important term, its breach does not entitled the injured party to terminate the contract, but confines him to a remedy in damages. Warranty is defined in the Sale of Goods Act 1979 in s61(1) as a term 'collateral to the main purpose of (the) contract, the breach of which gives rise to a claim for damages, but not a right to reject the goods and treat the contract as repudiated.'

A further category has, however, been recognised. Certain terms cannot be classified as conditions or warranties, but whether they are to be treated as conditions or warranties depends on the nature of the breach. Such terms are called 'innominate terms'. This approach was adopted in the earlier cases of *Bettini* v *Gye* (1876) and *Poussard* v *Spiers* (1876). A further example is the case of *Aerial Advertising Co* v *Batchelor's Peas Ltd* (1938). But the concept of the innominate term was first expressly recognised by the Court of Appeal decision in *Hongkong Fir Shipping Co Ltd* v *Kawasaki Kishen Kaisha Ltd* (1962). In the course of his judgment Diplock LJ (as he then was) said that many contractual undertakings could not be classified as conditions or warranties. 'Of such undertakings all that can be predicated is that some breaches will and others will not give rise to an event which will deprive the party not in default of substantially the whole benefit which it was intended that he should obtain from the contract ...' In *Bunge Corporation, New York v Tradax Export SA* (1980) Lord Scarman said that 'Unless the contract makes it clear, either by express provision or by necessary implication arising from its nature, purpose and circumstances ... that a particular stipulation is a condition or only a warranty, it is an innominate term the remedy for a breach of which depends on the nature, consequences and effect of the breach.'

A contractual term is then a condition if the parties expressly intended it to be so, or if it is classified as such by statute, or judicial decision; otherwise whether it is treated as a condition or merely as a warranty depends on the nature, extent and consequences of the breach.

In the present problem Xavier wishes to terminate the contract. Linus has clearly been in breach of the provisions set out. The question is: are any of these breaches to be regarded as a breach of condition? Each of the provisions must be considered in turn.

The provision for punctual payment:

It is provided that this 'is deemed to be of the essence of the contract'. The actual breach of this provision is trivial – Linus was two days late in paying last month's rent – but if the term is a condition any breach, however trivial, would justify Xavier in treating it as a repudiatory breach, and entitle him to terminate the contract.

Time is often of the essence in commercial contracts – see, for example, *The Mihalis Angelos* (1971). But a failure to make a punctual payment would not necessarily be considered to be repudiatory in a contract such as the present one: *Financings Ltd v Baldock* (1963). Clearly the nature of the breach here is not one that could be regarded as depriving Xavier of the substantial benefit of the contract. However, in *Lombard North Central plc v Butterworth* (1987) where there was a similar clause, the Court of Appeal held that even though the failure to pay promptly was not repudiatory, the clause had the effect of making failure to pay on time a breach of condition. In view of that decision, whilst it is harsh, it seems inescapable that Xavier would be able to rely on the breach by Linus as constituting a breach of condition, and thus entitling him to terminate the contract.

The provision with regard to disconnecting the power supply:

This clause is described as a 'condition'. This is not conclusive; the court would have to be satisfied that the parties intended to use the word in the technical sense. In *Schuler AG v Wickman Machine Tool Sales Ltd* (1974) one particular clause was called a condition and no other term in the 20 clauses was described as a condition. It was urged that because that particular clause was described as a condition any breach of it by the one party entitled the other party to terminate the contract. This argument was rejected by the House of Lords. Lord Reid held that the use of the word 'condition' was perhaps a strong indication that the parties intended the clause to be a condition in the technical sense, but it was not conclusive evidence. Their Lordships were able to come to the conclusion that the technical use of the word was not intended by a consideration of the contract as a whole. A further clause in the contract provided for notice to be given as a 'material breach'. This enabled the House of Lords to interpret the word in a non-technical sense. Lord Reid did say, however, that, but for this further clause, he would have found difficulty in reaching this conclusion.

The question here is not without difficulty. It seems unreasonable for Xavier to be held entitled to terminate the contract because of one failure by Linus to disconnect the power supply. But this would follow if this provision is interpreted as a condition, and it is so described. There is not the escape from that conclusion by a clause similar to the one in *Schuler*. There does not appear to be any provision for notice to Linus requiring him to remedy or desist from the breach. Accordingly it is submitted that this provision too would be regarded by the court as a condition, the breach of which would entitle Xavier to terminate.

The provision regarding faults and repairs:

This provision appears to be one which cannot be categorised as being a condition or a warranty. It is typically a clause which would require consideration of – in Lord Scarman's words – 'the nature effect and consequences of the breach'. It is therefore an innominate term. The breaches of this provision that have occurred are not of sufficient gravity to justify treating them as breaches of condition. Xavier would not be able to rely on them to justify termination.

In conclusion it is submitted that although Xavier cannot rely on the third provision as entitling him to terminate he can do so by virtue of the breaches of the first two provisions. It must be admitted that this conclusion could be regarded as over-technical, but the authorities do not appear to allow for any alternative.

# 5    MISREPRESENTATION

5.1    Introduction

5.2    Key points

5.3    Analysis of questions

5.4    Questions

## 5.1 Introduction

It has already been noted that the law makes a distinction between terms of the contract and mere representations. Statements made prior to the formulation of a contract, while they may not be considered important enough to be classified as terms, will nevertheless have some bearing on whether or not the contract is concluded and, possibly, what form that contract takes. If such a statement were to turn out to be incorrect, it is apparent that serious loss could be sustained by the injured party. The main problem is what, if any, remedy lies in respect of incorrect terms which induced a contract, but are not incorporated into it? The courts developed the concept of misrepresentation, originally only insofar as common law was prepared to give a remedy (for the tort of deceit) only where the misrepresentation was fraudulent. Equity took things a stage further by developing the remedy of rescission for both fraudulent and innocent misrepresentation. But like all equitable remedies the 'right' to rescission might be lost in a number of differing ways; there were also severe restrictions on the remedies for innocent misrepresentation. The advent of the Misrepresentation Act in 1967 solved a number of these problems.

## 5.2 Key points

It is important that the student understand the following:

a) *Definition of misrepresentation*

For an untrue statement to constitute an actionable misrepresentation it must have the following characteristics.

i)   The misrepresentation must be of fact

An expression of opinion, or belief incapable of actual proof, cannot be actionable. There is some authority, however, for the belief that to hold oneself out as holding a particular belief or opinion may amount to a misrepresentation, if it is a question of record that can be proved (or disproved).

Similarly statements as to future intention are not considered factual, but it is possible to cross the borderline; (for instance, in a prospectus for a potential company) and state intentions which have never been seriously envisaged. This would be misrepresentation. Statements of law are not factual; the main problem is distinguishing law from existing fact.

Silence is normally not considered a misrepresentation. However, there are many exceptions to this rule, with which the student should, of course, be familiar. Silence which amounts to a half truth is, for example actionable. So is remaining silent, if an earlier misstatement is discovered. There are a whole group of contracts, known as uberrimae fidei, where there is a positive duty of disclosure.

ii) The misrepresentation must have induced the contract

Reliance on the statement is obviously not present where the party to whom it was addressed was ignorant of the statement's existence. Nor could the misrepresentation be said to have induced the contract if the party to whom it was addressed, despite being aware of it, formed his own judgment as to the matter.

b) *Forms of misrepresentation*

There are now four main categories of misrepresentation. They are:

i) Fraudulent misrepresentation

In *Derry* v *Peek* (1889) 14 App Cas 337, it was stated that a mis-representation is fraudulent if it is made with knowledge of its falsity, or without belief in its truth, or recklessly not caring whether it is true or false.

A person misled by fraudulent misrepresentation has three options:

• affirm the contract and claim damages for the tort of deceit;
• rescind the contract and claim damages; or
• plead the fraud as a defence to any action against him for breach of contract.

ii) Negligent misstatements at common law

Following *Hedley Byrne* v *Heller* [1964] AC 465 it became clear that where there was a 'special relationship' between the parties then there was special liability for negligent misstatements. The special relationship arose when the representor had, or purported to have, some skill or knowledge not available to the other party, and who was aware that the other party would rely on the representation.

The remedy for the injured party in such cases lay in damages.

iii) Representations under the Misrepresentation Act 1967

Section 2(1) of the Act provides:

'... if the person making the misrepresentation would be liable to damages in respect thereof had the misrepresentation been fraudulently made, that person shall be so liable notwithstanding that the misrepresentation was not made fraudulently, unless he proves that he had reasonable ground to believe and did believe up to the time the contract was made that the facts represented were true.'

The effect of *Hedley Byrne* (see (ii) above) was quickly overshadowed by the fact that s2(1) provided, for the first time, a statutory remedy for negligent misrepresentation.

iv) Innocent misrepresentation

The Act has only to a very limited extent altered the position with regard to innocent misrepresentation. Section 2(2) now provides for an award of damages in lieu of rescission, though this is subject to certain limitations, the main restriction being that the award of damages is at the court's discretion rather than a remedy as of right. Also it should be noted that the award of damages is an alternative only, it is not possible to rescind and obtain damages.

c) *Remedies*

i) Damages

It should be remembered that originally the liability for fraudulent misrepresentation was tortious, the measure of damages was a tortious one, and that this has apparently extended into the provisions of the Misrepresentation Act 1967, insofar as this provides for damages as a remedy. It seems that where, for example, damages are awarded under s2(1) the measure of damages will be a tortious one not contractual.

ii) Rescission

This has already been noted as being available for any of the categories of misrepresentation. There are however a number of circumstances in which the injured party will lose the right to rescind (for further details see textbook) and so it has a limited usefulness as a remedy.

## 5.3 Analysis of questions

Looking at past papers of the University of London, it is clear that there is at least one question involving misrepresentation most years; although 1988 and 1994 were the odd year out; so it is not safe to assume automatically that there will be such a question on the paper. On the rare occasions misrepresentation has been combined with another topic the most likely possibility is exclusion clauses (see Question 3 of the 1983 paper) or remedies generally, possibly linked with breach of contract in the wider sense (see Question 5 of the 1984 paper, and Question 3 of the 1990 paper, both of which follow) or both breach *and* exclusion clauses (see Question 3 of the 1991 paper).

## 5.4 Questions

QUESTION ONE

Ian, an investment broker, was approached by Victor who asked him whether he should invest in Wander Electronics Ltd. Ian said 'You certainly should, Lord Wellybob is a director. It is a very sound company. It is my view that it will go from strength to strength. In fact, I own 5,000 shares myself which I can let you have.' Victor then bought the shares for £10,000. The company went into liquidation a month later. The shares are now worthless. It now turns out (a) that Lord Wellybob resigned from his directorship a week after Ian's statement was made; and (b) that Ian's statement regarding the prospects of the company was based on a report in a financial journal which was intended to refer to Wonder Electronics Ltd but gave the name of Wander Electronics by a printing error.

Advise Victor.

University of London LLB Examination
(for External Students) Elements of the Law of Contract June 1984 Q5

*Skeleton Solution*

• Terms or mere representations – which are Ian's pre-contractual statements?
• Characteristics of an actionable misrepresentation.
• Which of Ian's three relevant statements will qualify?
• Remedies: (a) damages; (b) rescission; available for different categories of misrepresentation. Limitations on remedies.

*Suggested Solution*

One must advise Victor whether he has any claim against Ian for the loss he has suffered as a result of purchasing the shares in Wander Electronics Ltd, either for breach of contract or misrepresentation.

As to breach of contract, to succeed Victor would have to establish that the statements made by Ian were incorporated as terms of the contract of sale between them. The test as to whether pre-contractual representations have become terms is one of contractual intention, considered objectively: *Heilbut, Symons & Co v Buckleton* (1913) and *Oscar Chess Ltd v Williams* (1957). It is submitted that the statements made by Ian cannot be objectively regarded as having been or intended to be of contractual effect; they are not couched in contractual language and it is unlikely that Victor could assert to the satisfaction of the court that he understood them to be contractual promises. One must therefore look next at the law of misrepresentation.

For the purposes of misrepresentation, the following three statements made by Ian are relevant:

a)  that Lord Wellybob was a director;

b)  that the company was very sound;

c)  that in his view it would go from strength to strength.

There are four elements to an actionable misrepresentation, namely that the statement was:

i)  false;

ii)  one of fact;

iii) addressed to the party misled; and

iv) induced the representee to enter into the contract.

Plainly in respect of all three statements, element (iii) is satisfied since the statements were addressed direct to Victor; it is elements (i), (ii) and (iv) which required discussion.

Dealing first with the statement that Lord Wellybob was a director, when made this statement was true, as he only resigned from Wander one week later. If, as appears to be the case, Victor purchased the shares very shortly after Ian's statements about Wander and before Wellybob's resignation, there is no element of falsity. On the other hand, if the resignation was after the statement was made and before the contract was concluded Ian's statement will be regarded as a continuing representation which was falsified by subsequent events and which Ian was under a duty to correct: *With* v *O'Flanagan* (1936). On this latter hypothesis, element (i) is present; (ii) clearly is, it is manifestly a representation of fact and providing under (iv) Victor can show that the statement was one of the reasons for his buying the shares then the requirement of inducement will be satisfied. He need not show that it was the sole or even principal reason for his buying the shares: providing it was a reason, that will suffice: *Edgington* v *Fitzmaurice* (1885).

As to statement (b), this is a clear false representation of fact which it must be inferred induced Victor to buy the shares and is therefore an actionable misrepresentation. It is submitted that the same is true of (c). Certainly Ian used the words 'It is my view ...' which suggests that the representation was one of opinion not fact and would therefore not be actionable: *Bisset* v *Wilkinson* (1927), but this is one of those cases where a representation of opinion carries with it an implied representation of fact. Ian is an investment broker and might reasonably be assumed to know something about the health of Wander. To assert the opinion that the company will go from strength to strength carries with it an implied representation that Ian knows facts to justify that opinion: *Smith* v *Land and House Property Corporation* (1884) and *Brown* v *Raphael* (1958). He does not and, again, inducement is clearly there, and in consequence Ian is liable also on an implied representation of fact.

Given that Ian is liable for misrepresentation for statements (b) and (c) and possibly also for (a) as well, one must next consider the remedies available to Victor.

Turning first to the remedy of damages, its availability or otherwise to Victor depends upon the nature of the misrepresentation committed by Ian ie whether it was fraudulent, negligent or innocent only.

Fraud was defined by Lord Herschell in *Derry* v *Peek* (1889) as meaning that the representor made the false representation (1) knowingly or (2) without belief in its truth; or (3) recklessly, careless whether it be true or false. Fraud must be strictly proved and the burden of proof is high: it requires evidence of actual dishonesty. There is no evidence here strong enough to allege fraud against Ian.

As to negligence, liability in damages for negligent misrepresentation is created by s2(1) of the Misrepresentation Act 1967, and to escape liability the representor must prove that he had reasonable grounds to believe and did believe up to the time the contract was made that the facts represented were true; one notes that the burden of proof is on the representor. On the facts Ian might well not succeed in discharging this burden. it is not enough for him to repeat to clients requiring skilled advice information (inaccurate as it turns out) gathered by him from a financial journal without at least making it clear what his source was). It was not reasonable for him to make the unqualified representations that he did, and he would probably be held liable under s2(1).

Under s2(1) Victor would be entitled to damages calculated according to the tortious out of pocket rule rather than the contract loss of bargain principle: *Andre et Cie SA v Ets Michel Blanc & Fils* (1979) and *Chesneau v Interhome* (1983), not following the dictum of Lord Denning MR in *Jarvis v Swan's Tours* (1973) and the decision of Graham J in *Watts v Spence* (1976). *Doyle v Olby* (1969) decided that the out of pocket rule applied to actions for fraudulent misrepresentation and *Andre* and *Chesneau* applied this decision to claims under s2(1).

The result is that Victor can recover from Ian the difference between the price paid for the shares, viz £10,000 and their true value, which was probably nil, so Victor would be awarded damages of around £10,000.

One might also add the Victor may well be able to establish that a special relationship existed between himself and Ian giving rise to liability for the tort of negligent misstatement, per *Hedley Byrne & Co Ltd v Heller & Partners Ltd* (1964). Ian was a skilled professional man acting in the course of his business upon whose advice it was reasonable for Victor to rely. *Esso Petroleum Ltd v Mardon* (1976) is authority that pre-contractual representations are capable of giving rise to this head of tortious liability. But note that it is clear from *Mariola Marine Corporation v Lloyds Register of Shipping* (1990) and *Caparo Industries plc v Dickman and Others* (1990) that there must be a special relationship or such proximity between the parties as to make reliance on the statement reasonably forceable.

However, it is doubtful whether this additional head of claim would add anything to Victor's existing rights under s2(1) of the 1967 Act. The facts giving rise to liability are broadly the same in each case and the measure of damages is the same too; on the other hand the burden of proof under a *Hedley Byrne* claim would lie on Victor, whereas under s2(1) Ian would have (in effect) to disprove negligence. So although Victor might additionally rely on *Hedley Byrne*, at the end of the day it may have little bearing on the outcome of the case.

In the event that Ian did discharge the burden of proof under s2(1) and showed that the misrepresentations were innocent only, then Victor would have no right to damages, but the court could make an award in his favour under s2(3) in lieu of allowing him to rescind the contract, as indeed it can where negligence is found. However, in awarding damages under s2(2) the court must have regard to any award already made under s2(1). No assistance is given by s2(2) as to how damages are to be calculated thereunder, but it is suggested that they should be assessed so as to compensate the representee for the financial loss he suffers as a result of not being permitted to rescind.

Financial remedies apart, rescission is always prima facie available for any misrepresentation whatever its nature, subject to a number of bars which may prevent the representee exercising this right including (inter alia) the fact that restitutio in integrum is impossible and, in cases other than fraud, the court's power under s2(2) to award damages in lieu, referred to above (see *Production Technology Consultants v Bartlett* (1988)).

Despite Wander having gone into liquidation, restitutio is still possible since the diminution in value of the subject matter of the contract is not a bar to rescission: *Adam v Newbigging* (1888). However, Victor cannot recover both the damages under s2(1) canvassed above and the purchase price since he would, in effect, be recovering twice over. It is submitted that in the present case the court might well regard financial compensation as a sufficient remedy and declare the contract subsisting under s2(2) with, perhaps, a further small award thereunder to compensate Victor for any further loss he might suffer from not being allowed to rescind.

## QUESTION TWO

Percy replied to Victor's advertisement for the sale of his small printing business. Victor has been ill for the last year and the business has been run by a manager. When Percy came to see him, Victor said that the business was 'in excellent order'. When Percy asked to seek the books Victor said 'You can see them if you wish but I assure you that profits have regularly topped £500 per week. Demand is exceptionally high and likely to remain so for the foreseeable future.' The figure quoted was in fact correct but recent figures indicated a likely downturn in business.

Victor's accountant had recently written to the firm warning of the need to invest heavily in new technology if the business was to survive.

Percy went ahead and bought the business which is now about to collapse unless there is substantial investment.

Advise Percy.

University of London LLB Examination
(for External Students) Elements of the Law of Contract June 1986 Q6

*Skeleton Solution*

• Pre-contractual statements: terms or mere representations?
• Statement 1 – a trade 'puff'?
• Statement 2 – silence amounting to misrepresentation?
• Statement 3 – statement of opinion?
• Fraud: burden of proof.
• Remedies: damages; rescission.

*Suggested Solution*

Victor has made certain statements to Percy in connection with the purchase of the business. Firstly, it is necessary to discuss whether these statements are terms of the contract or mere representations. The primary consideration is the intention of the parties: *Heilbut, Symons & Co v Buckleton* (1913); *Oscar Chess Ltd v Williams* (1957); *Dick Bentley Productions Ltd v Harold Smith (Motors) Ltd* (1965). The court will have regard to a number of factors; the stage at which the statements were made, whether the statements were followed by a reduction of the terms to writing, whether the person making the statements had special knowledge as compared to the other party.

It is submitted that, in view of the nature of the present statements, the court is more likely to construe them as representations rather than as contractual terms. It is, therefore, necessary to consider whether the statements amount to actionable misrepresentations. It is convenient to analyse the statements into three; the statement that the business was 'in excellent order', the assurance as to profits, and the forecast as to demand. Each statement will be considered in turn.

The statement that the business was 'in excellent order' seems, at first sight, to be what is regarded as a 'mere puff'; a simple laudatory statement made about the business will not be construed as a representation: *Dimmock* v *Hallett* (1866). In the present context, however, this statement might amount to more than a mere puff, particularly in light of the warning Victor had received from his accountant.

The statement as to profits is literally correct. Whilst silence of itself does not amount to a representation, the failure to disclose the recent figures would appear to make that statement a misleading half-truth: *Dimmock* v *Hallett* (1866). Furthermore, even if the recent figures only emerged after the statement was made, the failure to disclose the likely downturn in business will make the statement a representation: *With* v *O'Flanagan* (1936). The fact that Percy did not avail himself of the opportunity of inspecting the books does not matter: *Redgrave* v *Hurd* (1881).

The third statement involves a forecast of future demand. Whilst this might be regarded as a mere statement of opinion, which is not construed as a representation *Bisset* v *Wilkinson* (1927), an expression of opinion does amount to a representation where the person giving the opinion is in a position to know and could not have reasonably held that opinion *Smith* v *Land and House Property Corporation* (1884). In *Esso Petroleum Co Ltd* v *Mardon* (1976) the Court of Appeal held that a forecast made by the petrol company was, in view of their special skill and knowledge, a warranty. However, it has been argued here that in the present context the statement will amount to a representation, not a contractual term. It might be suggested that, in view of Victor's illness, which necessitated the business being run by a manager, Victor's statement is only an expression of opinion, as he had at the relevant time no special knowledge. This suggestion cannot be supported; Victor is the proprietor of the firm which had received a warning from the accountant.

Accordingly, though there may be some doubt as to the first statement, it does appear that there have been representations, which are false. Provided that they induced Percy to buy the business, in the sense that they were one reason for his doing so: *Edgington* v *Fitzmaurice* (1885), an action for misrepresentation will be available to him.

We next must consider the remedies Percy could seek. This depends on whether the misrepresentations were fraudulent, negligent or innocent.

There is not sufficient evidence here to establish fraud. The essence of fraud is dishonesty, as the speech of Lord Herschell made clear in *Derry* v *Peek* (1889), and the burden of proving fraud is on Percy. On the facts given it does not appear that he could discharge that burden.

For Percy to be able to claim damages the provisions of s2(1) of the Misrepresentation Act 1967 must be invoked. Section 2(1) will entitle Percy to damages unless Victor can prove that he not only believed in the truth of the representation, but had reasonable grounds for doing so, up to the time the contract was made. Despite his absence from the business through illness, it seems likely that Victor cannot discharge the burden of proof imposed on him by the Act. In particular, by ignoring, or not making himself aware of the accountant's warning, Victor is deprived of the averment that his belief is based on reasonable grounds. Support for this view can be gained from the majority judgments of the Court of Appeal in *Howard Marine & Dredging Co Ltd* v *A Ogden & Sons (Excavations) Ltd* (1978). In assessing damages the tortious measure would be employed: *Sharneyford Supplies Ltd* v *Edge* (1985).

One might add that Percy would be unlikely to maintain a claim in negligence at common law; the special relationship required by *Hedley Byrne & Co Ltd* v *Heller & Partners* (1964) does not appear to exist between the two parties. But, as it has been submitted that Percy has a claim under s2(1) of the 1967 Act, this is of little concern.

In addition to a claim for damages Percy will be entitled to rescission of the contract, whether the misrepresentations were negligent or innocent. They will be innocent only if Victor has proved his belief on reasonable grounds as required by s2(1). The fact that the contract between the parties has been executed is no bar to rescission, s1(b). The court has a discretion under s2(2) to award damages in lieu of rescission, but nothing here suggests why the court would exercise that discretion. Provided that there are no other bars to rescission, affirmation, delay or the acquisition of third party rights, Percy would succeed in obtaining rescission. Note that in the case of *Production Technology Consultants* v *Bartlett* (1988) in which the plaintiff had, by reason of delay, lost his right to rescind the contract; the right to damages in lieu remained unaltered.

QUESTION THREE

'The remedies for misrepresentation are now just as good as the remedies for breach of contract.'

Discuss.

University of London LLB Examination
(for External Students) Elements of the Law of Contract June 1990 Q3

*Skeleton Solution*

• Remedies for breach of contract especially damages.
• Loss of bargain.
• Reliance loss.
• Restitution.
• Remedies for misrepresentation, especially rescission and possibly damages.
• Evaluation of the merits of the various remedies.

*Suggested Solution*

This question self-evidently requires a discussion of the remedies for misrepresentation and the remedies for breach of contract. However, it is not sufficient merely to set out the respective remedies; an evaluation of the remedies and a comparison of their utilities must be made.

The question can usefully be answered by firstly setting out the remedies for breach of contract and then examining those for misrepresentation in order to discuss the given quotation.

*Breach of contract*

The basic common law remedy for breach of contract is an award of damages. The plaintiff is only entitled to terminate the contract – Treitel and Atiyah employ the expression 'rescission for breach' – where the breach is one of condition. The purpose of an award of damages is to compensate the plaintiff for the loss he has sustained. The types of loss for which damages can be recovered are: (a) loss of bargain; (b) reliance loss; and (c) restitution.

## a) *Loss of bargain*

The purpose of an award of damages for loss of bargain is to put the plaintiff 'so far as money can do it ... in the same situation as if the contract had been performed'; *Robinson* v *Harman* (1848). This is subject to the overriding limitation that the damages are not too remote. The leading cases in this context are: *Hadley* v *Baxendale* (1854); *Victoria Laundry (Windsor) Ltd* v *Newman Industries Ltd* (1949); and *The Heron II* (1969). The principle derived from these cases is that the plaintiff is entitled to be compensated for such loss as was reasonably within the contemplation of the parties.

## b) *Reliance loss*

As an alternative to loss of bargain the plaintiff is entitled to be compensated for the wasted expenditure he has incurred in the performance of the contract. The purpose here being to put the plaintiff in the position he would have been in if the contract had never been made: see *Anglia Television Ltd* v *Reed* (1972). Again this is subject to the principle regarding remoteness of damage.

## c) *Restitution*

Under this heading the defendant may be compelled to restore to the plaintiff the benefit he has received under the contract.

(The equitable remedies for breach of contract are an order for specific performance and an injunction, but discussion of these remedies is beyond the scope of this question.)

## *Misrepresentation*

The remedies for misrepresentation and rescission and, in certain circumstances, damages.

## a) *Rescission*

Rescission is an equitable remedy, which involves restoring the parties to the position they were in before the contract was concluded. It is available for all types of misrepresentation, whether fraudulent, negligent or innocent – these latter two are defined below.

Misrepresentation renders a contract voidable. The plaintiff can elect to affirm or rescind the contract. This remedy is often a satisfactory one for the plaintiff, it is indeed a drastic remedy. However, there are certain bars to the right to rescind. The right can be lost: (i) by affirmation of the contract by the plaintiff – *Long* v *Lloyd* (1958); (ii) where restitutio in integrum is not possible – *Clarke* v *Dickson* (1858); (iii) by the intervention of third party rights – *Phillips* v *Brooks Ltd* (1919); and (iv) by the lapse of time – *Leaf* v *International Galleries* (1950).

As has been seen the right to rescind for breach of contract only obtains where there has been a breach of condition. Before the Misrepresentation Act 1967 it was doubtful if the right to rescind for misrepresentation survived if the misrepresentation had become a term of the contract. Section 1(a) of the Act provides, however, that a person is entitled to rescind notwithstanding that the misrepresentation has become a term of the contract, if he would otherwise be entitled to rescind without alleging fraud. In some sense, therefore, rescission for misrepresentation is a more powerful remedy.

Because rescission may prove to be a drastic remedy the court is given a discretion under s2(2) of the Act, other than where the misrepresentation is fraudulent, to declare the contract subsisting and award damages in lieu of rescission if of the opinion that it would be equitable to do so.

## b) *Damages*

The entitlement to damages depends on the nature of the misrepresentation. Damages in the tort of deceit are available for fraudulent misrepresentation. The defendant may be held liable for all the loss flowing from the fraudulent misrepresentation even if this could not have been foreseen: *Doyle* v *Olby (Ironmongers) Ltd* (1969). Aggravated damages may be recoverable: *Archer* v *Brown* (1985).

Prior to the Misrepresentation Act where a misrepresentation was not fraudulent it was regarded as innocent, and for an innocent misrepresentation damages were not available. All that could be granted was the award of an indemnity, reimbursing the plaintiff for the expenses the contract itself had required him to incur: *Whittington* v *Seale-Hayne* (1900). This often posed a difficulty for the plaintiff. Unless he could prove fraud his only remedy would be rescission, and this right he might have lost through no fault of his own – for example by the intervention of third party rights. Moreover fraud is difficult to prove, see the stringent requirements set out by Lord Herschell in *Derry* v *Peek* (1889).

This situation was altered by the Misrepresentation Act. Under s2(1) where a person has entered into a contract after a misrepresentation has been made to him, and has suffered loss as a result, and the person making the misrepresentation would have been liable in damages if the misrepresentation had been fraudulent, he will still be liable even though it was not fraudulent, unless he proves that he had reasonable ground to believe and did believe up to the time the contract was made, that the facts represented were true. Thus, in comparison with an allegation of fraud, the onus of proof is reversed. Where the defendant is not able to discharge this onus, his misrepresentation is termed, for convenience, negligent misrepresentation, and this may incur liability in damages.

Some doubt was caused as to the measure of damages under s2(1). There are authorities suggesting that the contractual measure applies, which would compensate the plaintiff for his loss of bargain. However the more generally held view is that damages are to be assessed on the tortious basis, the purpose of which is to put the plaintiff in the position he would have been in if the wrong had not been committed: *Andre & Cie SA* v *Ets Michel Blanc & Fils* (1977); *Sharneyford Supplies Ltd* v *Edge* (1987).

Parallel with this statutory innovation the House of Lords developed liability at common law for the tort of negligent misstatement in *Hedley Byrne & Co* v

*Heller & Partners* (1964). Liability here, however, depends on there being a 'special relationship' between the parties, which is not required under s2(1).

In the absence of the *Hedley Byrne* situation, where the defendant discharges the onus imposed on him by s2(1), the misrepresentation is innocent and he will not incur liability in damages, but only for the payment of an indemnity.

It remains to say that where the court exercises its discretion under s2(2), and awards damages in lieu of rescission, the measure of damages is not clear. It is suggested that the award may well constitute an amount to compensate the plaintiff for the loss of his right to rescind.

In conclusion the remedies for misrepresentation may not be as good as the remedies for breach of contract where the right to rescind has been lost, where the representation is innocent and with regard to the measure of damages.

QUESTION FOUR

Does the law provide an adequate solution to the injustices that result when a person is induced to enter into a contract with another as a result of a misrepresentation of fact which does not constitute a term of the contract?

University of London LLB Examination
(for External Students) Elements of the Law of Contract June 1992 Q4

*Skeleton Solution*

- Rescission.
- Bars to rescission:
  - affirmation;
  - lapse of time;
  - impossibility of restitution;
  - third party rights.
  - s1 Misrepresentation Act 1967.
- Damages:
  - fraud;
  - s2(1) Misreprestentation Act 1967.

*Suggested Solution*

The possible remedies for an actionable misrepresentation are (a) rescission, and (b) damages – though, as will be seen, damages may not always be available and the injured party may be limited to a claim for indemnity.

a) *Rescission*

Rescission, setting the contract aside and restoring the parties to their previous position, is a possible remedy for the party who was induced to enter into the contract as a result of misrepresentation of fact. This would in most instances prove an adequate remedy for the injured party, but certain bars to rescission might deprive him of this remedy. The bars to rescission are: (i) affirmation; (ii) lapse of time; (iii) impossibility of restitution; and (iv) the intervention of third party rights.

i) Affirmation

If the injured party has affirmed the contract, that is continued with the contract after he has discovered the falsity of the representation, rescission will be denied him: *Long* v *Lloyd* (1958). However, he will not be deprived of the right to rescind because, knowing of the facts which gave rise to the right to rescind, he proceeded with the contract, unless he also knew that he had the right to rescind: *Peyman* v *Lanjani* (1985).

ii) Lapse of time

In *Leaf* v *International Galleries* (1950) the plaintiff discovered the falsity of the representation five years after the purchase of the picture. Denning LJ observed that the buyer had accepted the picture, had had ample opportunity for examination of it, and time to see if the representation was fulfilled. Five years having elapsed without notice of rejection he could not then claim to rescind.

iii) Impossibility of restitution

When a party exercises his right to rescind he must be in a position to to put the parties into their original state before the contract: *Clarke* v *Dickson* (1858). Destruction or alteration of the subject matter would deprive him of the right. The mere fact, however, that the subject matter has decreased in value would not operate as a bar to rescission; that might well be the very reason why the injured party wishes to exercise the right: *Armstrong* v *Jackson* (1917).

iv) Intervention of third party rights

This situation most commonly arises where the owner of goods has been induced to part with them as a result of the misrepresentation (usually fraudulent) of the other party to the contract. The contract is voidable at the instance of the original owner of the goods, but he must avoid the transaction before an innocent third party has acquired the goods for value: *Phillips* v *Brooks* (1919). (See also s23 Sale of Goods Act 1979.)

In the normal course of events the party electing to rescind must communicate his intention to do so to the other contracting party. Where he cannot find that other party the taking of all possible steps to regain the goods might constitute effective rescission: *Car and Universal Finance Co Ltd* v *Caldwell* (1965).

Two further bars to rescission have been removed by the Misrepresentation Act (MA) 1967. Under s1 it is not a bar to rescission that the representation has become a term of the contract, or that the contract has been executed.

The remedy of rescission might operate harshly against the party guilty of the misrepresentation, if such misrepresentation were innocent. Under s2(2) MA 1967 the court has the discretion to award damages in lieu of rescission for a misrepresentation, otherwise than fraudulent, if it considers it equitable to do so.

b) *Damages*

The availability of damages depends on the nature of the misrepresentation. Damages would be available if the misrepresentation were fraudulent; the injured party would sue in tort for deceit. The measure of damages is the tortious one: *East* v *Maurer* (1991), but it is not open to the tortfeasor to claim that he could not reasonably have foreseen the the loss incurred: *Doyle* v *Olby (Ironmongers) Ltd* (1969). The burden of proving fraud is a difficult one to discharge – see *Derry* v *Peek* (1889) for the requirements – but the necessity of alleging fraud is obviated by s2(1) MA 1967 (see below).

Prior to MA 1967 only two categories of misrepresentation were recognised in our law; fraudulent and innocent. For an innocent misrepresentation damages were not available. Section 2(1) introduced the 'fiction of fraud' whereby even if the misrepresentation were not fraudulent, the person induced by it might recover damages, unless the person making the representation proves that he had reasonable ground to believe and did believe up to the time the contract was made that the facts represented were true. This section reverses the onus of proof; if fraud is alleged the onus of proof is on the person alleging it.

It has now been established by the Court of Appeal that the measure of damages under s2(1) is the same as that for fraud: *Royscot Trust Ltd* v *Rogerson* (1991).

If the party making the representation discharges the burden imposed on him by s2(1) the misrepresentation might be termed wholly innocent, and the injured party would not then be entitled to damages, but only to an indemnity, that is the expenses he lost which the contract obliged him to incur: *Whittington* v *Seale-Hayne* (1900).

Whilst MA 1967 has removed some of the anomalies in the remedies available for misrepresentation certain difficulties remain. An innocent party might lose the right to rescind through no fault of his own, and in the event of the person making the misreresentation proving what is required of him under s2(1), he would not be entitled to damages. Even if he does obtain damages the measure of damages is the one in tort, not in contract, so that he would not recover for loss of expectation.

# 6 EXCLUSION CLAUSES

6.1 Introduction

6.2 Key points

6.3 Analysis of questions

6.4 Questions

## 6.1 Introduction

Exclusion or exemption clauses are, as the names suggest, attempts by one party or other to exclude (wholly or partially) liability for the happening of certain events. The courts have always been wary of such clauses and this is reflected in common law on the topic. More recently the Unfair Contract Terms Act (UCTA) 1977 marks the beginning of present statutory controls. The provisions of common law and statute co-exist insofar as they apply to many contracts.

Note also that EC Directive 93/13 (on unfair terms in contracts) is now in the process of implementation in this country. The main thrust of the Directive is that any term not individually negotiated by the parties is to be regarded as unfair if it creates inequality which operates to the detriment of the consumer. Like all presumptions this is capable of rebuttal – the burden of proof being on the party wishing to depend on the term.

Thus it is necessary to be familiar not only with common law rules, but also statute (including the EC Directive) regarding the legal effect of exclusion clauses.

## 6.2 Key points

It is important that the student understands the following:

a) *Incorporation into a contract*

In common law there are two main ways in which an exclusion or limitation clause can be incorporated into the contract. The first is by giving the contracting party adequate notice of the clause, so that he is aware that it is going to be a term of the contract. The other second method of incorporation is by signature.

i) Where incorporation is by notice there are three main situations:

• Notice by display

There are so many possibilities here, from notices on the back of a hotel door, or in a cloakroom, or a multi-storey car park, that it is impossible to list all the places where such a notice might be seen. Whether or not such notices have contractual force depends on whether they are clearly exhibited in such a position that they might be seen before the contract is finalised.

• Notice in a document

Where an exclusion clause is contained in a document, the first, and main question is whether that document is contractual. The document might be a ticket or a set of conditions of sale. The main test seems to be whether a reasonable person might expect to find 'terms and conditions' including the possible statement of any exclusion clauses, contained in such a document.

It is also relevant to ask whether any advance notice was given of the clause – obviously if the other party is aware of the existence of the clause he is much more likely to be bound by it. If the clause is very unusual, it may be difficult to establish that it has been incorporated into a contract, merely because it is included in a document. Usually the more unusual or unreasonable the clause, the more the other party's attention should have been drawn to it.

- Notice by course of dealing

  When two people have in the past dealt together several times and always on broadly similar terms, it is possible to imply that one party must be aware of the existence of an exclusion clause, simply because of these past dealings. It does not matter if one party does not know exactly what the exclusion clause says, if he is aware of it, and has had ample opportunity to find out what its provisions are. The very fact that he has carried on dealing, implies his acceptance of the exclusion clause. The main requirement is that the parties previous dealings should be both consistent and regular.

ii) Rules have always existed in common law that merely to sign a document will signify acceptance of the terms incorporated into it. This was so regardless of whether the party had read the document or not. The harshness of this rule is mitigated by a number of exceptions, most notably if either: the other party misrepresents what is in the document; or, if the plea of non est factum might apply (see also Chapter 8).

b) *Interpretation of the clause*

i)   The contra proferentem rule

     Literally translated this phrase means that the clause will, if there is any ambiguity be construed against the interests of the person seeking to rely on it. Thus, where a clause fails to deal with a particular matter, or is vague or uncertain, no account will be taken of the purported exclusion.

ii)  Fundamental breach and breach of a fundamental term

     These two are not quite the same thing. A fundamental term has never been fully defined; but its main characteristic will obviously be that it goes to the heart of the contract. Consequently, a breach of a fundamental term must inevitably be a fundamental breach. However, other minor terms in the contract might be breached in such a way as to cause a fundamental breach also.

     However it occurs, when there is a fundamental breach, it will be a matter of construction whether an exclusion clause is drafted sufficiently widely to apply to a fundamental breach. It certainly seems that through exclusion clauses to avoid liability (or limit it) for fundamental breach are theoretically possible; the courts will approach such clauses very cautiously and construe them strictly.

iii) Negligence

The UCTA 1977 (see below) now makes exclusion clauses purporting to exclude liability for negligence largely ineffective. Even where the Act does not apply, however, the courts, in interpreting such clauses at common law impose very strict rules. They require, in particular, clear unambiguous wording and specific reference to negligence.

c) *The Unfair Contract Terms Act 1977*

The name of the act is perhaps misleading because it does not cover all contracts and it does not cover all unfair or unreasonable terms. It seeks to cover terms which are concerned with restricting liability or excluding it altogether, in tort only.

The Act does not change, to any degree, the law as to incorporation or interpretation, both of which are, as we have seen, subject to common law rules.

The Act is concerned to protect primarily the person who deals as a consumer. This means that with the exception of s6 (which implies certain terms into sale of goods and hire purchase contracts) the Act applies only where one of the parties is dealing in the normal course of business, with a party who is a private individual who does *not* deal in the course of a business. This means, inevitably, that there are other contracts which are not covered by the Act at all, or where the exclusion clause will be covered only by the 'reasonableness test' as set out by the Act.

Basically, the effect of the Act is to render some types of exclusion clause completely void. In particular:

Section 2(1) covers any attempt to exclude liability for death or personal injury caused by negligence and declares such clauses ineffective.

Section 2(2) covers clauses excluding liability for negligently caused loss or damage (other than death or personal injury) and subjects them to a reasonableness test.

Section 3 similarly imposes a reasonableness test on clauses purporting to exclude contractual liability.

The reasonableness test referred to is very similar in its criteria to the common law rules which already existed before the Act. The principal section in the Act covering the reasonableness test is s11; which itself refers to further more detailed criteria in Schedule 2 of the Act. Section 11(5) places the burden of proof in establishing that an exclusion clause is reasonable on the person relying on it.

Section 11(4) specifies certain criteria which are relevant particularly to limitation clauses rather than exclusion clauses. In general both the Act and common law are more favourable to limitation clauses and they are perhaps, easier to enforce.

d) *The Unfair Terms in Consumer Contracts Regulations 1994*

As mentioned in 6.1 (above) these came into effect as of 1 July 1995. Effectively the Regulations will govern terms in a contract where one party is a seller or supplier in the course of business and the other party a consumer, though it should be noted that terms which define the subject matter and/or adequacy of the price are specifically excluded from the ambit of the Regulations.

'Unfair' is not defined specifically, though Schedule 2 of the Regulations lists a long, but not exhaustive, group of examples of such unfair terms. Essentially unfair terms will be those not individually negotiated between seller and consumer and which show, in some respect, evidence of bad faith on the part of the stronger party. Fairly obviously, exclusion clauses will come high on the list of potentially unfair clauses.

If a clause is adjudged 'unfair', it will not be binding on the consumer, though the contract as a whole may not be affected if it is capable of perfomance independently of the clause(s) concerned.

## 6.3 Analysis of questions

There has been a question on exclusion clauses in about half of the past papers. Each of the questions has followed a fairly similar format raising the triple issue of incorporation, interpretation and impact of the UCTA 1977.

On looking at the various questions more closely, it will be seen that it is quite common to need some knowledge of the interaction between UCTA and the Sale of Goods Act 1979. (See also Chapter 18.)

It is also possible to see, for example in Question 3 of the 1983 paper and Question 3 of the 1991 paper, how the topic of misrepresentation might quite conveniently (for the examiner, if not for the student!) be combined with a discussion of exclusion clauses (see Chapter 5 for misrepresentation).

Inevitably also, since not all exclusion clauses are valid, the problems may require the student to consider what remedies might be available to the injured party should the exclusion clause fail. (See Chapters 14 and 15 for more details as to remedies.)

## 6.4 Questions

QUESTION ONE

Urban, a window cleaner, hired a ladder from Vitus Equipment Hire Ltd to use while painting the outside of his house. He paid a deposit of £20 and was given a receipt on which was stated: 'Conditions of hire. Vitus accepts no responsibility for any loss or damage suffered as a result of the use of the equipment. Hirers use the equipment at their own risk.' Because of a defective rung on ladder, Urban fell off it and landed on an expensive radio that he was listening to while he worked. Urban suffered a broken leg and the radio was badly damaged.

Advise Urban. How would your answer differ if he had hired the ladder for use in cleaning windows and had been doing that when the accident happened?

University of London LLB Examination
(for External students) Elements of the Law of Contract June 1988 Q3

*Skeleton Solution*

• Receipt – incorporation of 'conditions of hire' into contract?

- Construction of clause – does it cover what happens?
- Provisions of UCTA 1977 – effect on clause?
- Hire of ladder in second variation – would U still be a consumer?
- Reasonableness test.

## Suggested Solution

### Incorporation

Where, as in the present case, the relevant document has not been signed by the party concerned, it has to be determined whether or not the party sought to be bound by the exclusion clause has been given reasonable notice of it: *Parker v South Eastern Railway* (1877). To answer this, one has to decide if the receipt can be considered to be a contractual document and if notice of it was given before the contract was concluded. In *Chapelton v Barry Urban District Council* (1940) a receipt furnished on the hire of a deck chair was held not to be a contractual document. But cloakroom tickets and railway tickets have been held to have contractual effect: *Alexander v Railway Executive* (1951); *Thompson v London, Midland & Scottish Railway Co* (1930). Much depends on the nature of the particular transaction. Whilst it is not possible to give a categorical answer, it is submitted that, given the type and cost of the equipment in this problem, the receipt could be expected to have contractual effect, provided that it was given to Urban before the conclusion of the contract. An exclusion clause will not be deemed to be incorporated if notice of it is given after the contract has been concluded: *Olley v Marlborough Court Hotel* (1949); *Thornton v Shoe Lane Parking Ltd* (1971). It is not clear from the facts that have been given when the contract between Urban and the Company was concluded, but it is assumed for the sake of argument that the receipt was given prior to or simultaneously with the conclusion of the contract.

If the clause was incorporated into the contract it is necessary to proceed to the next stage of investigation.

### Construction of the exclusion clause

Two aspects have to be considered: firstly, whether the defect in the ladder was caused by the negligence of the Company; and secondly, what other breach of contract the Company has committed.

There is a clear authority for the proposition that where a party can be held liable on some ground other than negligence the clause will be construed as excluding liability on that ground and not for negligence: *Alderslade v Hendon Laundry* (1945); *Gillespie Brothers v Roy Bowles Transport* (1973); *Hollier v Rambler Motors* (1972). As there is another ground on which the Company can be held liable it is submitted that the contra proferentum rule would be applied here and that the clause would not cover liability for negligence. Even if it did, as far as Urban's personal injuries are concerned, the clause would be ineffective by virtue of s2(1) Unfair Contract Terms Act. However, as there is no indication either way as to negligence on the part of the Company, this aspect cannot be pursued further.

The Company has hired the ladder to Urban in the course of a business. Under s9(2) Supply of Goods and Services Act 1982, as recently amended by the Sale and

Supply of Goods Act 1994, there is an implied condition that the ladder is of satisfactory quality. The Company appears clearly to be in breach of this implied term. They may also be in breach of the condition that the ladder is fit for a particular purpose which is implied by s9(5) of that Act, but this does not take the matter any further.

The clause appears wide enough to cover this breach. It is now settled law that there is no breach of contract so 'fundamental' that liability for its breach cannot be excluded as a matter of law; the question is always one of construction. The authority for this is three decisions of the House of Lords: *Suisse Atlantique Société D'Armament Maritime* v *NV Rotterdamsche Kolen Centrale* (1967); *Photo Production Ltd* v *Securicor Transport Ltd* (1980); *George Mitchell (Chesterhall) Ltd* v *Finney Lock Seeds Ltd* (1983). In *Suisse Atlantique* it was observed that as a rule of construction an exclusion clause should not, in the absence of clear words, be applied to breaches which tend to defeat the main purpose of the contract. But the clause here has been drafted in very wide terms and it would be difficult to argue that it could not be applied to the breach.

## The Unfair Contract Terms Act

The Act does apply here as the liability which the Company seeks to exclude is a business liability: s1(3).

As has already been noted, if the defect in the ladder arose from the negligence of the Company, the exclusion of liability in respect of Urban's broken leg would be totally ineffective. Liability for negligence in respect of the damage to Urban's radio could only be excluded in so far as the clause satisfies the requirement of reasonableness: s2(2). This requirement is discussed below.

Liability for negligence is doubtful, but the Company is clearly in breach of the implied conditions referred to above. It remains to consider the effect of the Act in this regard.

By virtue of s7(2), liability in respect of the ladder's quality or fitness for any particular purpose cannot be excluded as against a person dealing as a consumer. Under s12(1) a party deals as a consumer if he neither makes the contract in the course of a business nor holds himself out as doing so, and the other party does make the contract in the course of a business. It seems clear that, if Urban hired the ladder to use while painting his house, he was dealing as a consumer, and that, therefore, the Company's attempt to exclude liability for its breach of contract would be rendered ineffective under s7(2). The Company would consequently be liable to Urban for the damages he has suffered.

If Urban had hired the ladder for use in cleaning windows, and had been doing that when the accident happened, the question arises as to whether he would then be regarded as dealing as a consumer. Prima facie it would appear that he would then be deemed to have made the contract in the course of a business. This, however, is not beyond doubt in view of the decision in *R & B Customs Brokers Co Ltd* v *United Dominions Trust Ltd* (1988), where the Court of Appeal held that where a transaction was only incidental to a business activity, a degree of regularity was required before the transaction could be said to be an integral part of the business and so carried on in the course of that business. If the hiring of the ladder is considered merely incidental to Urban's business, and there is insufficient regularity in his making such hirings, then he may still be regarded as dealing as a consumer, with the consequences that have been mentioned.

However, it is arguable that the hiring of a ladder by a window cleaner is an integral and not an incidental part of his business, and that Urban would not be regarded as dealing as a consumer. In that event the relevant section of the Act is s7(3), which provides that the Company's liability can be excluded only in so far as the clause satisfies the requirement of reasonableness.

The requirement of reasonableness laid down in s11(1) is that the exclusion clause shall have been fair and reasonable 'having regard to the circumstances which were, or ought reasonably to have been, known to or in the contemplation of the parties when the contract was made'. Reasonableness has therefore to be judged by reference to the time of contracting. Under s11(5) the burden of proving that the clause is reasonable is on the Company. For the purposes of s7(3), inter alia, s11(2) requires that regard shall be had to the matters specified in Schedule 2 to the Act, in order to determine the reasonableness or otherwise of the clause. The matters specified in Schedule 2 which are relevant to this problem are: (a) the relative strength of the bargaining positions of the parties; (b) whether Urban received an inducement to agree to the clause, or in accepting it had an opportunity to enter into a similar contract with someone else, but without having to accept a similar clause; and (c) whether Urban knew or ought reasonably to have known of the existence and extent of the term. In the *George Mitchell* case (above) it was indicated that the courts would also take into account the resources of the parties concerned, and the availability of insurance to the party seeking to rely on the clause. See also the recent case of *Smith* v *Eric S Bush* (1989).

It is submitted that little guidance can be obtained from other decisions on very different facts as to whether the present clause meets the requirement of reasonableness. It is at least arguable that, given the wide nature of the clause and the probable inequality of relative bargaining strength, the clause would not be regarded as meeting the requirement. In that event the clause would be ineffective and the Company would be liable to Urban for the damages he has suffered, even if he is not considered to be dealing as a consumer.

QUESTION TWO

Cecil, a travel agent, ordered a word processor from Beta Ltd for his office. He signed the order form, which provided that Beta Ltd would replace or repair free of charge any goods sold by them which proved to be defective within nine months of purchase but were otherwise not to be under any liability whatsoever for loss or damage caused by defects in the goods.

After Cecil had used the word processor for a month he was so pleased with it that he bought a similar one for his personal use at home. The order form contained the same provision as before concerning Beta Ltd's liability for defective goods.

Shortly afterwards the word processor in Cecil's office developed a fault which caused the loss of the entire records of holiday bookings for July 1989. Cecil had to hire extra staff to do the work of reconfirming the bookings. Soon afterwards the word processor in Cecil's home suffered an electrical breakdown. Cecil received a severe electric shock and was unable to work for six weeks.

University of London LLB Examination
(for External Students) Elements of the Law of Contract June 1989 Q7

*Skeleton Solution*

- Incorporation by signature.
- Effect of UCTA depends on whether Cecil is a 'consumer'.
- Purchase (1) probably not a consumer – use of the reasonableness test;
- Purchase (2) deals as a consumer – effect of s6(2) UCTA on clause.
- No evidence of negligence.
- Relevant sections of SGA 1979 as to satisfactory quality of goods.

*Suggested Solution*

This question involves a discussion of the effect of the exclusion clause, and in particular the validity of that exclusion clause under the Unfair Contract Terms Act 1977.

The two purchases made by Cecil, the one for his office and the one for his home, will be discussed in that order.

The purchase for his office:

The exclusion clause is clearly incorporated into Cecil's contract with Beta Ltd. He signed the order form containing the clause: *L'Estrange* v *Graucob* (1934). This does not require further discussion.

Beta Ltd are in breach of their contract with Cecil. As they have sold the word processor in the course of a business there is the implied condition in the contract under s14(2) Sale of Goods Act 1979, as amended by the Sale and Supply of Goods Act 1994, that it is of satisfactory quality. As the word processor developed a fault shortly after its purchase there appears to be a clear breach of this implied condition. What must now be considered is whether, as a matter of construction, the clause covers this breach. As a result of the breach Cecil has suffered considerable loss, but it is now settled that there is no breach of contract so 'fundamental' that liability for its breach cannot be excluded as a matter of law: the question is always one of construction: *Suisse Atlantique Société D'Armament Maritime* v *NV Rotterdamsche Kolen Centrale* (1967); *Photo Production Ltd* v *Securicor Transport Ltd* (1980). The clause clearly covers the breach and would, at common law, exclude liability for the consequential loss sustained by Cecil.

The further question remains, however, as to the validity of the clause under the Unfair Contract Terms Act 1977. The Act applies in the present situation by virtue of s1(3)(a) as Beta Ltd's liability for its breach of contract arises 'from things done ... in the course of a business'.

The validity of a clause excluding or restricting liability for breach of a seller's obligations arising from, inter alia, s14(2) Sale of Goods Act 1979 depends on whether or not the purchaser is 'dealing as a consumer'. At first sight, as Cecil has purchased the article for use in his office, s12(1) UCTA would seem definitive that, as he made the contract in the course of a business, he was not dealing as a consumer. However, the position is not beyond all doubt in view of the decision of the Court of Appeal in *R & B Customs Brokers Co Ltd* v *United Dominions Trust Ltd* (1988). It was held in that case that where a transaction was only incidental to a business activity a degree of regularity was required before the transaction could be said to be an integral part of the business, and so carried on in the course of that business. It is, however, highly likely that the purchase of a word processor, now normal office equipment, would be regarded as an integral part of Cecil's business and not merely incidental to that business. Cecil would not, therefore be considered to be dealing as a consumer.

Under s6(3) of the Act, as against a person dealing otherwise than as a consumer liability for Beta Ltd's breach of contract can only be excluded or restricted in so far as the exclusion clause satisfies the requirement of reasonableness. The question is: does the present clause satisfy this requirement?

The requirement is set out in s11(1) of the Act, which provides that the test is that the clause shall have been a fair and reasonable one 'having regard to the circumstances which were, or ought reasonably to have been, known to or in the contemplation of the parties when the contract was made'. Under s11(5) the burden of proving that the clause is a reasonable one is on Beta Ltd. Section 11(2) provides that, in determining whether the clause is a reasonable one for the purposes of s6(3), regard shall be had to the 'Guidelines' set out in Schedule 2 to the Act. These guidelines refer to such matters as the bargaining strength of the parties, and whether the customer had received an inducement to agree to the clause, or whether, in accepting it, had an opportunity to enter into a similar contract without having to accept a similar term. In *George Mitchell (Chesterhall) Ltd* v *Finney Lock Seeds Ltd* (1983) it was indicated that the courts would also take into account the resources of the parties concerned, and the availability of insurance to the party seeking to rely on the clause. Most recently, in *Smith* v *Eric S Bush* (1989), Lord Griffiths said that in deciding whether an exclusion clause met the requirement of reasonableness these matters should always be taken into account. See also *Flamar Interocean* v *Denmac Ltd* (1990) in which the question of availability of insurance was discussed in the context of the reasonableness test.

Without all the facts before one it is difficult to give Cecil firm advice as to whether or not the present clause would meet the requirement of reasonableness. There does not appear to be any reason to think that the parties were of unequal bargaining strength. It can also, perhaps, be assumed that Cecil could have entered into a similar contract without having to accept a similar clause. On balance, therefore, it can be tentatively concluded that the clause would be effective, as it would meet the reasonableness requirement. Even if it does not, it is submitted that the cost of hiring extra staff would be regarded as too remote, in accordance with the principles relating to remoteness of damage in contract.

The purchase for Cecil's home:

It can be assumed that the clause was also incorporated into this contract.

Under s12(1) Cecil would be regarded as 'dealing as a consumer' if:

a) he neither made the contract in the course of a business nor held himself out as doing so;

b) Beta Ltd did make the contract in the course of a business; and

c) the goods in question were of a type ordinarily sold for private use or consumption.

Clearly (b) is satisfied. It appears that (a) would also be satisfied subject to the reservation that, as Cecil had made the previous purchase for his office, there is the possibility that he might be deemed to have held himself out as having made this contract in the course of a business. With regard to (c) it is submitted that in the present day word processors are ordinarily sold for private use or consumption.

If Cecil is dealing as a consumer in the second contract the exclusion clause is totally ineffective under s6(2) of the Act, and Beta Ltd will be liable to him for the damages he has sustained.

One further point remains to be noted. Under s2(1) of the Act the exclusion or restriction of liability for death or personal injury resulting from negligence is rendered totally ineffective, and Cecil has suffered personal injury. However, there is no evidence either way as to negligence on the part of Beta Ltd, so this aspect cannot be further pursued.

QUESTION THREE

T, a pilot, agreed to sell his second-hand estate car to U, a self-employed plumber, for £6,000. T assumed that U was going to use the car in the course of U's plumbing business, although he knew that U had a number of convictions for burglary. In fact U bought it as a get-away car. Whilst U and his wife, V, were on a shopping trip, a wheel came off and U and V were injured. As a result of the accident U was unable to work for six weeks. He lost £4,000 from his plumbing business and £5,000 which he would have earned from burglary. The sale agreement in respect of the car contained the following clauses:

'46. The Vehicle is sold as seen with no undertaking about suitability or condition.'

'47. There is no liability in respect of any damage, harm or injury which arises from the use of the vehicle.'

Advise U. What difference, if any, would it make to your advice if T had sold the vehicle in the course of T's business?

*University of London LLB Examination*
*(for External Students) Elements of the Law of Contract June 1992 Q1*

*Skeleton Solution*

• Effect of exclusion clauses if the sale is a private one.
• Effect of the clauses if T sold the vehicle in the course of his business.
• Relevance of U's intention to use vehicle for an illegal purpose.

*Suggested Solution*

*The situation if the sale were a private one*

On the assumption that the accident was caused by a defect which existed in the vehicle at the time of the sale it must be considered whether such defect constitutes a breach of contract by T. The statutory implied term as to 'satisfactory quality' imposed by s14(2) Sale of Goods Act 1979, as amended by the Sale and Supply of Goods Act 1994, does not apply in these circumstances as such term is implied only where ' the seller sells goods in the course of a business'.

It appears that the exclusion clauses were incorporated into the contract, as it is stated that the sales agreement contained the clauses. As a matter of construction the clauses also appear to have covered the defect. The breach does appear to have been 'fundamental', but it is now settled law that the question as to whether or not an exclusion clause covers the breach is a matter of construction of the clause: *Suisse Atlantique* (1967); *Photo Production Ltd* v *Securicor Transport Ltd* (1980).

U is accordingly advised that, if the sale were a private one, he has no cause of action against T.

## The situation if T had sold the vehicle in the course of his business

In this event the implied condition as to satisfactory quality provided for in s14(2) Sale of Goods Act would apply. This section provides that 'Where the seller sells goods in the course of a business, there is an implied condition that that the goods supplied under the contract are of satisfactory quality ...'. (The exceptions to this do not appear to apply). Goods are of 'satisfactory quality' under s14(2A) 'if they are as fit for the purpose or purposes for which goods of that kind are commonly bought as it is reasonable to expect having regard to any description applied to them, the price (if relevant) and all other relevant circumstances.' A purchaser of a second hand car should expect defects to develop sooner or later: *Bartlett* v *Sydney Marcus* (1965), but it is submitted that the nature of the incident indicates that the car was not usable at the time it was sold: see for example *Crowther* v *Shannon Motor Co* (1975). A car that is not usable is clearly not of satisfactory quality.

Clauses 46 and 47 purport to exclude the statutory liability. The effectiveness of these clauses must be now examined in the light of the Unfair Contracts Act (UCTA) 1977. It appears that U made the contract in the course of a business and was accordingly not dealing as a consumer s12 UCTA. If, as the scenario suggests, T sold the car in the course of his business, effectively both U and T would be dealing as businesses and not as business/consumer. This limits the effect of the purported exclusion clause(s). Under s6(3) UCTA the relevant liability can only be excluded only in so far as the clauses satisfy the requirement of reasonableness. Under s11(1) regard must be had 'to the circumstances which were, or ought reasonably to have been, in the contemplation of the parties when the contract was made'. Regard must also be had to the matters specified in Schedule 2 to the Act. The 'Guidelines' set out in Schedule 2 do not assist in the present problem in the absence of further information as to the matters to be considered. In *George Mitchell Ltd* v *Finney Lock Seeds Ltd* (1983) the limitation clause was held not to be reasonable because it was the practice of the seller not to rely on such a clause; in a contrasting case the clause was held to be reasonable in view of the quality and price of the goods concerned: *R W Green Ltd* v *Cade Bros Farms* (1978). We do not have any information here, however, as to the business practice of T or the price of the vehicle. The seriousness of the defect, however, would suggest that the clauses would not meet the reasonableness requirement. It must be noted that the onus of proving that the clauses meet the reasonableness requirement is on T (s11(5) UCTA). It is submitted, therefore, that

T would be liable for breach of the implied condition of satisfactory quality. Whether or not he could be sued on this account is considered below.

It is not clear whether T was negligent in selling the car with the defect in question. If he were, then a court might well decide that the clauses in the sale agreement do not cover negligence: *Alderslade* v *Hendon Laundry Ltd* (1945); *Smith* v *South Wales Switchgear* (1978). Even if they do, as far as the personal injuries are concerned, s2(1) UCTA would render the clauses totally ineffective. It must be noted that U's wife, V, was not a party to the contract and therefore the clauses cannot be imposed on her.

### The relevance of U's intention to use the car for an illegal purpose

T assumed that U was going to use the vehicle for a legitimate business; the mere fact that he knew U had criminal convictions does not make him a party to the illegality. U intended to use the vehicle for an illegal purpose and bought it for that purpose. It is therefore necessary to consider whether U could recover for that financial loss. Where a party has the intention of committing an unlawful act at the time of contracting it is submitted that it would be against public policy to permit him to enforce the contract: see *Coral Leisure Group* v *Barnet* (1981). Even if T were liable for negligence in selling the car it is contended that to allow U to frame his action in tort would constitute an evasion of the illegality rule and thus would similarly be against public policy.

In conclusion, it would appear, therefore, that U has no cause of action against T. It is, in consequence, unnecessary to consider whether he could recover for his financial loss. If T were negligent V, U's wife, would have a claim in tort against him.

# 7  INCAPACITY

## 7.1 Introduction

In this country everyone is assumed to have the right to make contracts as they wish. A few categories of persons and organisations are said to be under a disability, though it might be more true to say that with the exception of corporations (see post) the status of these groups is rather one of privilege than incapacity.

The groups concerned comprise: minors, persons of unsound mind and drunken persons and in a rather different category, corporations.

The first three groups are not so much incapable of making valid enforceable (by them) contracts as privileged in that though they may make, and enforce such contracts as they wish others may not be able to enforce certain types of contract against them. As a matter of self-defence some traders and businesses refuse to deal, particularly with minors and so the myth has grown that minors cannot make valid contracts. In many ways the law treats the first group (minors, those of unsound mind and those who are drunk) in a similar manner, while corporations are in a rather different situation.

## 7.2 Key points

It is important that the student understands the following:

a) *Minors*

Anyone is a minor who is under 18. The contracts such a person makes may, for practical purposes be divided into two groups:

i)   contracts for necessaries which are valid and enforceable by both sides; and

ii)  all other contracts (for non-necessaries) which are voidable at the option of the minor.

The definition of a 'necessary' contract is a difficult one, since the concept of what is necessary will vary with the minor concerned. Section 3(3) SGA 1979 says, for example, that necessaries are goods 'suitable to the condition of life of the ... (minor) and to his actual requirements at time of sale and delivery'. Thus, even if the goods concerned fall into the category of necessary in the normal way of things; if the minor already has an adequate supply of those items they will not so qualify in this case. The range of contracts which would fall within the category of necessary is potentially very wide: food, clothing and accommodation, naturally, but also education, apprenticeship and other 'beneficial contracts'. The full potential of this last has never been properly explored. For example, in common law as long ago as 1694 (*Darby* v *Boucher* (1694) 1 Salk 279) that loans to purchase necessaries where taken out by a minor, were not, in themselves contracts for necessaries. But it seems now, purely on the grounds of common sense that this may no longer be the case.

All contracts for necessaries are fully enforceable both by and against the minor, assuming of course, that the contract is valid in every other way.

All contracts made by a minor for anything other than necessaries are voidable. These are contracts which may be repudiated by the minor, provided he does so before reaching 18 or within a reasonable time thereafter. Should a minor repudiate a contract he has made, he will cease to have future liability on the contract, but remains bound to meet obligations which have accrued to date.

Note that s1(a) of the Minors Contracts Act 1987 restores a minor's right to ratify a contract on coming of age. Should he choose to do so, he cannot afterwards repudiate the contract on the grounds that he was a minor when he made it.

This ability of minors to repudiate a contract, with a possibility of having derived benefit from it before the act of repudiation was obviously unfair to the other party. In Equity there existed the power to order the minor to return goods, money or other benefit received by him under a repudiated contract. This equitable remedy has now been specifically incorporated into s3 of the Minors Contracts Act 1987. The remedy thus given by s3 is, however, at the courts discretion, and not available 'as of right'.

b) *Persons of unsound mind*

There are two possible ways to define such a person. If a person is certified by two doctors as being incapable of dealing with his property, then under the Mental Health Act 1983 Part VII any contract to dispose of property by the person concerned will be set aside by the courts. The affairs of the mentally disturbed person will usually be delegated to a representative who will, under the Act be accountable to the courts, for any contract he may make.

There are, however, people who are mentally disturbed who have not been so certified. In their case much the same rules apply as to minor, ie contracts for necessaries will be binding on them; other contracts may be repudiated by the mentally disturbed person if:

i) the other party knew of the disorder;

ii) the nature of the mental disorder meant that the affected party was unaware of the effect of the contract.

c) *Persons who are drunk*

If a person is so drunk that he was incapable of understanding the contract and the other party knew this, he may on regaining sobriety apply to have the contract set aside. Should he ratify the contract when sober he will then be bound by it and will in any case be liable to pay a reasonable price on all contracts for necessaries.

d) *Corporations*

It is most usual to think of corporations in the context of commercial companies, but the definition also includes local authorities, nationalised industries and so on. Corporations are essentially organisations created (either by statute or Royal Charter) of two or more persons associating to carry out transactions of a particular kind.

When incorporated, the purpose of the corporation will be stated: either in its Charter, or in the case of statutory corporations in the Memorandum of Association. These objectives may be far ranging and disparate or very narrowly defined, depending on the type of corporation. A corporation which acts beyond its stated objectives is said to be acting 'ultra vires' and is outside its authority. Any contract so made will be unauthorised and consequently invalid. It should be noted, however, that the difficulty of defining exactly what contracts are intra vires is softened by the rule that *any* contract that is 'reasonably incidental' to the stated objective, even though not specifically authorised will be acceptable as being within the corporation's powers. Note that the Companies Acts of 1985 and 1989 have cut down the effect of the doctrine of ultra vires. The effect of the latter Act in particular has been to virtually abolish the doctrine with a very few exceptions.

## 7.3 Analysis of questions

Considering the relatively minor part this topic plays in the overall syllabus, there have been a surprising number of questions over the last twelve years of London University's Elements of the Law of Contract papers.

Nearly all have, however, combined the topic with something else.

Sometimes the question is of the type: 'write brief notes on ...' and then some aspect of incapacity will be incorporated along with a random mixture of other topics (see Question 9(3) on the 1983 paper). This arbitrary mix of topics is the type of question most difficult to predict and fortunately it seems to have gone out of fashion in recent years.

In other question the question of minors' contracts is combined quite effectively with the issue of restraint of trade clauses (see Question 4 on the 1984 paper).

The questions quoted below are fairly typical: all are on the question of minors' contractual capacity, which is the commonest area for questions. They are a mixture of problems and essay, reflecting the difference in approach between different years. For the most recent example, see Question 3 of the 1994 paper (chapter 20).

## 7.4 Questions

QUESTION ONE

Referring to infants' contracts it has been said that 'The law on this topic is based on two principles. The first, and more important, is that the law must protect the infant against his own inexperience ... the second principle is that the law should not cause unnecessary hardship to adults who deal fairly with infants.' (Treitel)

Explain how the law gives effect to these principles and consider how, if necessary, the law might usefully be reformed.

University of London LLB Examination
(for External Students) Elements of the Law of Contract June 1986 Q9

*Skeleton Solution*

• General common law rules that an infant is not bound to certain contracts.
• Minors are bound by contracts for necessaries – definition?
• SGA s3(3) consolidates some of the common law.
• Types of contract voidable at option of infant.
• Contracts declared 'absolutely void' by statute.
• Liability of minors in tort.
• Equitable redress.
• Potential reforms.

*Suggested Solution*

The first principle which Treitel mentions is given effect to by the general common law rule that an infant is not bound by certain contracts. The common law, in this respect, is reinforced by the Infants Relief Act 1874. The second principle finds expression in the rules that certain contracts with infants are valid, others are merely voidable at the instance of the infant, and an infant may incur some liability in tort, quasi-contract and in equity. To reconcile these two principles does create some problems for the law, though perhaps on a smaller scale than prior to 1969, when the Family Law Reform Act of that year reduced the age of majority from 21 to 18.

*Valid contracts*

An infant is bound by contracts for necessaries. Necessaries include goods and services which are fit to maintain the infant in the station of life to which he is accustomed: *Peters* v *Fleming* (1840). Necessary goods are defined by s3(3) Sale of Goods Act 1979 as 'goods suitable to the condition in life of the minor ... and to his actual requirements at the time of sale and delivery'. The onus of proof is on the supplier to show that the goods are capable of being necessaries (*Ryder* v *Wombwell* (1869)) and that the goods purchased actually were necessary at the time of purchase (*Nash* v *Inman* (1908)).

It is not entirely clear whether an infant is bound by an executory contract for necessary goods. Section 3(2) of the Sale of Goods Act provides that an infant must pay a reasonably price for 'necessaries sold and delivered'. And necessaries are defined in s3(3) in relation to the time of sale and delivery. Is the infant liable if the goods have been sold, but not yet delivered? The answer depends on whether the infant is liable re, that is because he has been supplied or consensu, that is because he has contracted. The wording of s3 suggests that the infant is liable re, because he has been supplied. Conflicting views were expressed in *Nash* v *Inman* (1908). Fletcher Moulton LJ said that the infant was liable because he had been supplied, not because he had contracted. Buckley LJ held, however, that the infant was liable because he had contracted. In *Roberts* v *Gray* (1913) it was held that an infant was bound by an

79

executory contract for services and education and it is difficult to see how a valid distinction can be drawn between goods and services on this point.

An infant cannot be made liable on a loan to him to purchase necessaries, s1 Infants Relief Act, but if the loan is actually spent on necessaries equity will allow recovery of the money so spent: *Marlow* v *Pitfield* (1719).

Contracts for service, apprenticeship and education are binding on the infant if the contract as a whole is for his benefit, even if certain clauses in it are harsh: *Clements* v *London and North Western Railway* (1894). In *De Francesco* v *Barnum* (1890) the infant was not bound because the overriding effect of the contract was held to be oppressive. The binding effect of service contracts has been extended to contracts for the exercise of a profession: *Doyle* v *White City Stadium* (1935); *Chaplin* v *Leslie Frewin (Publishers) Ltd* (1966); *Denmark Productions Ltd* v *Boscobel Productions Ltd* (1969). The law distinguishes between an infant who earns his living by the exercise of a profession and one who earns his living by trading, because in the latter case he risks his capital. 'The law will not suffer him to trade, which may be his undoing': *Whymall* v *Campion* (1738).

## Voidable contracts

Certain contracts subsist unless and until avoided. In the case of infants' voidable contracts only the infant may avoid them. The kinds of contract that are voidable at the instance of the infant are:

i)   contracts concerning real property;

ii)  contracts involving shares in companies;

iii) partnership agreements; and

iv)  marriage settlements.

These contracts would not be considered as for necessaries, but to consider them void might well work injustice to the other party, as they involve reciprocal liability extending over a period of time.

The rules relating to infants' voidable contracts are: (a) that he must repudiate before or within a reasonable time of attaining majority; and (b) the effect of repudiation is that he is relieved of obligations arising after the time of repudiation, but remains bound to meet obligations which have already arisen and cannot recover money paid prior to that time: *Steinberg* v *Scala (Leeds) Ltd* (1923).

## Void contracts

Section 1 of the Infants Relief Act provides that contracts entered into by infants for 'the repayment of money lent or to be lent' or for 'goods supplied to be supplied (other than ... necessaries)' and 'all accounts stated' shall be 'absolutely void'.

The effect of the words 'absolutely void' is not entirely clear. Generally money paid under a void contract can be recovered, but in *Valentini* v *Canali* (1889) an infant was denied recovery and in *Pearce* v *Brain* (1929) it was held that an infant plaintiff could not recover unless there had been a total failure of consideration. Normally, too, property does not pass under a void contract but in *Stock* v *Wilson* (1913) Lush J expressed the view, obiter that property in non-necessary goods obtained by an infant is passed on delivery.

## Liability of infants in tort

An infant cannot be sued in tort for an act which was within the contemplation of the void contract: *Jennings* v *Rundall* (1799). If, however, the wrongful act is of a kind not contemplated by the contract, the infant may be exposed to tortuous liability: *Burnard* v *Haggis* (1863).

## Liability of infants in equity

The court may have power to order restitution against the infant where the infant still has the property in his possession.

In *Stock* v *Wilson* where the infant misrepresented his age to obtain property he was held liable to account for the proceeds of the sale of the property by him to a third party. The infant cannot, however, be held to account for money which he has dissipated.

## Proposed reforms

In 1967 the Latey Committee on the Age of Majority (Cmnd 3342) recommended that the Infants Relief Act should be totally repealed. It proposed that all contracts should be unenforceable against an infant, subject to the infant being liable to account to the adult party for any money, goods or other benefit received. These proposals have not been implemented.

The Law Commission suggested in 1982 (Working Paper No 81) that infants should have full contractual capacity at the age of sixteen. Under that age an infant should not be liable on, but able to enforce his contracts with an adult party. The adult party should be entitled to recover any property transferred to an infant under sixteen and which has not been paid for. But the adult party should not be entitled to recover the price, or money lent or to assert any other remedy to enforce the contract.

QUESTION TWO

Simon is seventeen. He lives in an isolated village and has recently been offered a job as a sales assistant in the nearest town, which is 15 miles from the village. As there is no bus service, he agreed to buy a used car from Finan Motors for £500. Two days later he discovered that he would be able to get a lift to work from a friend. He then told Finan Motors that he no longer needed the car and would not collect it or pay for it.

Simon also bought a personal stereo and a set of golf clubs from General Trading plc. He has paid for the stereo but not the clubs. Because of a fault the stereo has damaged an irreplaceable tape of great sentimental value.

Consider Simon's rights and liabilities in respect of the car, the stereo and the golf clubs.

University of London LLB Examination
(for External Students) Elements of the Law of Contract June 1988 Q6

## Skeleton Solution

- Purchase 1: the car – necessary or not – executory contracts – effect of SGA s3(2).
- Purchase 2: the stereo – not necessary – infant may repudiate by other party bound.

- Purchase 3: the golf clubs – not necessary – repudiation by minor – equitable restoration – Minors Contract Act 1987 s3(1).

## Suggested Solution

This question requires discussion of the contractual capacity of minors.

Simon, a minor has entered into three contracts. Firstly, for the purchase of a second hand car, secondly, for the purchase of a personal stereo and thirdly, for a set of golf clubs. It is necessary to examine each of these contracts in turn.

a) *The purchase of a second hand car*

A minor is bound by a contract for necessary goods. Necessary goods were defined in the common law as 'such articles as are fit to maintain the particular person in the state, station and degree ... in which he is' (*Peters* v *Fleming* (1840)). Section 3(3) of the Sale of Goods Act 1979 defines necessaries as 'goods suitable to the condition in life of the minor ... and to his actual requirements at the time of the sale and delivery'. The onus would be on Finan Motors to prove that the car was not only capable of being a necessary but was so in Simon's particular case: *Nash* v *Inman* (1908).

There seems little doubt, in the circumstances, that the car is a necessary. If the car had actually been delivered to Simon he would be bound by the contract. However, Simon has repudiated the contract before the car has been delivered to him and the question is: can the minor be held to an executory contract? This question has not been finally resolved. In *Nash* v *Inman* (1908) Fletcher-Moulton LJ held that the minor was liable re, because he had been supplied, and not consensu, because he had contracted. His Lordship held further that a minor was incapable of contracting, and that the law only imposed an obligation upon him to pay if the necessaries had actually been delivered to him. In the same case, however, Buckley LJ held that a contract for necessaries was one that a minor could make. He held that a minor had a limited capacity to contract. The contention that a minor is only bound if the goods have actually been delivered to him is also supported by the definition of necessaries in the Sale of Goods Act quoted above. Under s3(2) of the same Act the minor is only obliged to pay a reasonable price for the necessaries, which may not be the contract price.

These statutory definitions suggest that a minor is only bound if he has actually been supplied with the necessary goods, and that the minor would not be bound by an executory contract. However, there is authority to the contrary. In *Roberts* v *Gray* (1913) the defendant, who was a minor, desired to become a professional billiard player and made a contract with Roberts under which the parties agreed to accompany each other on a world tour and to play matches together. Roberts expended a great deal of time and trouble and incurred certain liabilities in the course of preparing for the contract. Gray repudiated the contract while it was still largely executory and Roberts obtained damages for breach of contract. In the Court of Appeal Hamilton LJ said:

'I am unable to appreciate why a contract which is in itself binding, because it is a contract for necessaries ..., can cease to be binding merely because it is executory ... If the Contract is binding at all it must be binding for all such remedies as are appropriate of it.'

In Cheshire, Fifoot and Furmston's *Law of Contract* it is observed that the contract in *Roberts* v *Gray* (1913) was more closely analogous to beneficial contracts of service, which are binding even though not completely executed. It is also observed that all the authorities relied upon by the court in *Roberts* v *Gray* (1913) concern beneficial contracts of service. Treitel has the view that it is difficult to justify the distinction between necessary goods and beneficial contracts of service. Treitel (ibid) considers that the reasons for holding a minor liable and for limiting his liability are the same in both cases.

The position is therefore still open to argument. However, it is submitted that Treitel's view is the better one. If that is so, Simon would be bound by the contract and therefore liable in damages to Finan Motors for breach of contract. It is clear that the suppliers could not obtain an order for specific performance against him.

b) *The purchase of the stereo*

It seems clear that the stereo is not a necessary. Whilst Simon, therefore, would not be bound by the contract the other party, General Trading plc is bound by the contract: *Bruce* v *Warwick* (1815). General Trading plc appear to be in breach of contract. More particularly they are in breach of s14(2) of the Sale of Goods Act, as recently amended by the Sale and Supply of Goods Act 1994 – the implied condition that the goods supplied under the contract are of satisfactory quality. (The provision is the Infants Relief Act 1874 which made certain contracts with minors 'absolutely void' has now been repealed by the Minors Contract Act 1987.) General Trading plc are therefore liable in damages to Simon. They would therefore be liable for the cost of the tape that has been damaged: such damage would be reasonably foreseeable, see *Hadley* v *Baxendale* (1854), etc. We are informed that the tape was of great sentimental value. Whether this would increase the damages available to Simon is however doubtful. It is not immediately apparent that such increased damages would have been reasonably foreseeable. It could be argued, though, that as General Trading plc could have foreseen the kind of damage, they are not absolved from liability merely because they could not foresee the extent of the damage: *H Parsons (Livestock) Ltd* v *Uttley, Ingham & Co Ltd* (1978). It is also possible that Simon's claim for the loss of an article of sentimental value is closely akin to claiming damages for distress. In *Bliss* v *South East Thames Regional Health Authority* (1987) Dillon LJ stated that damages for distress were limited to cases 'where the contract which has been broken was itself a contract to provide peace of mind or freedom from distress.' A similar view was taken by the Court of Appeal in *Hayes* v *James & Charles Dodd* (1988). It does not appear that the purchase of the stereo was such a contract and that therefore a claim in respect of the sentimental value of the tape could not be supported, as the damages would be too remote.

As the contract for the stereo has already been performed Simon cannot recover back the money he paid for it: *Corpe* v *Overton* (1833).

c) *The purchase of the golf clubs*

It seems clear that the golf clubs are not necessaries. The supplier can therefore not claim either the contract price or a reasonable price from Simon. Simon can, however, be held liable to restore the golf clubs to General Trading plc. Such liability was imposed in equity before the Minors Contract 1987. Section 3(1) of the Act now gives the court a discretion to order the minor to transfer to the adult party any property acquired by the minor under a contract which was not enforceable against him. There seems to be no reason why the court would not exercise its discretion in favour of General Trading plc and order Simon to transfer the golf clubs back to them.

QUESTION THREE

Consider the rights and liabilities of Jason, who is 17, in respect of the following transactions:

i) he bought a pair of gold cufflinks costing £200 from Harold, but has not paid for them;

ii) he bought an exercise bicycle from Kenneth and paid for it, but has now decided that exercise is a waste of time and wants to have his money back;

iii) he agreed to work as an assistant in Simon's shop but left after one week because the hours were too long. The contract with Simon provided that it could only be terminated by six months' notice on either side.

University of London LLB Examination
(for External Students) Elements of the Law of Contract June 1990 Q7

*Skeleton Solution*

- Minors, contractual capacity.
- Contracts for necessaries.
- Beneficial contracts, contracts of service.
- Other contracts.
- Remedies for the other party.

*Suggested Solution*

Jason, being under the age of 18, is a minor in law – s1 Family Law Reform Act 1969. This question, therefore, raises the issues of the contractual capacity of minors. Jason has entered into three contracts: (i) the purchase of the cufflinks from Harold; (ii) the purchase of the exercise bicycle from Kenneth; and (iii) the agreement to work as an assistant in Simon's shop. These three transactions will be considered in turn.

*The purchase of the cufflinks*

A minor is bound by a contract for necessary goods – described in *Peters* v *Fleming* (1842) as 'such goods as are fit to maintain the particular person in the state, station and degree ... in which he is'. Section 3(3) Sale of Goods Act 1979 defines 'necessaries' as 'goods suitable to the condition in life of the minor ... and to his actual requirements at the time of the sale and delivery'.

There is a paucity of modern authority as to the nature of necessaries. In *Peters* v *Fleming* (1840) jewellery supplied to the son of a wealthy man were found to be necessaries, but in *Ryder* v *Wombwell* (1869) the court set aside the verdict of a jury that similar items were necessaries. It is, perhaps, doubtful whether these two mid-nineteenth century cases can provide much guidance in the present day.

The onus is on Harold to show that the cufflinks were necessaries. He would have to prove not only that they were capable of being necessaries, but that they actually were necessaries in Jason's case: *Nash* v *Inman* (1908). It seems unlikely that Harold could discharge this onus – it is difficult to conceive that gold cufflinks costing £200 could be regarded as necessaries for a 17 year old.

If they are not necessaries the contract is unenforceable against Jason. The purchase price cannot be recovered from him. However, Harold is not without a remedy. Equity provides the remedy of restitution where non-necessary goods were sold and transferred to a minor who was guilty of fraud. At common law restitution can also be ordered in certain cases of quasi-contract. This remedy is now also afforded by statute: s3(1) Minors' Contracts Act 1987 gives the court a discretion to order the minor to transfer to the plaintiff any property acquired by the minor under a contract which was not enforceable against him. There does not appear to be any reason why the court should not exercise its discretion in favour of Harold and order Jason to restore the cufflinks to him.

The possibility should briefly be considered that, by virtue of Jason's particular circumstances, these articles are considered to be necessaries, although – as has been indicated – this is thought to be unlikely. If they are necessaries s3(2) Sale of Goods Act provides that the minor must pay a reasonable price for them. This may not be the contract price, but there is insufficient information to determine what it might be.

### The purchase of the exercise bicycle from Kenneth

The question here again is whether this article can be considered to be a necessary. A helpful authority is, possibly, *Clyde Cycle Co* v *Hargreaves* (1898), which concerned the purchase of a racing bicycle by an apprentice. This was held to be a necessary. However, too much reliance should not be placed on that case. It is not conclusive with regard to the present problem; much depends on the price of the exercise bicycle and on Jason's particular requirements.

It is necessary to consider both possibilities; that the bicycle is not a necessary and that it is.

If it is not a necessary the contract would not be enforceable against Jason. But it appears that he has already paid for it. He cannot recover the money paid simply on the ground that he was not bound by the contract because of his minority. Treitel cites three authorities in support of this proposition: *Wilson* v *Kearse* (1800); *Corpe* v *Overton* (1833) and *Ex parte Taylor* (1856). The right to reject the goods and reclaim the purchase price would have to be based on ground that were also available to an adult.

If the bicycle is a necessary then Jason is bound by the contract, subject to the aforestated provision in the Sale of Goods Act that he would have been required to pay only 'a reasonable price', not necessarily the contract price. But what a reasonable price might have been is of academic interest: he has made the payment and, as indicated by the above three authorities, once the minor has performed the contract, he cannot recover the money.

### The contract to work for Simon

This is a contract of service, and the rule in this regard is that a minor is bound by beneficial contracts of service. The test is this: if the contract is to the minor's benefit as a whole, he will be bound by it, notwithstanding that it contains certain provisions that are to his disadvantage: *Clements* v *L & N W Ry* (1894); *Doyle* v *White City Stadium Ltd* (1935): he will not be bound by a service contract if it is on the whole harsh and oppressive: *De Francesco* v *Barnum* (1890).

It is difficult to be certain whether or not Jason's contract with Simon would fall into the latter category. No information is given as to the hours of work, the other conditions of the employment and his remuneration. It is conceivable that the mere requirement of six months' notice from a minor performing a menial task would persuade the court that the contract is harsh and oppressive. In that event the contract would not be binding on Jason, and his leaving would not incur him in any liability.

Even if the contract is binding on Jason the remedy available to Simon is somewhat limited. He could not obtain an order which would have the effect of compelling Jason to return to work. The courts have long refused to order specific peformance of contracts involving personal service, and such an order is prohibited by s16 Trade Union and Labour Relations Act 1974. Simon would be confined to a claim for damages for the breach of contract and, in view of the nature of the employment and the plaintiff's duty to mitigate his loss, such claim would only realise an extremely modest amount, indeed the damages might only be nominal.

# 8 MISTAKE

## 8.1 Introduction

There are a number of possible ways of classifying mistake and different authorities use different terminology.

For convenience it is probably easiest to divide mistake initially according to the rules of common law and of equity.

At common law the effect of an operative mistake is to render the contract void ab initio, no matter how blameless the parties are or how the mistake arose. No obligations can arise under such a contract, nor can title in goods pass.

In equity, on the other hand, a contract affected by mistake may be voidable at the option of the mistaken party. Until such time as the mistaken party chooses to avoid the contract property will pass and obligations arise. Note that as will be discussed later in the chapter on Remedies, the right to rescind may be lost if the subject matter of a contract affected by mistake has passed to a bona fide purchaser for value and without notice of the circumstances of mistake.

Within the categories of mistake at common law and mistake in equity there are further categories and terminology; some of which will be noted in the key points that follow.

## 8.2 Key points

It is important that the student understands the following:

a) *Mistake at common law*

The two main groups of mistakes comprise:

i) mutual mistake; and

ii) unilateral mistake.

Some authorities further subdivide still further and refer to common mistake where two parties share an erroneous belief, mutual mistake where the two parties are at cross purposes and unilateral mistake (as above).

For convenience it is proposed to accept the twofold division with definitions as shown below, but the fact that this alternative terminology and definition exists should not be forgotten.

i) Mutual mistake can therefore be defined as occurring where the two parties have reached genuine agreement, but under some common misapprehension as to a fact which lies at the heart of the contract; and

ii) unilateral mistake occurs where although apparently the parties have agreed, in fact there is no genuine agreement between them and accordingly, no binding contract.

b) *Mutual mistake*

The concept of mutual mistake was extensively explored by the House of Lords in *Bell* v *Lever Bros Ltd* [1932] AC 161. In the course of this case the point was made that wherever possible the courts will seek to uphold contracts rather than to have them declared invalid and that, therefore, for a contract to be declared void for mistake, the mistake must be some false and fundamental fact which strikes to the very root of the contract. There are various forms which a mutual mistake may take. The commonest are:

i) a mistake as to the quality of the subject matter;

ii) a mistake as to the existence of the subject matter;

iii) mistake as to title.

The two most recent cases in this area are: *Associated Japanese Bank* v *Credit du Nord* (1988) and *Rover International* v *Cannon Film Sales (No 3)* (1989), but the whole area of mistake is rich in case law and in particular there is a very great deal of litigation in the area of these three types of mutual mistake. The student should obviously be familiar with the major cases.

c) *Unilateral mistake*

In such cases the mistake is either made only by one party, or possibly, though less likely, each party has made a different mistake and they are at cross purposes.

It is for the mistaken party to prove that the circumstances were such, that it is impossible to infer any sort of agreement between the parties; either because of ambiguity surrounding the making of the agreement or because the other party has knowingly formed a contract different from the terms intended by the other.

The mistake is most likely to take one of three forms.

i) Where the parties are completely at cross purposes.

This is to be decided by an objective test, ie would the reasonable person in possession of the full facts assume that both parties were in full agreement and intended the contract to take the same form. If this is not the case, there will be no concluded contract. The effect of such an objective test is that negligence or carelessness may have a bearing on whether a person can be concluded to have entered into a contract.

ii) Where there is a mistake as to the terms of the contract.

Here the test is subjective because the type of situation when this happens is when the other party is aware that a mistake has been made, and still enters into the contract, knowing one party has mistaken one or more terms. However, it should be noted that at common law, both parties are presumed to have equal bargaining power and be generally of equal status. In fact the maxim is caveat emptor! Thus, it is not that one party is mistaken as to the nature of the subject matter for example, but that the seller is aware that the other party is mistaken as to the terms on which that subject matter is being offered.

iii) Where a mistake as to identity has occurred.

Normally it will be true to say that identity of one or other parties is irrelevant.

Only where one party is adamant that he wishes to deal with one party and one only will it be fundamental to the contract to prove that: since he mistook the identity of the person he did deal with, then the contract should be set aside.

Thus, to succeed, the burden is on the party alleging mistaken identity to prove that (a) there existed a genuine third party with whom he wished to trade and (b) that the mistake really was as to identity not attributes.

d) *Non est factum*

The basic rule at common law is that anyone who signs a document is bound by it. In some cases, however, where a person by signing a document, finds himself unwittingly involved in a contract the nature of which he had mistaken; it may be possible for him to avoid liability under the contract by raising the plea of 'non est factum' (literally: not my deed). The plea is not open to all. A person must establish themselves to be (by reason of blindness, illness, illiteracy or whatever) incapable of reading and sufficiently understanding the document. They must be able to prove that they were unable, because of this incapacity to detect the fundamental difference between what they believed the document to be and what it actually was. Even in claiming such disability, the party pleading non est factum must prove that he was in no way negligent or careless in signing – the test being an objective one, bearing in mind that the number of precautions a reasonable blind person or sick person might take are, of necessity, limited. The recent case of *Lloyds Bank plc* v *Waterhouse* (1990) examines the defence of non est factum in some detail.

e) *Common law and equity*

Common law has traditionally taken a very narrow view that if the mistake is an operative one it will make a contract void. This in itself has been subject to considerable criticism, partly because of the difficulty of defining 'operative' in this context and partly because it involves a very drastic, 'all or nothing' decision and makes it impossible to salvage anything from the contract.

Consequently, over the years, mistake has been held in equity only to render a contract voidable. This means that while, among other remedies, rescission may be available to the injured party, equally he may choose to affirm the contract and seek compensation for the mistake. Also, since rescission is an equitable remedy and therefore at the courts' discretion, it may be easily lost, for example where third party rights become involved.

Note also that because some mistakes, though by no means all, are actively induced by misrepresentation, the improved availability of rescission as a remedy for misrepresentation means that there is less need today to apply to have a contract declared void at common law for mistake (see also, Chapter 5 on Misrepresentation).

## 8.3 Analysis of questions

Mistake raises so many complex issues, it is perhaps not surprising that there has been a question on some aspect of mistake in the London University past papers every year since 1983, sometimes more than one. In 1983 for example there was one question: Question 6 on common and on unilateral mistakes and also a part question, Question 9(ii) on non est factum.

Mistake is a topic where it is not easy to predict how the examiner will phrase his questions. In the London University papers there is an almost equal mix of problems, essay questions and two-part questions with one (short) essay required for one half and an answer to a problem for the second half.

It is worth noting that often, where there are problem type questions, they are split to give a wider range of coverage in different scenarios. See for example Question 6 on the 1983 paper, Question 5 on the 1987 paper, and Q5 on the 1991 paper. It is also becoming common to see questions like questions 2 and 6 (below) as to the comparative approaches of common law and equity.

Of the questions quoted below, four are typical problem type questions, the other two indicative of the sort of essay requirement the student is likely to meet. By comparing them, especially the problems, it is possible to see how much they overlap.

## 8.4 Questions

QUESTION ONE

P and Q are rival art dealers who live in the same town. In August 1988, while P was on holiday in Spain, he acquired what he honestly believed was a valuable painting by Goya. On returning home he offered the painting for sale. Q, after having viewed the painting and also believing it to be a Goya, sent his agent, W, to buy the painting, instructing him to pose as Sir Charles Trevelyan. P sold the painting to W for £250,000, pleased at last that he was attracting wealthy clientele. Q subsequently resold the painting for £300,000 to S who also believed it was a Goya. Last month all the parties discovered that they were mistaken and that the painting is in fact a missing part of Guernica by Picasso and that the art world has been searching for this painting for years. It is worth £2,000,000.

Advise P.

University of London LLB Examination
(for External Students) Elements of the Law of Contract June 1989 Q5

*Skeleton Solution*

• Mistake as to identity – void at common law for mistake? – relevant case law for and against – equitable remedy of rescission unlikely to be of use to P.

- Mutual mistake – mistake as to quality of subject matter – void at common law for mistake? – relevant case law for and against – equitable rescission not available – third party rights.

### Suggested Solution

This question involves discussion of two areas of mistake; mistake as to identity, and mutual mistake.

### The mistake as to identity

P sells the painting to W (Q's agent) in the mistaken belief that the buyer is Sir Charles Trevelyan. It seems clear that P has been induced to sell the painting to W by a fraudulent misrepresentation. Whilst the remedy of rescission may be available for such misrepresentation, in this case a third party has acquired rights to the painting, and this is a bar to rescission. (Whether P has an action for damages in the tort of deceit against Q or his agent is beyond the scope of this question.)

It will not therefore avail P merely to establish that the contract was voidable. P would wish to establish that the contract between himself and W was void at common law for mistake. If he can establish this, then neither W nor S will have acquired rights under the contract and he will be entitled to assert ownership of the painting. The question is: can he be successful in this contention?

In *Lewis* v *Averay* (1972) Lord Denning said that:

'When a dealing is had between a seller ... and a person who is actually there present before him, then the presumption in law is that there is a contract, even though there is a fraudulent impersonation by the buyer representing himself as a different man than he is.'

The Court of Appeal derived support from the long-standing decision in *Phillips* v *Brooks Ltd* (1919) where the principle was held to be that the fact that one party is mistaken as to the identity of the other does not mean that there is no contract, or that the contract is a nullity and void from the beginning. This principle appears also to have been accepted by the Court of Appeal in *King's Norton Metal Co Ltd* v *Edridge, Merret & Co Ltd* (1897).

However, there are decisions which appear to be contrary to these authorities, and these must be briefly examined. *Ingram* v *Little* (1961) is difficult to reconcile with either *Phillips* v *Brooks* (1919) or *Lewis* v *Averay* (1972). Although it is a Court of Appeal decision it is submitted that, in view of the criticisms directed against it in *Lewis* v *Averay* (1972) and the balance of authority against it, it must be considered of doubtful authority or as turning on its own facts. *Cundy* v *Lindsay* (1878), where the contract was found to be void for mistake can be distinguished. The parties there were not inter praesentes and the decision can be explained on the ground that the offer was made to one person and accepted by another: this is the explanation given by Lord Denning in the Court of Appeal hearing in *Gallie* v *Lee* (1969). The same explanation can be given for the case of *Boulton* v *Jones* (1857).

P must be advised therefore that he would be highly unlikely to be able to persuade a court that the contract with W was void for mistake at common law. The equitable remedy of rescission would not avail him for the reason previously given.

## The mutual mistake

The actual purchaser of the painting was Q and both he and P were operating under the mistaken belief that the painting was a Goya, whereas it was, in fact, by Picasso. This can be characterised as a mistake as to quality. It appears that this type of mistake rarely makes the contract void at common law. The decision of the House of Lords in *Bell* v *Lever Brothers Ltd* (1932) seems to confine operative mistake as to quality to very narrow limits. In *Bell* v *Lever Brothers Ltd* (1932) Lord Atkin said that:

'... a mistake will not affect assent unless it is the mistake of both parties and is as to the existence of some quality which makes the thing without the quality essentially different from the thing it was believed to be.'

At first sight the mistake here does seem to meet even this restrictive requirement. But, in his speech, Lord Atkin gave a number of examples of mistake as to quality which his Lordship averred would not affect the validity of the contract. One example is the purchase of a picture which both parties believe to be work of an old master, but which turns out to be a modern copy. This is analogous to the situation here. But this example is cogently criticised by Treitel. He argues that a mistake of this nature stands on a different level from Lord Atkin's other examples. In *Leaf* v *International Galleries* (1950) the purchaser bought a painting under the mistaken belief that it was the work of Constable. There are dicta in that case to the effect that this mistake would not have rendered the contract void. But, as Treitel observes, these dicta are not conclusive; the decision did not turn on that point, the plaintiff only claimed rescission for misrepresentation.

In cases prior to *Bell* v *Lever Brothers Ltd* (1932) the courts, whilst recognising that mistake as to quality could make a contract void, have not been ready to do so, see *Kennedy* v *Panama Royal Mail Co* (1867); *Smith* v *Hughes* (1871). In cases since, *Harrison & Jones* v *Bunten & Lancaster* (1953) and *F E Rose (London) Ltd* v *W H Pim Junior & Co Ltd* (1953) instance further examples that the courts are not over-ready to find a mistake as to quality to be operative.

In *Nicholson and Venn* v *Smith-Marriott* (1947) the court would have been prepared to find the contract void for mistake, but the decision did not turn on that point. More recently in *Peco Arts Inc* v *Hazlitt Gallery Ltd* (1983) it was a term of the contract that the subject matter was a drawing by a particular artist, but it was, in fact, a copy. The seller conceded that the price was paid 'under a common mistake of fact'; however, the only issue before the court was whether the claim was statute-barred.

In the recent case on this area of the law, *Associated Japanese Bank (International) Ltd* v *Credit du Nord SA* (1988), Steyn J conducts a searching examination of the authorities and in particular of the facts of and speeches in *Bell* v *Lever Brothers Ltd* (1932). It has been suggested, most notably by Lord Denning in *Solle* v *Butcher* (1950) and in *Magee* v *Pennine Insurance Co Ltd* (1969), that the effect of the decision in *Bell* was to eliminate the possibility of mutual (common) mistake rendering a contract void at common law. Steyn J concludes that such interpretation does not do justice to the speeches in that case, and that such mistake could have this effect, albeit in wholly exceptional circumstances. Steyn J would have been prepared to find that the contract before him was void for mistake as to quality, but again the matter was decided on other grounds. See also the latest case of *Rover International* v *Cannon Film Sales (No 3)* (1989).

In view of the uncertainty of the law in this area one cannot with any degree of confidence advise P that he would be successful in a contention that the contract whereby he sold the painting would be found void for mistake.

Nor will equity come to his assistance. It has been established in *Solle* v *Butcher* (1950) and *Magee* v *Pennine Insurance Co Ltd* (1969) that even where the contract is valid at law equity may be able to provide relief by granting the remedy of rescission; see also *Grist* v *Bailey* (1967). However, this remedy has been barred, as S, a third party has acquired rights.

Finally an anomaly has to be noted. Q might be able to have the contract with S set aside by the exercise of the equitable jurisdiction. It would seem less than just for him to obtain the remedy denied to P. But perhaps the court would take cognisance of Q's conduct, and on those grounds refuse him equitable relief.

QUESTION TWO

'If the parties to a contract are labouring under a common mistake of fact when the contract is made the contract is valid but equity may set it aside.'

Explain and comment.

University of London LLB Examination
(for External Students) Elements of the Law of Contract June 1988 Q4

*Skeleton Solution*

• *Bell* v *Lever Bros* effect on common mistake.
• Types of mistake:
  – mistake as to existence of subject matter;
  – mistake as to title;
  – mistake based on false assumption;
  – mistake as to title.

• Contracts void at common law for mistake.
• Contracts likely to be set aside in equity, equitable remedies.

*Suggested Solution*

The assumption behind the quotation in this question is that the landmark decision of the House of Lords in *Bell* v *Lever Brothers Ltd* (1932) has virtually eliminated the possibility of common mistake rendering the contract void at common law. It is submitted that the statement in the quotation is misleading, and in order to support this submission it will be convenient to examine common mistake under four headings.

a) Mistake as to the existence of the subject matter.

b) Mistake as to title.

c) Mistake based on a false and fundamental assumption.

d) Mistake as to quality.

a) *Mistake as to the existence of the subject matter*

A contract will be void if the subject matter of the contract never existed or had ceased to exist at the time the contract was concluded. With regard to sale of goods s6 Sale of Goods Act 1979 provides:

'Where there is a contract for the sale of specific goods, and the goods without the knowledge of the seller have perished at the time when the contract is made, the contract is void.'

At common law *Couturier* v *Hastie* (1856) is authority for the view that mistake as to the existence of the subject matter makes the contract void. Whilst the concept of the mistake was not the basis of the judgment in that case, indeed the word 'mistake' was not used in the judgments, there are clear indications in the decisions that the contract would be void for mistake. In his speech in the House of Lords, Lord Cransworth LC said that the whole question turned upon the construction of the contract which was entered into between the parties. The Lord Chancellor said that the contract plainly imported that there was something which was to be sold at the time of the contract, and something to be purchased. As no such thing existed, the Lord Chancellor clearly implied that the contract was void.

In *McRae* v *Commonwealth Disposals Commission* (1951) the High Court of Australia was able to distinguish the facts before it from *Couturier* v *Hastie* (1856). There it was held that, as a matter of construction of the contract, there was an implied undertaking that the tanker existed. Whether or not *McRae* v *Commonwealth Disposals Commission* (1951) can be reconciled with *Couturier* v *Hastie* (1856) is still a matter for argument. An explanation of the decision in *McRae* v *Commonwealth Disposals Commission* (1951) is given by Steyn J in *Associated Japanese Bank* v *Credit du Nord SA* (1988) where His Lordship suggested that a party should not be able to rely on a common mistake where he had no reasonable grounds for the belief.

b) *Mistake as to title*

In *Cooper* v *Phibbs* (1867), A agreed to take a lease of a fishery from B though, contrary to the belief of both parties at the time, A was tenant for life of the fishery and B apparently had no title at all. This mistake rendered the contract void. Lord Atkin in *Bell* v *Lever Brothers Ltd* (1932) thought that mistake as to title corresponded to mistake as to the existence of the subject matter.

c) *False and fundamental assumption*

There are circumstances where the parties share a false and fundamental assumption going to the route of the contract, and because of that mistake, the contract will be void. In *Griffith* v *Brymer* (1903) the parties had entered into an agreement for the hire of a room to view the coronation procession of King Edward VII. However, the decision to operate on the King, which caused the cancellation of the procession, had been taken prior to the conclusion of the contract. It was held that the agreement was made on a missupposition of facts which went to the whole root of the matter the contract. (It is perhaps doubtful whether this decision can stand with *Bell* v *Lever Brothers Ltd* (1932).) In *Scott* v *Coulson* (1903) a contract for the assignment of a policy of life insurance concluded on the shared mistaken belief that the assured was still alive was held to be void for mistake. In *Galloway* v *Galloway* (1914) a separation deed entered into by the parties on the mistaken assumption they had a valid marriage was also held to be void. The above three cases were heard before *Bell* v *Lever Brothers Ltd* (1932). However, in *Sheik Brothers Ltd* v *Ochsner* (1957) a contract was held to be void for mistake because of an initial commercial impossibility. The case was decided under s20 Indian Contract Act 1872 but the Privy Council expressly applied the principles laid down in *Bell* v *Lever Brothers Ltd* (1932).

### d)  *Mistake as to quality*

It does appear that mistake as to quality will rarely make the contract void at common law: see the authorities prior to *Bell* v *Lever Brothers Ltd* (1932) of *Kennedy* v *Panama Royal Mail Co* (1867) and *Smith* v *Hughes* (1871). The decision in *Bell* turned on the question of mistake as to quality, and it is suggested in Cheshire, Fifoot and Furmston's *Law of Contract* that if the mistake in that case did not make the contract void, it would be difficult to envisage circumstances in which a contract would ever be void for mistake as to quality. In *Associated Japanese Bank* v *Credit du Nord SA* (1988) Steyn J suggested that this conclusion did not do justice to the speeches in *Bell* v *Lever Brothers Ltd* (1932) Lord Atkin had held in *Bell* v *Lever Brothers Ltd* (1932) that:

'... a mistake will not affect assent unless it is the mistake of both parties and is as to the existence of some quality which makes the thing without the quality essentially different from the thing it was believed to be.'

Since the decision in *Bell* v *Lever Brothers Ltd* (1932) it has proved difficult for the courts to find a contract void for mistake as to quality: *Leaf* v *International Galleries* (1950); *Harrison & Jones* v *Bunten & Lancaster* (1953). In *Nicholson and Venn* v *Smith-Marriott* (1947) and in *Peco Arts Inc* v *Hazlitt Gallery Ltd* (1983) the court would have been prepared to find the contracts in those cases void for mistake as to quality, but in neither case did the decision turn on that point.

In *Associated Japanese Bank* v *Credit du Nord* (1988) Steyn J would also have been prepared to find the contract void for mistake as to quality, but again His Lordship decided the matter on other grounds. In the course of his judgment Steyn J suggested a number of guiding principles.

i)   The first imperative was that the law ought to uphold rather than destroy apparent contracts.

ii)  The common law rules as to a mistake regarding the quality of the subject matter, like the common law rules regarding commercial frustration, are designed to cope with the impact of unexpected and wholly exceptional circumstances on apparent contracts.

iii) Such a mistake must be substantially shared by both parties, and must relate to facts as they existed at the time the contract was made.

iv)  As established by *Bell* v *Lever Brothers Ltd* (1932) the mistake must render the subject matter of the contract essentially and radically different from the subject matter which the parties believed to existed.

v)   A party cannot be allowed to rely on a common mistake where the mistake consists of a belief which is entertained by him without any reasonable grounds for such a belief. With regard to the latter point Steyn J referred to *McRae* v *Commonwealth Disposals Commission* (1951).

Whilst there are circumstances in which a contract will be held to be void at common law for mistake, such circumstances appear to be limited and somewhat uncertain. Even where the contract is not void at common law, however, equity may be able to provide relief. In *Solle* v *Butcher* (1950) Lord Denning MR said that:

'A contract is also liable in equity to be set aside if the parties were under a common misapprehension either as to the facts or as to their relative and respective rights, provided that the misapprehension was fundamental and that the party seeking to set it aside was not himself at fault.'

The correctness of the decision in *Solle* v *Butcher* (1950) has been doubted, see for example *Amalgamated Investment & Property Co Ltd* v *John Walker and Sons Ltd* (1976). However, the equitable jurisdiction has become firmly established. The principles of *Solle* v *Butcher* (1950) have been considered and applied in the later cases of *Grist* v *Bailey* (1967), *Magee* v *Pennine Insurance Co Ltd* (1969) and *Laurence* v *Lexcourt Holdings Ltd* (1978). According to that jurisdiction a contract may be voidable for common mistake in equity even though it is valid at law. The courts can impose terms on which equitable relief is granted.

Whilst the equitable remedy of rescission is available for common mistake, the remedy is subject to certain bars. The right to rescind may be barred if:

i) the contract has been affirmed;

ii) third party rights have intervened;

iii) there has been delay;

iv) restitution has become impossible.

QUESTION THREE

a) A contracts to buy a house from B which both parties believe to be let to T, a tenant protected by the Rent Acts (a fact which would depress the value of the property). B has now discovered that T died the day before the contract was signed.

Advise B. Would you advice differ if A had since sold the property at a great profit?

b) Victor sells a painting to Peter for £50. It is in fact a masterpiece worth £50,000.

Advise Victor. How would your answer differ, if at all, if Peter had been an art expert?

University of London LLB Examination
(for External Students) Elements of the Law of Contract June 1983 Q6

*Skeleton Solution*

• Mistake, types: common, unilateral, etc.

- Mistake in common law, equity.
- Remedies.
- Other factors, eg fraud, misrepresentation.

*Suggested Solution*

a) B has sold a house to A at an undervalue, owing to a common mistaken belief that it was occupied by a protected tenant. One must consider the effect of this mistake (i) at law and (ii) in equity.

An operative common mistake at law renders a contract void. However, since the decision of the House of Lords in *Bell* v *Lever Bros* (1932) it is clear that only a common mistake of a most exceptional kind will be so operative, and in no reported case since then has the plea of common mistake at law succeeded. Indeed, Lord Denning MR has sought fundamentally to restate the law of mistake and has said that the true interpretation of *Bell* is that contracts are never void for common mistake at law: *Solle* v *Butcher* (1950) and *Magee* v *Pennine Insurance* (1969). It may be respectfully questioned whether his Lordship's view is correct, given that in *Bell* although the decision on the facts was that the contract was not void, their Lordships were at pains to seek to define the circumstances in which a common mistake would be operative at law. It was their failure clearly or succinctly so to do which has led to the law developing in a different direction since *Solle*.

That different direction is the new wide-ranging, flexible and discretionary doctrine of mistake in equity. It is exemplified by *Grist* v *Bailey* (1967) where a vendor and purchaser believed that the house to be sold was occupied by a protected tenant, which belief was incorrect. Goff J held the contract to be valid at law but, applying *Solle*, set it aside in equity. This case, *Solle* itself and *Magee* lead one irresistibly to the conclusion that here there was no mistake sufficient to render the contract void within the ratio of *Bell*, and it is to equity that B must look for relief.

In *Solle* Denning LJ (as he then was) held that a contract will be rescinded in equity for common mistake where the parties are under a fundamental common misapprehension either as to facts or as to their relative and respective rights, providing the party to set aside the contract is not at fault. It is submitted that this case falls squarely within that principle and in the absence of any evidence that B was in some way at fault concerning the mistake, B will be able to rescind the contract of sale.

*Solle* has been criticised as being an extension of equitable intervention, unwarranted by *Bell*, which was a case in which both mistake at law and in equity were concerned. Nevertheless the ratio of *Solle* has been acted upon and applied in a number of subsequent cases, eg *Magee*, *Grist* and *Laurence* v *Lexcourt Holdings Ltd* (1978) and short of its being overruled at some future time by the House of Lords, it must be accepted as being a settled part of English law.

Finally, the new equitable jurisdiction has been held to empower the courts not merely to grant rescission, but in addition to fix terms for so doing.

In *Grist* the vendor was permitted to rescind on condition that he should offer to sell the property to the purchaser at the market price with full vacant possession. The likelihood is that in allowing B to rescind the contract the court would require him to make a similar offer to A.

On the footing that A sold the house before B sought to rescind the contract, it is submitted that B would be remediless. Where a bona fide third party purchaser has intervened, rescission is no longer possible because a third party purchaser cannot be prejudiced by a voidable transaction of which he was unaware. Thus B's right to rescind the contract depends upon his discovering the mistake and moving swiftly to rescind before A had dealt with the house.

b) Victor has made a bad bargain with Peter by selling the painting to Peter at a gross undervalue. It is assumed that Victor did not intend so to do, but entered into the contract under an erroneous belief as to the painting's value, though one does not know if Peter shared that belief. One must thus consider whether the doctrine of mistake either at law or in equity will enable Victor to escape from the transaction, having regard to whether Peter was or was not a party to the mistake.

First, if there was a common mistake as to the origin and value of the painting, is the contract void at law? There is some relevant authority dealing with the opposite case, that is where a painting is believed to be an old master but is in fact a modern copy: in *Leaf* v *International Galleries* (1950) the court held such a contract to be valid and binding, affirming a view first expressed by Lord Atkin in *Bell* v *Lever Bros* (1932) that a mistake of this nature would not vitiate the contract. The principle applies with equal force to the case in hand, being the converse situation, and there is therefore no operative common mistake at law. This conclusion is reinforced by the post-*Bell* cases, eg *Solle* v *Butcher* (1950) and *Magee* v *Pennine Insurance* (1969) where the courts have been concerned very narrowly to limit mistake at law, if not dismiss it altogether.

Might there then be relief in equity for common mistake, having regard to the new equitable doctrine flowing from *Solle* v *Butcher* (1950)? At first sight it would be an attractive answer to say 'yes', given that there has been a serious mistake as to the value of the painting. However, notwithstanding the extended scope of the new equity, it is submitted that one must advise Victor, regrettably, that it would not avail him in this case. It only assists where there has been a fundamental common misapprehension as to facts, whereas the mistake in question is more properly described as one as to value. The law of mistake does not rescue parties from bad bargains, as is clear from *Bell* v *Lever Bros* (1932) itself, and Peter could therefore keep the painting.

Secondly, if the mistake was on Victor's part alone ie unilateral only, again it is submitted that Victor is without a remedy. Unless Victor can show that his erroneous belief was in some way caused or contributed to by Peter then the latter is entitled to take advantage of Victor's ignorance and to obtain the bargain that he did. In *Riverlate Properties Ltd* v *Paul* (1975) the Court of Appeal made it clear that there must be some element of fraud, misrepresentation or sharp practice to justify rescission for unilateral mistake. The facts fall considerably short of establishing this and in consequence equity will not assist Victor. A fortiori, if there is no relief in equity, the contract is valid at law unless Victor can establish that there was a mistake as to the terms of the contract known to Peter, *Smith* v *Hughes* (1871) and *Colin* v *Hartog & Shields* (1939). There is no evidence to show this, thus the contract cannot be impugned.

On the hypothesis that Peter was an art expert, the conclusion reached above in relation to unilateral mistake would still apply. The mere fact that he possessed expert knowledge and Victor did not cannot of itself affect the validity of the transaction. In English law there is no concept of fair bargaining or the like; each contracting party must look after his own interests and is under no obligation to draw to the other's attention facts of which he may be unaware.

QUESTION FOUR

A, who is emigrating to Australia in three months, invites his two work colleagues, B and C, to his house. A offers to sell his favourite painting to B for £1,000 which B accepts. Both A and B believe the painting is by a little known French artist and is probably worth between £1,000–£2,000.

A also offers to sell his two dining candlesticks to C for £500, which offer C accepts. C believes the candlesticks are gold and worth about £3,000. A knows C believes the candlesticks are gold but he knows that they are only cheap imitations.

A few days later, B and C decide to have their new purchases valued. B took the painting to an art-dealer who identified it as a Manet and offered B £250,000 for it, but B refused to sell. C showed his candlesticks to an expert who informed him that they were made of a very cheap metal and were probably worth about £20 each.

C immediately took the candlesticks around to A's house and demanded his money back which A refused. C also told A about the news that B had received at the art dealer's.

Advise the parties as to their rights and liabilities.

University of London LLB Examination
(for External Students) Elements of the Law of Contract June 1992 Q7

*Skeleton Solution*

• Common mistake as to quality:
  – the common law;
  – equity.

• Unilateral mistake:
  – the common law;
  – equity.

*Suggested Solution*

It is most convenient to deal with the contracts between A and B, and A and C in turn.

*The contract between A and B*

In this situation both A and B share the same mistake. It is, therefore, a case of

99

mutual mistake: the expression 'common mistake' is more frequently employed and will be used hereafter.

The common mistake is one as to quality. It is necessary to examine the effect of the mistake at common law and the effect in equity.

The effect of operative mistake at common law is to render the contract void. The decision in *Bell* v *Lever Brothers Ltd* (1932) has confined operative mistake as to quality within very narrow limits. In his speech Lord Atkin said:

'... a mistake (as to quality) will not affect assent unless it is the mistake of both parties, and is as to the existence of some quality which makes the thing without the quality essentially different from the thing as it was believed to be.'

Lord Atkin gave examples of mistakes as to quality which would not have this effect; one such example was the purchase of picture which both parties believe to be the work of an old master, and it turns out to be a modern copy. This is the converse of the situation before us.

In *Associated Japanese Bank Ltd* v *Credit du Nord S A* (1989) Steyn J examined the speeches in Bell v Lever Brothers and concluded that certain commentators were in error in concluding that the decision in that case precluded the possibility of a mistake as to quality ever rendering the contract void at common law; he did say, however, that such a situation would be rare.

Cases in which mistake as to quality did not affect the contract at common law might be mentioned: *Harrison & Jones Ltd* v *Bunten and Lancaster Ltd* (1953); and *Leaf* v *International Galleries* (1950), though the case was not argued on that point. It is significant that in the recent case of *Harlingdon & Leinster Enterprises* v *Christopher Hull Fine Art* (1990), where the paintings which were the subject matter of the sale turned out to be forgeries, the question of mistake was not even mentioned.

In the above cases the mistake made the article less valuable than it was believed to be; here the situation is the converse, but the principle must be the same. Consequently the mistake does not make the contract void at common law.

Nor, it is submitted, would A be able to invoke the assistance of equity. Rescission has been granted in equity in cases of common mistake: *Solle* v *Butcher* (1950); *Grist* v *Bailey* (1967); *Magee* v *Pennine Insurance Co Ltd* (1969). But here there seems no equitable reason why B should be compelled to surrender his good fortune; see the remarks of Russell LJ in *Riverlate Properties Ltd* v *Paul* (1975) to the effect that for equity to compel a man to abandon a good bargain would run counter to the attitudes of much of mankind. His Lordship was speaking in the context of unilateral mistake, but his remarks seem appropriate in the present situation.

*The contract between A and C*

Here the mistake is unilateral. C believes the candlesticks are gold and valuable. A knows that they are only cheap imitations. We are also informed that A knows of C's belief. The case of *Smith* v *Hughes* (1871) is particularly relevant here. The defendant thought that he was buying old oats, the plaintiff knew that the oats were new. Hannen J said:

'In order to relieve the defendant it was necessary that the jury should find not merely that the plaintiff believed the defendant to believe that he was buying old oats, but that he believed the defendant to believe that he, the plaintiff, was contracting to sell old oats ...'

If we apply that statement to the present problem, in order to find for C, it would have to be shown that A had the belief that C thought that he (A) was contracting to sell gold candlesticks. This does not appear to have been the position.

C cannot, therefore, claim that the contract is void at common law because of his mistake.

Equity here would also prove of no assistance to C. Rescission is not an available remedy for unilateral mistake: *Riverlate Properties Ltd* v *Paul*.

QUESTION FIVE

D was an antiques dealer specialising in the sale of china. D put cups, saucers and other items in his shop window with lengthy descriptions on the price tags.

a)  A cup and saucer were described as early Swansea and the price was £150. D and E, who bought them from D, both believed that they had been accurately described but in fact they proved to be excellent fakes.

b)  A tea pot was offered for sale at £200. F, believing that it was early Welsh Blue, agreed to purchase it. In fact it was Staffordshire Blue and worth much less. D knew of F's mistake but had said nothing.

c)  G walked into the shop and offered D £3,500 for a Nantgarw tea set. D agreed to sell it. G offered to pay by cheque which D refused to accept without some proof of identification. G had pretended to be Sir Robert Slip and G gave his address as Slip Hall. D checked the local trade directory and found that Sir Robert Slip lived at the address given. G also produced a Racing Club membership card containing G's photograph and with the subscription Sir Robert Slip. D allowed G to take the china. G sold the Nantgarw to H, another antique dealer, before D learned that the cheque had 'bounced'.

Advise D.

University of London LLB Examination
(for External Students) Elements of the Law of Contract June 1991 Q5

*Suggested Solution*

• Mutual or common mistake.
• Unilateral mistake.
• Mistake as to identity.
• Sale of goods by description.

*Suggested Solution*

Each of D's three contracts must be examined in turn.

a)  *The contract with E*

Both parties conclude the contract in the mistaken belief that the articles are

'Early Swansea' but are in fact fakes. This is an instance of mutual mistake as to quality.

At common law the effect of operative mistake is to render the contract void. Mutual mistake, where it operates, nullifies consent. However the operation of mistake as to quality has been confined to very narrow limits at common law, particularly by the decision in *Bell* v *Lever Bros Ltd* (1932). Earlier cases had also set narrow confines within which mistake as to quality was operative: *Kennedy* v *Panama etc Royal Mail Co* (1867); *Smith* v *Hughes* (1871).

In *Bell* Lord Atkin said that a mistake as to quality would render a contract void where it was a mistake of both parties which was 'as to the existence of some quality which makes the thing without the quality essentially different from the thing it was supposed to be'. Lord Atkin gave a number of examples in his speech of contracts that would not be avoided, including the example of the purchase of a painting which both buyer and seller believe to be an old master, but is in reality a copy. This example is closely analogous to the present problem. Treitel (*Law of Contract*) believes that this type of case stands on a different level from Lord Atkin's other examples, and that in such a situation the contract should be held void. Some support for this view can be derived from *Peco Arts Inc* v *Hazlitt Gallery Ltd* (1983), though the only issue there was whether the claim was statute-barred. Authority supporting the contention that the contract here would not be held void include dicta in *Leaf* v *International Galleries* (1950) and the decision in *Harrison & Jones Ltd* v *Bunten & Lancaster Ltd* (1953).

In *Associated Japanese Bank (International) Ltd* v *Credit du Nord SA* (1989) Steyn J reviewed the authorities on the question of mistake as to quality and concluded that, contrary to some of the interpretations of *Bell* v *Lever Bros Ltd*, there was a narrow but perceptible area in which such mistake rendered the contract void. In the present context the balance of authority would suggest that the contract between D and E does not fall within this area and would not therefore be void for mistake at common law.

Equity may provide E with a remedy. Where the mistake is not such as to render the contract void at common law, equity may nevertheless set it aside and thus, in this instance, relieve E of the hardship: *Solle* v *Butcher* (1950); *Magee* v *Pennine Insurance Co Ltd* (1969).

E would have a further remedy. The cup and saucer were described as 'early Swansea' and it appears that there were lengthy descriptions on the price tags. It would seem, therefore, that D is in breach of the condition, implied by s13 Sale of Goods Act 1979, that the goods would correspond with the description. D is an antiques dealer and E, apparently, a private buyer (cf *Harlingdon and Leinster Enterprise Ltd* v *Christopher Hull Fine Art Ltd* (1990) where both parties were dealers).

b)  *The contract with F*

The contract appears to have been entered into as a result of the unilateral mistake on the part of F. The general rule is that a party is bound despite his mistake, if 'whatever (his) real intentions may be, he so conducts himself that a reasonable man would believe that he was assenting to the terms proposed by the other party, and that other party upon that belief enters into a contract with him ...' – *Smith* v *Hughes* (above). On the authority of that case it is submitted that the contract would not be void at common law.

Nor can it be said with any certainty that equity would intervene. Rescission for unilateral mistake will only be granted if the one party had contributed to the other party's mistake: *Riverlate Properties Ltd* v *Paul* (1975). The problem does not clearly indicate whether D did so contribute. That he might have done so appears from the information that the articles in question had lengthy descriptions on the price tags attached to them. In this event equity would come to the aid of F, either by granting rescission or by refusing D specific performance.

A further possibility should be mentioned: if the tea pot was described as early Welsh Blue D would be liable for breach of s13 Sale of Goods Act as set out in part (a) above.

c) *The contract with G*

This is an instance of mistake as to identity where the parties are inter praesentes. D could not aver that he intended to contract only with a specific named party, Sir Robert Slip, and derive support from the decisions in *Boulton* v *Jones* (1857) or *Lake* v *Simmons* (1927). The facts are closely analogous to those in *Phillips* v *Brooks* (1919) and particularly *Lewis* v *Averay* (1972), in both of which cases the contract was held not to be void for mistake. Authority to the contrary might be found in *Ingram* v *Little* (1961), but this case must be of doubtful authority since the decision in *Lewis* v *Averay*.

Assuming that H was a bona fide purchaser, he acquires good title, and D cannot found a claim against him. D's only remedy is an action in damages against G for fraudulent misrepresentation.

QUESTION SIX

'A rigid doctrine of mistake in contract at common law is being replaced by excessively flexible principles of equity.'

Discuss.

University of London LLB Examination
(for External Students) Elements of the Law of Contract June 1993 Q2

*Skeleton Solution*

• Types of mistake – unilateral mistake and mutual (common) mistake.
• The effect of operative mistake at common law.
• Operative unilateral mistake at common law.
• Operative mutual mistake at common law.
• Equitable remedies.

## Suggested Solution

### Mistake at common law

'If mistake operates at all it operates so as to negative or in some cases to nullify consent' (per Lord Atkin in *Bell* v *Lever Brothers Ltd* (1932)).

A mistake which negatives consent falls within the category of unilateral mistake. Where unilateral mistake operates the result is to show that there was no true agreement between the parties. Mistake which nullifies consent refers to the category of mutual or common mistake (the terms mutual and common are used interchangeably here). In the case of mutual mistake there has been agreement between the parties, who have shared the mistake, but that mistake relates to so fundamental a matter that the effect of it is to nullify the consent that has been arrived at.

Where mistake does operate at common law the effect of it is to render the contract void. But mistake at common law operates within narrow limits.

### Unilateral mistake

The limits within which unilateral mistake operates at common law was expressed by Blackburn J in *Smith* v *Hughes* (1871) as follows:

'If, whatever a man's real intention may be, he so conducts himself that a reasonable man would believe that he was assenting to the terms proposed by the other party, and that other party upon that belief enters into the contract with him, the man thus conducting himself would be equally bound as if he had intended to agree to the other party's terms.'

Unilateral mistake has been held to operate, so as to render the contract void, but in limited circumstances. In *Hartog* v *Colin & Shields* (1939) the mistake negatived consent where the one party knew from the previous negotiations that the offer in question could not have been intended. Where the parties are at cross-purposes as to the subject matter of the contract this mistake may also negative consent: *Raffles* v *Wichelhaus* (1864); *Scriven Bros & Co* v *Hindley & Co* (1913); *Falck* v *Williams* (1900).

A problematic area has been the one of mistake as to identity. There are cases where the mistake by one party as to the identity of the other has been held to render the contract void: *Cundy* v *Lindsay* (1878); *Ingram* v *Little* (1961); *Lake* v *Simmons* (1927). But these were in special circumstances. The general rule appears to be that mistake as to identity may render the contract voidable, but would not render it void: *Phillips* v *Brooks* (1919); *Lewis* v *Averay* (1972). In a recent case, *Citibank NA* v *Brown Shipley & Co Ltd* (1991), Waller J stated the principle that a mistake as to identity renders the contract void *only* 'where the findings of fact are: (i) A thinks he has agreed with C because he believes B, with whom he is negotiating, is C; (ii) B is aware that A did not intend to make any agreement with him; and (iii) A has established that the identity of C was a matter of crucial importance.'

### Mutual mistake

The decision in *Bell* v *Lever Brothers* (above) has been regarded as having confined the doctrine of mutual (common) mistake within very narrow limits. Lord Denning MR has stated that, as a result of that decision, 'A common mistake, even on a most fundamental matter, does not make a contract void at law: but it makes it voidable in equity.' See *Magee* v *Pennine Insurance Co Ltd* (1969). In *Associated Japanese Bank (International) Ltd* v *Credit du Nord SA* (1988) this view was criticised by Steyn J as not doing justice to the speeches in *Bell*. In those speeches, notably those of Lords Atkin and Thankerton, it was recognised that certain types of mutual mistake could render a contract void, although in very limited circumstances.

The circumstances in which mutual mistake could render a contract void include mistake as to the existence of the subject matter: *Couturier* v *Hastie* (1856) – see also s6 Sale of Goods Act 1979. A party will not, however, be able to plead mistake where there are no reasonable grounds for his belief: *McRae* v *Commonwealth Disposals Commission* (1951).

Mistake may also render a contract void in the somewhat unusual situation where a party negotiates for the acquisition of rights to property which he already owns: *Cooper* v *Phibbs* (1867).

There are decisions to the effect that a contract will be declared void where the parties shared the same false and fundamental assumption. The earlier cases include; *Scott* v *Coulson* (1903), *Galloway* v *Galloway* (1914), and *Griffith* v *Brymer* (1903). But these cases are all prior to *Bell* v *Lever Brothers*, and their authority is perhaps doubtful. However, there are also Privy Council decisions post *Bell* to this effect: *Sheikh Brothers Ltd* v *Ochsner* (1957); *Norwich Union Fire Insurance Society* v *Price* (1934).

It would seem that a mistake as to quality rarely, if ever, renders a contract void at common law. In *Bell* Lord Atkin said that such a mistake 'will not affect assent unless it is the mistake of both parties, and is as to the existence of some quality which makes the thing without the quality essentially different from the thing as it was believed to be.' There are numerous cases where the mutual mistake as to quality did *not* render the contract void: *Kennedy* v *Panama etc Royal Mail Co* (1867); *Leaf* v *International Galleries* (1950); *Harrison & Jones* v *Bunten & Lancaster* (1953); and, of course, *Bell* v *Lever Brothers* itself. But it is difficult to find a clear and satisfactory decision where the mistake as to quality was of such a nature that the court was able to find that the contract was void ab initio. Such a decision was reached in *Nicholson and Venn* v *Smith-Marriot* (1947), but was said to be wrong by Denning LJ in *Solle* v *Butcher* (below). In *Peco Arts Inc* v *Hazlitt Gallery Ltd* (1983), where a drawing was said to be by a named artist and turned out to be a copy, the seller conceded that the price had been paid under 'a common mistake of fact': but the decision was on the question of limitation of action.

In *Associated Japanese Bank* v *Credit du Nord* (above) Steyn J would have been prepared to find that the mistake as to quality rendered the contract void, but the actual decision turned on another point. Steyn J did state that 'the common law rules as to a mistake regarding the quality of the subject matter, ... are designed to cope with the impact of unexpected and wholly exceptional circumstances on apparent contracts.'

It is, therefore, apparent that a rigid doctrine of mistake has developed at common law. It remains to consider how this doctrine has been tempered by principles of equity.

*Mistake in equity*

The leading case is the decision of the Court of Appeal in *Solle* v *Butcher* (1950). The mistake in that case was one as to quality and, in the light of common law doctrine, that mistake could not have been held to render the contract void, but the equitable remedy of rescission was held to be available to the plaintiff. 'A contract', said Denning LJ, 'is ... liable in equity to be set aside if the parties were under a common misapprehension either as to the facts or as to their relative and respective rights, provided that the misapprehension was fundamental and that the party seeking to set it aside was not himself as fault.'

The decision in *Solle* v *Butcher* was followed by Goff J in *Grist* v *Bailey* (1967) and the principle re-affirmed by the Court of Appeal in *Magee* v *Pennine Insurance Co Ltd* (above).

It has been queried whether the decision in *Solle* v *Butcher* is consistent with *Bell* v *Lever Brothers*. See the observations of Buckley LJ and Sir John Pennycuick in *Amalgamated Investment & Property Co Ltd* v *John Walker & Sons Ltd* (1976) and the dissenting judgment of Winn LJ in *Magee* v *Pennine Insurance*.

The equitable principle in relation to mutual mistake is, therefore, an uncertain one. Moreover it appears that rescission is not available for unilateral mistake, unless the one party contributed to the other's mistake: *Riverlate Properties Ltd* v *Paul* (1975). It is not easy to discern the equitable principle behind this distinction. Equity may also intervene by the refusal of the remedy of specific performance. And the courts do not always appear to have been consistent in this regard: contrast *Malins* v *Freeman* (1837) with *Tamplin* v *James* (1880).

It appears, therefore, that the rigidity of the common law doctrine of mistake all but precludes a plaintiff from relying on the mistake in order to avoid the contract. He would be better advised to seek relief in equity, but the flexibility of the equitable principles may lead to an uncertain outcome.

# 9 DURESS AND UNDUE INFLUENCE

9.1 Introduction

9.2 Key points

9.3 Analysis of questions

9.4 Questions

## 9.1 Introduction

As we have seen in earlier chapters, the law has never been particularly concerned with equality of the parties or their relative status. As a result of the early twin influences of laissez faire and the doctrine of freedom of contract the courts have never been prepared to intervene simply because a contract is unfair to one party. The law will, however, intervene if improper pressure has been put on the disadvantaged party to make the contract. It should be noted, however, that the pressure must be *improper*; simple competition between two parties is not enough. Inevitably in any agreement, although entered into voluntarily, the parties may have been influenced by their own personal financial status or market levels or other factors.

In the key points that follow, the commonest forms of such improper pressure are noted.

## 9.2 Key points

It is important that the student understands the following:

a) *Duress*

Traditionally common law defined duress within the very strict confines of actual or threatened physical violence to the victim. In particular common law did not recognise threats directed at goods or possessions as duress.

The presence of duress makes the contract voidable at the option of the victim. Starting in 1964, with the case of *Rookes* v *Barnard* [1964] AC 1129, however, there are a whole line of cases which have developed the law relating to duress, considerably. The *Rookes* v *Barnard* case revived and expanded the hitherto neglected tort of intimidation. In *Universe Tankships* v *ITF* [1982] 2 All ER 67, it was stated by Lord Scarman that 'duress if proved, not only renders voidable a transaction into which a person has entered under its compulsion, but is actionable as a tort, if it causes damage or loss', thus establishing the connection between duress and the tort of intimidation.

As a steady progress in after 1964 the courts have systematically extended the definition of duress to take into account the fact that certain forms of unethical commercial pressure could amount to economic duress. Again there is a long line of cases tracing this development and with which the student should be familiar.

As recently as 1989, in *Atlas Express Ltd* v *Kafco* [1989] 1 All ER 641 and in *Vantage Navigation Corp* v *Suhail & Saud Bahwan Building Materials, The Alev* [1989] 1 Lloyd's Rep 138 the concept of economic duress was discussed and it is apparent that the concept is still developing. The student should read further in a more detailed textbook.

Finally, it should be noted that it is not necessary to show that duress was the sole cause of the victim entering into the contract. Any form of pressure which is unlawful will be sufficient to constitute duress, the effect of which on a contract is, as stated before, to render it voidable.

b) *Undue influence*

As noted earlier, the common law definition of duress was an extremely narrow one.

Equitable rules developed a doctrine of undue influence in response to this. There are two main forms of undue influence: express and presumed.

Express influence means that the party seeking to avoid the transaction must clearly and specifically prove that as a result of improper pressure by the advantaged person, and *only* because of that, he was induced to make the contract. More frequently it is the second form of undue influence – that presumed from a special relationship which is involved.

The type of relationship in which such influence has been presumed is not a closed list – students should consult a textbook for details. However, the type of relationship tends to be where one party is better educated, or has some dominant psychological influence, or has a senior relationship to the other party. Hence solicitor and client, religious adviser and parishioner and parent and child are examples of the above influences.

Recent cases on undue influence include *O'Sullivan* v *Management Agency & Music International* (1985); *Goldsworthy* v *Brickell* (1987); *Midland Bank* v *Shephard* (1988); *Bank of Credit & Commerce International SA* v *Aboody* (1989) and a New Zealand case, *Shivas* v *Bank of NZ* (1990). The student should of course be familiar with these and other cases concerning undue influence.

The burden of proof is on the party seeking to enforce the contract, to rebut the presumption of undue influence. This is most often done by showing that the apparently 'influenced' person had independent, impartial advice before entering the contract.

Finally, note that because undue influence is an equitable doctrine, the right to have the contract set aside may be lost in a number of circumstances, most especially where there is undue delay or third party rights have arisen.

c) *Inequality of bargaining power*

In *Lloyds Bank* v *Bundy* [1975] QB 326, Lord Denning argued that duress and the various other forms of improper pressure all shared the same common feature that the parties were of unequal bargaining power. Similarly, a decade later in *Alec Lobb (Garages)* v *Total Oil* [1985] 1 All ER 303 it was sought to have a contract set aside on the grounds, inter alia, that the bargain was harsh and unconscionable.

It was argued that, because of the financial pressures suffered by the garage owner plaintiff and because of the oil company's superior economic footing, the parties were on an unequal footing and because of that inequality, the terms of the contract were unfair and unreasonable.

The Court of Appeal rejected the argument and stated that the question of unconscionable conduct and use of coercive power would only become relevant in 'exceptional cases'. Most recently of all in *National Westminster Bank v Morgan* [1985] 2 WLR 588 it was noted that because of increased legislative controls to protect the interests of consumers there was really no need in modern law for a doctrine of relief against inequality of bargaining power.

Thus, the concept of relief afforded by the courts to a plaintiff who claims he is a victim of unequal bargaining power now seems suspect. The courts recognise that it is rare in any transaction to find the parties on an exactly equal footing. Also, as already pointed out, the scope of duress has been widened very considerably and has reduced the need for a common law rule on inequality of bargaining power.

d) *Protection by statute*

As well as those statutes which, by their provisions protect individual consumers – such as the Sale of Goods Act 1979, or the Unfair Contracts Act 1977, or the Consumer Credit Act 1974 – it is worth noting in particular:

i)   Consumer Credit Act 1974 empowers a court to 'reopen' any contract which amounts to 'an extortionate credit bargain'; and

ii)  Fair Trading Act 1973 which controls practices which 'subject customers to undue pressure'.

## 9.3 Analysis of questions

Duress and undue influence have not been popular as topics for examination questions. It should be noted that the first question quoted (which was until 1991, the *only* question to feature duress) couples duress and non est factum (which was dealt with in Chapter 8: Mistake). This is in fact a very common way of linking the two topics. Since the material available on duress and undue influence has been rather limited it has never made a very suitable topic for a full question. Recently, however, an increase in the amount of material available has made inequality of bargaining power and economic duress suitable topics for questions (see especially Q2 1991, quoted below.) Often, where a question of the 'write short notes on ...' type appears, or a multi-part question, it is this type of question that sometimes has duress or undue influence as a topic. This is the type of mix of topics it is difficult to predict, often appearing to be quite arbitrary in choice by the examiner. Note, in the first question below that part (iii) relates to capacity (see Chapter 7).

## 9.4 Questions

QUESTION ONE

Explain the meaning and effect of:

i) undue influence;

ii) non est factum; and

iii) contracts for necessaries.

University of London LLB Examination
(for External Students) Elements of the Law of Contract June 1983 Q9

*Skeleton Solution*

Undue influence

• express influence – burden of proof;
• presumed influence – relationships – rebuttal;
• effect of undue influence on a contract;
• loss of right of rescission.

Non est factum

• incapacity of person raising plea;
• disparity between documents in reality and as believed to be by mistaken party;
• effect of negligence or carelessness;
• if plea successful – effect on contract?

Contracts for necessaries

• those affected: infants, of unsound mind and drunk;
• definition including SGA s3(3);
• executory contracts;
• must be, overall, beneficial to the infant.

*Suggested Solution*

i)  *Undue influence*

Undue influence is an equitable doctrine and is concerned with cases in which one party to a gift or contract has, or is in equity considered to have, used to his advantage some position of influence or dominance acquired or enjoyed by him over another. It may take one of two forms: (a) express influence or influence in fact; and (b) presumed influence.

Express influence arises where there is some degree of actual coercion or domination, falling short of duress at common law. In a leading case, *Williams* v *Bayley* (1866), a mortgage executed by a father in favour of some bankers so as to prevent his son being prosecuted for forgery was set aside in equity, the court having regarded the father as not having entered into the transaction as a free agent. With the development of 'economic duress' at common law, in *The Atlantic*

*Baron* (1979) and *Pao On* v *Lau Yiu Long* (1980), express influence is likely to be of decreasing importance. Where express influence is alleged, it must be proved by the party alleging it.

Undue influence is presumed where the parties are in a particular relationship of confidence, being usually but not necessarily a fiduciary relationship. Typical cases are parent and child, doctor and patient, trustee and beneficiary and solicitor and client. However, it is the nature of the confidential relationship which is important, as was emphasised in *Tate* v *Williamson* (1866), where undue influence was presumed in a transaction between distant relatives, and in *Lloyds Bank* v *Bundy* (1975) the presumption was held to arise in a banker and customer relationship. The presumption, however, cannot arise between husband and wife: *Hoes* v *Bishop* (1909). Or, if undue influence does exist as between husband and wife, the court will not recognise its effects. See *Bank of Credit & Commerce International* v *Aboody* (1989) where the Court of Appeal refused to interfere on the basis that the wife would probably have acted in the same manner anyway and no hardship had been caused.

Where undue influence is presumed, the court must be satisfied that the transaction was the result of the free exercise of an independent will by the vendor or transferor, the burden of proof being on the other party; he must rebut the presumption. Normally this will be done by showing that the vendor or transferor was independently advised, but this is not a necessary requirement: *Inche Noriah* v *Shaik Allie Bin Omar* (1929). However, its absence greatly increases the burden of the party seeking to rebut the presumption.

Undue influence renders a contract voidable in equity, not void at law, and the right to rescind the contract may be lost through affirmation or acquiescence: *Allcard* v *Skinner* (1887).

ii) *Non est factum*

Non est factum – 'it is not my deed' – is a common law doctrine under which a party executing a deed or signing a document may contend that it is not binding on him and void at law because he executed or signed it under a mistake.

Because of the sanctity of deeds and written contracts in English law, non est factum is a plea which is available only in exceptional cases. Originally only a blind or illiterate person could rely on the plea, and although the scope has been gradually extended, still the courts require some degree of disability or infirmity on the part of the signer. In *Gallie* v *Lee* (1971) the House of Lords was divided as to whether a person of full age and understanding could rely on the plea. Those of their Lordships who were not prepared to rule out this possibility expressed the view that it would only be in the most exceptional of cases that such a person could plead it.

*Gallie* v *Lee* clarified the law in two important respects. First it rejected the test laid down in *Foster* v *MacKinnon* (1869) that the mistake on the part of the signatory had to be a mistake as to the character of the document rather than its contents. The House of Lords held that the disparity between the document actually signed and the document as it was believed to be must be 'fundamental', 'radical' or 'very substantial'.

Secondly, their Lordships overruled *Carlisle and Cumberland Banking Co* v *Bragg* (1911) and held negligence or carelessness on the part of the signatory precludes a plea of non est factum.

### iii) *Contracts for necessaries*

Contracts for necessaries merit special treatment in English law where one party to the contract suffers from some form of incapacity, ie infancy, drunkenness or mental incapacity. Necessaries comprise strictly: (a) necessary goods, as defined in the Sale of Goods Act 1979 s3(3); and (b) necessary services, eg legal or medical services. However, in the context of infants the courts have on occasions extended 'necessaries' to include beneficial contracts of service under which an infant is or is learning skills to enable him to earn his living: *Roberts* v *Gray* (1913).

Section 3(3) of the 1979 Act defines necessary goods as 'goods suitable to the condition in life of the minor or other person concerned and to his actual requirements at the time of the sale and delivery'. Thus one must ascertain whether the goods themselves are capable of being necessaries, and then whether in fact they are necessaries for this particular purchaser, and it matters not that the seller was unaware that he was already adequately supplied with goods of the type in question: *Nash* v *Inman* (1908).

It is settled law that drunken or mentally disordered persons are not liable on executory contracts for the sale of necessary goods: *Re Rhodes* (1890). In the case of infants, the law is less certain. In *Nash* v *Inman* (1908) Buckley LJ was of the view that an infant had limited contractual capacity under the Sale of Goods Act and was thus liable ex contracta, whereas Fletcher Moulton LJ considered an infant's liability was re ie in quasi-contract. In the light of s3(2) of the 1979 Act, which refers to necessaries 'sold and delivered', of the desirability and logic of having one rule which applies to infants and drunken and mentally disordered persons, and also because there has (remarkably) been no reported case in which an infant has been held liable on an executory contract, it is submitted that the view of Buckley LJ is to be preferred.

As to infants' beneficial contracts of service, referred to as 'necessaries' in *Roberts* v *Gray* (1913) that case is authority that an infant may be liable where the contract is executory only. However, for the contract to be binding it must be shown that, having regard to all the terms of the contract, it is, overall, beneficial to the infant: *De Francesco* v *Barnum* (1890) and *Clements* v *LNW Ry Co* (1894).

QUESTION TWO

'I would suggest that ... there runs a single thread ... "inequality of bargaining power". By virtue of it, the English law gives relief to one who, without independent advice, enters into a contract upon terms which are very unfair or transfers property for a consideration which is grossly inadequate ...' Lord Denning in *Lloyds Bank* v *Bundy* (1975).

Discuss this statement.

Written by Editor

*Skeleton Solution*

• Duress.
• Undue influence.
• Statutory controls.
• Inequality of bargaining power.
• Denning's argument.
• Refutation of that argument.

*Suggested Solution*

The twin doctrines of laissez faire and freedom of contract have meant that the courts have never been particularly interested in the fairness or otherwise of a bargain or the relative status of parties to the contract. However, the very fact that for a valid contract to exist, the parties must voluntarily consent to the agreement means that the courts have been forced to recognise the fact that this reality of consent will not be present if one party has been subjected to improper pressure by the other. Note that it is important that the pressure must be 'improper', normal commercial competition is not at all the same thing.

The law recognises various kinds of improper pressure, falling within the following categories: duress, undue influence, inequality of bargaining power and certain forms of pressure proscribed by statute.

Duress, a common law concept, originally existed only within narrowly defined limits: *Skeate* v *Beale* (1840), though in modern times the doctrine has been extended and become more flexible. In particular the courts have developed a form of 'economic' duress in *Occidental Worldwide Investment* v *Skibs A/S Avanti* (1976); Kerr J declared that commercial pressure alone was not enough to constitute economic duress. 'The court must be satisfied that the consent of one party was overborne by compulsion so as to deprive him of any animus contrahendi.'

Much will obviously depend on the facts of the particular case whether this is so. See *North Ocean Shipping* v *Hyundai Construction* (1979), *Pao On* v *Lau Yiu Long* (1980) and *Universe Tankships* v *ITF* (1982).

The narrowness of the original concept of duress led to the development of undue influence. The basis of the doctrine was best explained in *Allcard* v *Skinner* (1887) and the rules of undue influence are based on manifest disadvantage of one party conferring benefit on the other. Undue influence may take two forms, that where the law *presumes* because of the relationship of the parties that undue influence exists and that which must be proved expressly.

Certain statutes, eg Consumer Credit Act 1974 and Fair Trading Act 1973 seek to control transactions where one party may be at a notable disadvantage to the other.

In *Lloyds Bank* v *Bundy* (1975) Lord Denning, after examining duress, the various forms of improper pressure and inconscionable bargains, sought to derive a general principle from these categories. He felt they all rested in inequality of bargaining power. 'By virtue of it' he said, 'English law gives relief to one who, without independent advice, enters into a contract on terms which are very unfair or transfers property for a consideration which is grossly inadequate, when his bargaining power is grievously impaired by reason of his own needs or desires, or by his own ignorance or infirmity, coupled with undue influence or pressures brought to bear on him by or for the benefit of the other.' The principle, said Denning, did not depend on any proof of wrongdoing, there was no need to establish improper pressure.

In subsequent cases Lord Denning went on to reiterate his view that the concept of inequality of bargaining power is recognised by English law: see *Clifford Davis* v *WEA Records* (1975) and *Levison* v *Patent Steam Carpet Cleaning* (1978).

But did others agree with him? Some support for Denning's argument is derived from the speech of Lord Diplock in *Schroeder Music Publishing* v *Macaulay* (1974), but it should be remembered that Diplock was dealing with the particularly narrow problem of standard form restraint of trade contracts.

Otherwise there has been little indication of judicial support. In *Bundy* (1975) itself the other members of the Court of Appeal based their decision on undue influence and did not find it necessary to comment on Denning's argument.

In *Pao On* v *Lau Yiu Long* (1980) Lord Scarman stated that if duress was not established, to treat the unfair use of a dominant bargaining position as a ground for invalidating a contract was 'unhelpful in the development of law' and a year later in *Burmah Oil* v *Bank of England* (1981) the court rejected the argument that inequality of bargaining power is of itself a ground of invalidity.

In *Lobb* v *Total Oil* (1985) the plaintiff sought to have the transaction set aside on the grounds, inter alia, that the bargain was harsh and unconscionable. It was argued that because of Total Oil's superior economic position and the financial pressures faced by the plaintiff, the parties were in a position of unequal bargaining power and the courts should apply criteria to assess whether the terms were fair and reasonable.

The Court of Appeal rejected this argument. Dillon LJ observed that it was seldom in any contract that the bargaining power of the two parties was absolutely equal. The courts, said Dillon LJ, 'would only interfere in exceptional cases where as a matter of common fairness it was not right that the strong should be allowed to push the weak to the wall'.

In *National Westminster Bank* v *Morgan* (1985) Lord Scarman pointing out the increasing growth of (particularly) statutory restrictions on freedom of contract declared: 'I question whether there is any need in the modern law to erect a general principle of relief against inequality of bargaining power.'

In conclusion, therefore, it may be said that Denning's proposal has found little support among the judiciary. The increasing importance attached to economic duress and the widening of the scope of this concept has largely, as Treitel points out, rendered Denning's 'golden thread' irrelevant. While it is true to say that most forms of duress and undue influence stem from the inequality of the parties, it is *not* true that the mere fact that the parties are not on an equal footing will give grounds for declaring the contract invalid.

QUESTION THREE

'The concept of economic duress is built on shaky foundations, since superior bargaining power always coerces.'

Discuss.

University of London LLB Examination
(for External Students) Elements of the Law of Contract June 1991 Q2

*Skeleton Solution*

• Concept of economic duress.

• Development.

• Limitations on the doctrine.

*Suggested Solution*

The concept of economic duress is of recent origin, receiving the first clear judicial recognition in *Occidental Worldwide Investment Corp* v *Skibs A/S Avanti, The Sibeon and The Sibotre* (1976) where Kerr J rejected the earlier narrow confines of duress and held that, in certain circumstances, a contract entered into as a result of economic pressure could be liable to be set aside. Kerr J emphasised, however, that mere commercial pressure, exerted by one party, was not in itself sufficient to constitute duress. He said that the court must 'be satisfied that the consent of the other party was overborne by compulsion so as to deprive him of animus contrahendi'. The concept of economic duress received further recognition in *North Ocean Shipping Co Ltd* v *Hyundai Construction Co Ltd, The Atlantic Baron* (1979) where Mocatta J held that a threat to break a contract could amount to duress.

The existence of the doctrine of economic duress has been affirmed by the Court of Appeal in *B & S Contracts and Design Ltd* v *Victor Green Publications Ltd* (1984), by the House of Lords in *Universe Tankships Inc of Monrovia* v *International Transport Workers' Federation* (1983) and by the Judicial Committee of the Privy Council in *Pao On* v *Lau Yiu Long* (1980). In two recent cases the doctrine has been regarded as firmly established. In *Vantage Navigation Corporation* v *Suhail and Saud Bahwan Building Materials, The Alev* (1989) Hobhouse J stated that the doctrine is 'now well established' and in *Atlas Express Ltd* v *Kafco (Importers and Distributors) Ltd* (1989) Tucker J observed that it was 'a concept recognised by English law'.

There is, it is submitted, still some uncertainty surrounding the operation of the concept. In *The Sibeon and The Sibotre*, it has been noted above, duress was distinguished from mere commercial pressure: it was necessary to show that the will of the party concerned had been overborne by compulsion. In *Pao On* the Judicial Committee of the Privy Council endorsed this approach. Lord Scarman said that there must be the presence of some factor 'which could be regarded as coercion of his will so as to vitiate his consent'. The factors to consider were:

i)   whether the person alleged to have been coerced did or did not protest;

ii)  whether he had an adequate legal remedy;

iii) whether he was independently legally advised; and

iv)  whether he subsequently took steps to avoid the contract.

This approach has been subsequently modified. In the *Universe Tankships* case Lord Scarman said that compulsion had been described in the authorities as coercion or the vitiation of consent. But his lordship went on to say that:

'The classic case of duress is, however, not the lack of will to submit but the victim's intentional submission arising from the realisation that there is no other practical choice open to him.'

Lord Scarman emphasised that the lack of choice could be proved in various ways, by protest, by the absence of independent advice, by the steps taken to avoid the contract, but none of these evidentiary matters went to the essence of duress. 'The victim's silence will not assist the bully, if the lack of any practicable choice but to submit is proved'. In the recent case of *Dimskal Shipping* v *ITWF* (1991) the House of Lords, discussing what constituted duress, stressed that while the 'pressure' complained of might be quite legal in Sweden where the act took place, it constituted duress under English law (by which the contract was governed) and was thus 'improper'.

It has been suggested that to regard these matters as merely 'evidentiary' creates considerable uncertainty in applying the doctrine (Andrew Phang, 'Whither Economic Duress' (1990) 50 MLR 107). Moreover whilst the decisions focus on the *illegitimacy* of the pressure there is some doubt as to what constitutes illegitimate pressure. In *Universe Tankships* Lord Scarman suggested that 'illegitimate' pressure could include pressure that was not 'unlawful' but this suggestion was not elaborated on.

The courts have often stressed the distinction between duress and commercial pressure. In *Lloyds Bank Ltd* v *Bundy* (1975) Lord Denning MR sought to merge the concept of duress with the broader doctrine of 'inequality of bargaining power'. Subsequently Lord Denning reiterated the view that English law recognised the doctrine in *Clifford Davis Management Ltd* v *WEA Records Ltd* (1975) and in *Levison* v *Patent Steam Cleaning Co Ltd* (1978). Some recognition appeared to be afforded to the doctrine by the speech of Lord Diplock in *Schroeder Music Publishing Co Ltd* v *Macaulay* (1974), but this was in the particular context of a restraint of trade clause in a standard form contract.

But this broad doctrine was doubted by the Privy Council in *Pao On* and expressly disapproved by the House of Lords in *National Westminster Bank* v *Morgan* (1985). Lord Scarman observed that the legislature had undertaken the task of enacting restrictions on freedom of contract, and he doubted whether the courts should assume the burden of formulating further restrictions. In the Court of Appeal, in *Alec Lobb (Garages) Ltd* v *Total Oil (Great Britain) Ltd* (1985) Dillon LJ, in rejecting the argument based on unequal bargaining power, noted that it was seldom in any negotiation that the bargaining position of the parties was absolutely equal.

Whilst the concept of economic duress does now appear to be firmly recognised in English law doubts remain, both as to the nature of the pressure required and as to the evidence necessary to prove the absence of choice.

# 10 PRIVITY OF CONTRACT

10.1 Introduction

10.2 Key points

10.3 Analysis of questions

10.4 Questions

## 10.1 Introduction

The traditional approach to rights and liabilities which are the subject of a contract is to assert that they can vest only in a party to the contract. This is because the law seeks only to enforce contracts supported by consideration. This approach has, on occasion, caused hardship and in recent years a departure may be witnessed from strict application of the rules of privity (see, for example, *Jackson* v *Horizon Holidays* (1975)).

## 10.2 Key points

It is important the the student understands the following:

a) *Circumstances outside the rule*

  i) Collateral contracts

    The concept of a collateral contract has already been mentioned (in Chapter 4: Contents of the contract) where, as in *Shanklin Pier* v *Detel Products* [1951] 2 KB 854 when A enters into a contract with B to undertake work, and as a consequence of that agreement B enters into a subsidiary or collateral contract with C for the supply of materials; when the materials prove defective it proved possible for A to sue C. The reasoning in the above case was that the plaintiffs had provided consideration to the defendants by making the opportunity for the contractors to purchase and use the defendants paint.

    Obviously in this type of contract, it is sometimes necessary to use very convoluted, not to say artificial reasons, to find the consideration moving from the plaintiffs.

  ii) Multi-partite agreements

    There are a number of possibilities here. For example, if a person joins a club or other unincorporated association, the contracts with all the other members, even though he may not know them or even be aware of the total membership. Another example of a multi-partite agreement is, of course, agency, when one person contracts as agent with a third party, on behalf of his principal. There may also be sub-agencies. Generally, if things go well, the agent(s) then drop out and are not privy to the contract and cannot sue or be sued on it. However, see the section on agency (in chapter 16) for more details.

b) *Attempts to impose liabilities on third parties*

As a general rule the contract will bind only those who are parties to it and cannot impose obligations on a third party. The reason is obviously, to impose obligations on a person via a contract to which he had never consented or perhaps never even knew about, would run contrary to the most fundamental doctrine of freedom of contract. There are, however, ways in which the common law has sought to circumvent this rule. For example, by using the law of tort, a person may be forced to adhere to the terms of another's contract. The *Lumley* v *Gye* case ((1853) 2 E & B 216), is still a good example despite its age – the plaintiff being able to sue the defendant for interference with contractual rights; after the defendant had induced an opera singer employed by the plaintiff to refuse to perform her contract for the plaintiff in order to go and work for the defendant.

Bear in mind that, even when the common law imposes no liability, equity may. In relation to negative covenants concerning the use of land, for example, equity imposes a duty on third party purchasers of affected land to observe such covenants. The leading case is *Tulk* v *Moxhay* (1848) 2 Ph 774. Even so, the rules relating to restrictive covenants are qualified by restrictions, the most notable being that in order to be bound the third parties must have 'notice' – again a harking back to the doctrine of freedom of contract.

There have been some rather desultory attempts to extend the equitable doctrine on restrictive covenants to cover contracts for hire of ships, but this has never really been systematically followed up in the English courts and it is probable that there is not really an equitable rule in existence on this matter.

c) *Attempts to impose benefits on third parties*

The main rule here is also known as the rule in *Tweddle* v *Atkinson*, after the leading case on the subject ((1861) 1 B & S 393). In that case it was stated that while one or two older cases might give the impression that a stranger to the consideration may maintain an action on it if he stood in a near relationship to the party furnishing consideration, that was no longer to be assumed to be possible. The rule laid down by *Tweddle* v *Atkinson* has become a standard common law rule – that no one who is not a party may sue on a contract.

d) *Creation of a benefit by equity*

Although in common law contractual rights cannot be bestowed on or enforced by a stranger to the contract, one way of getting around this rule is the equitable concept of a trust.

Two conditions are necessary for the courts to be persuaded that there really is a trust in existence and that this is not just some disguised attempt for a third party to enforce a contract:

i) there must be a clear intention to create a trust, though actual terminology is not vital;

ii) it should be apparent that, once set up, the parties had no intention of altering/reducing the subject matter of the trust.

Thus, although if A and B contract together to pay C £1,000, C cannot enforce the contract if they fail to do so; if A and B set up a trust then it would be possible not only for the trustees to sue, but C the beneficiary also, should the trust be broken.

e) *Statutory exceptions*

Certain specific exceptions to the doctrine of privity have been created by statute, such as price maintenance agreements and certain types of insurance contract.

Lord Denning also suggested that the wording of s56 LPA 1925 which declared: 'A person may take an interest in land or other property, or the benefits concerning land or other property, though he may not be named a party to the conveyance or other instrument' effectively destroyed the doctrine of privity. However, in 1968 the Lords rejected this view outright in *Beswick* v *Beswick* [1968] AC 58 and declared that s56 should not be taken outside its context and could have no application here.

## 10.3 Analysis of questions

There have been only five questions in the last twelve years of London University papers devoted exclusively to privity of contract. Four are quoted below and it will be seen that the essay-type question is most common and all cover some similar ground. However while the 1983 question requires the student to argue a particular proposition as to circumvention of the rule, the 1985 question requires a much more general overview of the doctrine, including some thoughts on reforms, while the 1990 and 1992 questions are a mix of both. The fifth question (Question 6 of the 1994 paper) is included in chapter 20.

It should be noted as well, that the subject can be combined with a number of other possible topics. Thus, in the 1987 paper from University of London Question 6 linked privity with exclusion clauses. To be sure the lion's share of the answer needed to cover exclusion clauses, but at least one quarter of it was concerned with enforcement of a contract by a third party.

Similarly in the same year, 1987, the question devoted mainly to remedies – Question 8 – had a part in which it was necessary to discuss, as a preliminary item, whether or not the remedy would be available at all to a stranger to the contract.

1990 provides another instance of combination of privity with remedies – primarily damages for distress and that question is quoted below.

## 10.4 Questions

QUESTION ONE

'The doctrine of privity of contract is largely academic at the present day, since the courts in practice do indirectly what the doctrine says cannot be done directly.'

Explain and comment.

University of London LLB Examination
(for External Students) Elements of the Law of Contract June 1983 Q8

*Skeleton Solution*

• History and development of doctrine of privity.

- Suggestions for reform, criticisms.
- Ways of circumventing doctrine, eg trusts, collateral contracts.
- Unsuccessful attempts by judiciary to further wider doctrine.
- Statutory exceptions.

## Suggested Solution

The doctrine of privity of contract is a settled and integral part of English law. However, it has long been apparent that the doctrine can operate harshly or inequitably or otherwise produce undesirable results, and in consequence the courts have in a variety of ways sought to avoid this by developing a number of exceptions or qualifications to it. In this essay these judicial innovations will be examined in order to see whether the doctrine has in consequence been deprived of all or most of its practical effect and become 'largely academic'.

The problem the courts have most often had to grapple with is that of a contract made for the benefit of a third party. The doctrine of privity means that the third party cannot enforce the contract against the promisor: *Tweddle* v *Atkinson* (1861) and *Beswick* v *Beswick* (1968). As long ago as 1937 the Law Revision Committee recommended the abolition by Parliament of this rule, but no steps have been taken to do this. Recently in *Woodar* v *Wimpey* (1980) three members of the House of Lords indicated, obiter, that the time had come for the courts to act, if Parliament would not, and to reverse the rule in *Tweddle* v *Atkinson* (1861). That is something which can only be done by the Lords, and if and until that happens, lower courts are bound by authority to deny the third party a remedy.

This rule has, however, been circumvented in reported cases in a number of ways:

i)  By granting specific performance at the suit of the promisee in favour of the third party, as in *Beswick* v *Beswick* (1968). But as exemplified by *Woodar*, for one reason or another specific performance may not always be available or appropriate. In *Beswick* v *Beswick* (1968) the plaintiff only succeeded because of her dual capacity as administratrix and third party.

ii) By holding that the promisor is the trustee of his contractual promise for the third party, thereby enabling the latter as beneficiary directly to enforce the trust, eg *Les Affreteurs Reunis* v *Leopold Walford (London) Ltd* (1919). However, this is a device which is not now favoured by the courts, as exemplified by *Re Schebsman* (1944), because it usually involved imputting to the promisor and promisee an intention to create a trust which they may well not have possessed.

iii) By, if the facts of the case permit, holding there to be a collateral contract with the third party, eg *Shanklin Pier* v *Detel Products* (1951). This convenience will, however, be available only in a small minority of cases.

Attempts have been made to establish broader exceptions of more general application; in particular by Lord Denning MR. These have, however, been censored or overruled by the House of Lords. In *Beswick* v *Beswick* (1968) in the Court of Appeal his Lordship took the view that the doctrine of privity was procedural only and could be overcome by the third party joining the promisee as a defendant in an action. On appeal the House of Lords rejected this.

In *Jackson* v *Horizon Holidays* (1975) his Lordship applied an alternative device, holding that the promisee could recover damages for and on behalf of the third party, and would hold them to the third party's order. His Lordship sought to rely on *Lloyds* v *Harper* (1880). In particular the judgment of Lush LJ as establishing this principle, but in *Woodar* v *Wimpey* (1980) the House of Lords (obiter) severely disapproved of this concept and was unanimously of the view that Lush LJ was concerned solely with a case of trust or agency and was not enunciating a principle of general application.

The continual existence and operation of the doctrine of privity can also be seen in cases dealing with the converse of the above, ie instances in which it is sought to impose burdens on persons not parties to the contract. Resale price maintenance cases such as *Taddy* v *Sterious* (1904) and *McGruther* v *Pitcher* (1904) illustrate that but for the intervention of the legislation by means of the Resale Price Maintenance Acts, the doctrine of privity would mean that manufacturers would be virtually powerless to impose or enforce resale price levels.

Similarly, save for the somewhat uncertain exception exemplified by *De Mattos* v *Gibbon* (1859) and *Lord Strathcona SS Co* v *Dominion Coal Co* (1926) and recently revived by Browne-Wilkinson J at first instance in *Swiss Bank Corporation* v *Lloyds Bank Limited* (1981) a purchaser of goods or chattels in English law appears to take them free of prior contractual rights as to their use. In *Port Line Ltd* v *Ben Line Steamers Ltd* (1958) Diplock J (as he then was) emphatically thought this was so, and expressed the view that the *Strathcona* case was wrongly decided.

The reason why a purchaser is not affected by prior rights is that the doctrine of privity holds that he cannot be bound by the terms of a contract to which he is not a party. He may view liability to the third party in Court, eg inducing breach of contract or unlawful interference with contractual rights, but in contract the doctrine of privity does not fetter him.

It is therefore respectfully submitted that the doctrine of privity cannot correctly be described as being 'largely academic'. It certainly would not have been in *Woodar* v *Wimpey* (1980) where if the House of Lords had agreed with the Court of Appeal and held the promisor to be in breach of contract, by rejecting the judgment of Lord Denning in *Jackson* their Lordships would have been bound to hold that the promisor could, in effect, breach with impunity his promise to pay a substantial sum of money to a third party, the contract no longer being specifically enforceable. True, as indicated, the courts have developed a number of devices to avoid some of the harsher consequences of the doctrine of privity, but some only, not all. That was why in *Woodar* three of their Lordships were in favour of radically revising the doctrine should some appropriate occasion arise in the future.

QUESTION TWO

'English law holds that no stranger to the consideration can take advantage of a contract, although it was made for his benefit.'

Explain and comment. To what extent do you consider that this statement presents an accurate picture of the legal position?

University of London LLB Examination
(for External Students) Elements of the Law of Contract June 1985 Q7

## Skeleton Solution

- The general rules as to privity – the basic case of *Tweddle* v *Atkinson* (1861) – developments.
- Ways to circumvent the rule – developments of equity – trusts – statutory exceptions.
- Reforms – 1937 LRC Report – responses.

## Suggested Solution

The statement refers to the doctrine of privity of contract and in considering it the following will be discussed:

a) the general rule;

b) exceptions to it; and

c) how the law may be developed in future cases.

### The general rule

The rule that a person cannot acquire enforceable rights under a contract to which he is not a party, even though it may have been made for his benefit, is considered to have been conclusively established in 1861 in the case of *Tweddle* v *Atkinson* (1861) where the fathers of a bride and groom agreed with each other to pay certain sums to the groom, adding that the groom should have the power to recover those sums by action if either failed to pay. The bride's father defaulted and the groom sued, but his action failed on the grounds (inter alia) that he was not a party to the contract.

The rule in *Tweddle* v *Atkinson* has been affirmed by the House of Lords on three separate occasions this century, namely *Dunlop Pneumatic Tyre Co Ltd* v *Selfridge & Co Ltd* (1915), *Scruttons Ltd* v *Midland Silicones Ltd* (1962) and *Beswick* v *Beswick* (1968). In the latter case their Lordships disagreed with the conclusion of the Court of Appeal that s56(1) of the Law of Property Act 1925 had abolished the doctrine of privity and expressed the view that the sub-section created only a limited exception in the law of real property. Although in *Woodar Investment Development Co Ltd* v *Wimpey Construction UK Ltd* (1980) certain remarks were made by their Lordships about the desirability of overruling *Tweddle* v *Atkinson* (1861), unless and until this is done by the House, or the legislature chooses to amend the law by statute, *Tweddle* v *Atkinson* (1861) is binding authority on all inferior courts that a stranger cannot sue on a contract to which he is not a party.

The practical consequences of the rule can often be that a considerable injustice is suffered. Not only can the third party not sue, the promisee also cannot sue to recover damages on behalf of the third party unless a relationship of trust or agency exists. In *Jackson* v *Horizon Holidays Ltd* (1975) Lord Denning held that *Lloyds* v *Harper* (1880) established the principle that a promisee who made a contract for the benefit of a third party can recover damages on the latter's behalf. This judgement was strongly disapproved by all five members of the House in *Woodar Investment Development Co Ltd* v *Wimpey Construction UK Ltd* (1980) and although *Jackson* v *Horizon Holidays Ltd* (1975) was technically not overruled, it seems inconceivable that it would be followed in future cases. Henceforth *Lloyds* v *Harper* (1880) is to be regarded as dealing with relationships of trust or agency only and, in consequence, the third party's loss will be uncompensated. In *Forster* v *Silvermere Golf and Equestrian Centre Ltd* (1981) Dillon J said this result was a blot on the law and most unjust; it remains, nevertheless, the law.

A means of avoiding this injustice and preventing the third party's loss not being remedied was utilised in *Beswick* v *Beswick* (1968) where the plaintiff, the promisee's widow, was able as his administratrix to obtain specific performance against the defendant, the promisor, in her own favour as third party beneficiary, thereby preventing the defendant from breaking his contract with impunity. However, specific performance is a discretionary remedy and not automatically granted, and although the court might be strongly minded to order it so as to prevent injustice occurring, it will not always be possible, eg as in *Woodar Investment Development Co Ltd* v *Wimpey Construction UK Ltd* (1980) where the contract had been terminated and was not capable of being specifically enforced.

*Exceptions*

Because of the injustice that may flow from a strict application of the rule in *Tweddle* v *Atkinson* (1861), there are many exceptions to it, statutory, equitable and at common law. Some are true exceptions and others are devices adopted by the courts to circumvent the rule.

Of the statutory exceptions, reference has always been made to s56(1) of the 1925 Act. Whilst their Lordships in *Beswick* v *Beswick* (1968) did not speak with one voice as to the true construction of that sub-section, the predominant view was that it only applied in the law of real property where there is a purported grant to or covenant with a named person who is not a party to the instrument.

Other important statutory exceptions are contained in the law of insurance, in particular the Married Women's Property Act 1882 s11, the Road Traffic Act 1972 s148(4), the Marine Insurance Act 1906 s14(2) and the Fires Prevention (Metropolis) Act 1774 s83. These, in one field of insurance or another, allow an action to be maintained on an insurance policy by a person who is not a party to it.

The most important equitable exception is that of a trust: where A makes a promise to B for the benefit of C, C can enforce the promise if B has been instituted trustee of the promise for C: *Tomlinson* v *Gee* (1756) and *Les Affreteur Reunis SA* v *Leopold Walford (London) Ltd* (1919). Whilst the concept of a trust of a contractual right is straightforward and comprehensible, determining in any particular case whether one has been created can be a question of considerable difficulty and leave much room for judicial ingenuity.

For a trust to be instituted the 'three certainties' must be present, ie of intention, subject matter and objects. In contract, it is the former that gives rise to the most difficulty, since it is rare for the promisor and promisee to make their intention clear in the terms of their agreement. Accordingly the question is often one of inference: whether one can impute to them an irrevocable intention to benefit the third party. Irrevocability is vital, since once a trust is created it is enforceable by the beneficiary and cannot be dissolved or determined by the settlor or the trustee or both.

The difficulty of deducing the parties' intentions have led to different conclusions being reached in cases involving broadly similar facts, eg *Re Flavell* (1883) and *Re*

*Schebsman* (1944). Taking a broad view of the trust cases it is probably fair to say that at one time the trust of a contractual right was a device commonly used to circumvent the doctrine of privity, but that often it was no more than device, and it involved attributing to the parties an intention they almost certainly never possessed. Now, by contrast, it seems no longer to be in favour.

Other exceptions, apparent or real, are the doctrine of agency, including the rules relating to undisclosed principals; collateral contracts, which may be used to 'construct' a contract (eg *Shanklin Pier* v *Detel Products* (1951)); and by established commercial practices which the courts are reluctant to upset, particularly the proposition that the bank is liable to pay on presentation by the seller of the proper shipping documents, although it is doubtful whether in terms of strict legal analysis a contract exists between them (eg *Hamzeh Malas & Sons* v *British Imex Industries Ltd* (1958)).

### Reform

As long ago as 1937, the Law Revision Committee in its 6th Interim Report recommended the abolition of the rule in *Tweddle* v *Atkinson* (1861) and that third parties should be entitled to enforce contracts made for their benefit, providing certain conditions were satisfied. Since then, two decisions of the House of Lords, *Scruttons* (1962) and *Beswick* (1968) have spurned this opportunity. However, in the latest privity case to reach their Lordships' House, *Woodar Investment Development Co Ltd* v *Wimpey Construction UK Ltd* (1980), there was a significant shift in judicial thinking. Although the point did not fall squarely for consideration, Lords Salmon, Keith and Scarman all said, obiter, that the time had come to reconsider and, probably reverse the rule in *Tweddle* v *Atkinson* (1861), and that if the legislature did not soon take this step then their Lordships' House should consider doing so. It seems, therefore, that the days of that rule may now be numbered.

### Conclusion

It is submitted that the statement is broadly correct, though it is a general rule subject to exceptions rather than being an absolute one. Further, it is a rule which, it appears, may now be retaining only a precarious foothold in English law.

QUESTION THREE

In January, in preparation for her daughter Bella's wedding in May, Mrs H agreed to hire J's vintage white Rolls Royce as the bridal car. She engaged K to take the wedding photographs and L to do the catering at the reception.

One week before the wedding J sold the Rolls Royce to M. M is also a photographer, and although he knew about the arrangements made by Mrs H he would not allow the Rolls Royce to be used for Bella's wedding unless he (M) was engaged to take the photographs in place of K.

Mrs H refused to employ M as the photographer and had to hire a modern limousine at a greater cost than the vintage Rolls Royce.

K's flash equipment failed during the service and Bella was heartbroken to find afterwards that there are no pictures of the actual marriage ceremony.

Mrs H, Bella and many more of the guests became ill after eating chicken at the reception which, unknown to L, was contaminated by salmonella.

Advise Mrs H and Bella.

University of London LLB Examination
(for External Students) Elements of the Law of Contract June 1990 Q6

## Skeleton Solution

- Privity of contract.
- Third party rights.
- Circumventing the doctrine of privity.
- Breach of contract.
- Damages for distress.

## Suggested Solution

The main issues raised here are those arising out of the doctrine of privity of contract. The question also requires some discussion of the availability of damages for distress for breach of contract.

The basic rule of privity was expressed in the following terms by Viscount Haldane in *Dunlop Pneumatic Tyre Co Ltd* v *Selfridge & Co Ltd* (1915):

'... in the law of England certain principles are fundamental. One is that only a person who is a party to a contract can sue on it. Our law knows nothing of a jus quaesitum tertio arising by way of contract.'

The consequences of the doctrine of privity of contract is that a third party cannot acquire benefits under a contract to which he was not a party, nor can a third party have obligations imposed on him by such contract. The doctrine has been characterised as 'a blot on our law and most unjust' by Dillon J in *Forster* v *Silvermere Golf and Equestrian Centre* (1981). Lord Scarman appeared to call for its abolition in *Woodar Investment Development Ltd* v *Wimpey Construction (UK) Ltd* (1980). As long ago as 1937 the Law Revision Committee (Cmnd 5449) recommended that where a contract expressly conferred a benefit on a third party it should be directly enforceable by the third party. However, these reforms have not as yet been implemented, though there are statutory exceptions to the privity rule and it may be possible to circumvent it.

Adverting to the particular problem, it is necessary to examine each of the contracts in turn.

## The contract with J for the hire of the Rolls Royce

J is clearly in breach of contract by selling the car to M. Mrs H can sustain an action against him for the breach. The remedy of specific performance is not, of course, available as performance is impossible: *Watts* v *Spence* (1976). Her remedy against J is a claim for damages. In accordance with the general principle that the purpose of an award of damages is to put her in the position she would have been in if the contract had been performed, she would be entitled to the difference between the contract price and the price she has to pay for the other vehicle. It is possible that she might have suffered distress at not being able to obtain the vintage Rolls Royce. The question of damages for distress is dealt with below.

M, to whom the Rolls Royce has been sold, knows of Mrs H's contractual rights, but refuses to allow her to exercise them unless he is engaged as the photographer. Because of the rules of privity of contract, this does not afford Mrs H any contractual claim against M: *Dunlop* v *Selfridge* (above). M is not a party to the contract between Mrs H and J and the obligations of that contract cannot be imposed on him at common law. Nor would equity impose any liability on him. The rule in *Tulk* v *Moxhay* (1848) appears to be confined to interests in land: the purported extension of that rule by the Judicial Committee of the Privy Council in *Lord Strathcona Steamship Co* v *Dominion Coal Co* (1926) has never been followed in the English courts and that decision must be regarded as doubtful authority; see the judgments of Diplock J in *Port Line Ltd* v *Ben Line Steamers Ltd* (1958) and Denning LJ in *Bendall* v *McWhirter* (1952).

The one possibility of circumventing the privity rule and fixing M with liability is in the law of tort which recognises liability for interfering with contractual rights: *Lumley* v *Gye* (1853); *British Motor Trade Association* v *Salvadori* (1949). (There are a number of trade union cases in this area of the law, but citation of them is beyond the scope of this question.) It is an essential ingredient of the tort that the wrongdoer knew of the contractual rights, but M possessed that knowledge and could not, it appears, escape liability.

*The contract with K for the wedding photographs*

It is assumed that the failure to take the photographs constitutes a beach of contract on K's part. Section 13 Supply of Goods and Services Act 1982 imposes a duty on the supplier of a service to carry out that service with reasonable skill and care. The question is: to whom, and to what extent, is he liable for that breach?

The question suggests that it is Bella, and not Mrs H, who has suffered distress as a result of the breach. Two points emerge for discussion; one, the extent to which a court will award damages for distress; two, who can sue for such distress.

Damages for distress have been awarded in cases involving contracts for a holiday: *Jackson* v *Horizon Holidays Ltd* (1975); *Jarvis* v *Swan's Tours Ltd* (1973). But an award of damages for distress is limited in certain classes of cases. In *Bliss* v *South East Thames Regional Health Authority* (1987) Dillon LJ held that such an award should be confined to cases 'Where the contract which has been broken was itself a contract to provide peace of mind or freedom from distress.' In *Hayes* v *James & Charles Dodd* (1988) Staughton LJ was of the opinion that the class might be somewhat wider than that 'But it should not include any case where the object of the contract was not comfort or pleasure or the relief of discomfort, but simply carrying on a commercial activity with a view to profit.'

A claim for damages for distress would, it is submitted, fall at least within the limits set by Staughton LJ. (By the same token Mrs H might well have a claim for damages for distress against J for his failure to supply the Rolls Royce.)

The question of who can sustain a claim for the distress against K must next be addressed. The privity rule is the clear difficulty in the way of an action by Bella. The rule that a benefit cannot be conferred on a third party was established in *Tweddle* v

*Atkinson* (1861) and affirmed by the House of Lords in *Beswick* v *Beswick* (1968). There is no evidence on the facts presented to indicate that Mrs H acted as Bella's agent, or that Bella was in any sense a party to the contract.

Nor can Mrs H sue for Bella's loss. In *Jackson* v *Horizon Holidays* (1975) Lord Denning held that the promisee could always sue for the third party's loss, but this view was expressly disapproved by the House of Lords in *Woodar* v *Wimpey* (1980). It must be concluded, therefore, that no claim will lie against K.

### The contract with L for the catering

The question suggests that there has been no negligence on L's part, so no action in tort will lie. So far as a contractual claim is concerned L appears to be in breach of the implied term in s14(2) Sale of Goods Act 1979, as amended by the Sale and Supply of Goods Act 1994, in that he has failed to supply goods of a satisfactory quality. Clearly Mrs H, as a party to the contract, can sue for damages for the illness she has suffered. What of Bella's illness? In *Woodar* v *Wimpey* (1980) Lord Wilberforce 'explained' the decision in *Jackson* v *Horizon Holidays* (1975). Although he rejected the view that the promisee can sue for the third party's loss, he was not prepared to part from the actual decision in that case. He said that it could be supported as a special type of contract, examples of which are persons contracting for family holidays or ordering meals in a restaurant, calling for special treatment – all the members of the family would be regarded as parties to the contract. Lord Russell appeared to hold that he did not criticise the outcome in *Jackson* because there the third party's loss was also the promisee's loss.

The strict application of the privity rule would debar Bella from a claim against L, and would also prevent Mrs H from suing for Bella's loss. However, the decision in *Jackson*, as justified by the House of Lords in *Wimpey*, permits the possibility that Bella can sustain an action on the basis that she too was a party to the contract with L, or that Mrs H can claim that Bella's loss was also her own. Whether this can be extended to the guests is extremely doubtful.

QUESTION FOUR

a)  Why does English law retain the doctrine of privity of contract?

b)  A owns a combine harvester. In May he enters into a contract with X in which he agrees to lease the machine to X for two weeks at the beginning of September for £2,000. X pays A a deposit of £500. In August A realises that his crops will fail and that he will have no need for the combine harvester so he sells it to Z who is aware of A's existing contract with X. In September X contacts A and then Z, but Z refuses to allow him to use the combine harvester. X cannot obtain the machine anywhere else at such short notice and faces losing all his crop if he is unable to harvest it by autumn.

Advise X of his rights against A and Z.

University of London LLB Examination
(for External Students) Elements of the Law of Contract June 1992 Q6

*Skeleton Solution*

a)  • Meaning of the privity rule.

   • Justification and criticisms of the rule.

b)  • X's rights against A.

   • X's rights against Z:

   – in contract;

   – in tort.

*Suggested Solution*

a) *Why does English law retain the doctrine of privity of contract?*

The doctrine of privity of contract has two aspects: the first is that a person who was not party to a contract cannot acquire rights under it; the second is that a person not party to the contract cannot have obligations imposed on him by that contract.

The doctrine has been much criticised, certainly in relation to the first aspect, and Lord Denning made frequent attempts to get rid of it, but at the time of writing it remains part of our law. The second aspect of the doctrine can be justified, but it is the refusal of our law to recognise third party rights in the conferring of benefits that is more difficult to justify. Treitel (Law of Contract, pp527–8) suggests four possible reasons for the retention of the doctrine. The first is that a contract is a personal affair, affecting only the parties to it; the second is that it would not be just to allow a person to sue on a contract when he could not be sued on it; the third is that to allow third party rights would interfere with the rights of the contracting parties to vary or rescind the contract; and the fourth possible reason is that the third party is often a mere donee and that it would be contrary to principle to allow him a contractual right.

A further feature of the privity of contract doctrine is that the promisee cannot sue for the third party's loss: see *Woodar Investment Development Ltd* v *Wimpey Construction Ltd* (1980) where the House of Lords disapproved the view of Lord Denning to the contrary in *Jackson* v *Horizon Holidays* (1975). In *Forster* v *Silvermere Golf and Equestrian Centre* (1981) Dillon J referred to this rule as 'a blot on our law and most unjust'.

Abolition of the rule that a third party cannot enforce the benefit was recommended by the Law Revision Committee in 1937 (6th Interim Report, 1937). And in *Woodar* v *Wimpey* Lord Scarman remarked that as the legislature had not acted to implement that recommendation the courts might have to. The Law Commission have recently published a consultation paper recommending that a third party should be able to enforce contractual promises subject to the promisor having the same defences and the same rights as to set-off and counter-claim as he would have against the promisee (See: 'Privity of Contract: Contracts for the Benefit of Third Parties' (Consultation Paper No 121, 1992)). The Commission recommends that parties to a contract should not be able thereby to impose duties on a third party.

In view of the judicial criticisms and repeated calls for the modification of the doctrine of privity of contract it is difficult to see why English law retains the doctrine.

b) *The problem*

    i) X's rights against A

In this problem X has certain rights and A has corresponding obligations arising out of the contract for the lease of the machine. A sells the machine to Z: by so doing he deprives himself of the ability to perform his contractual obligations and is, therefore, in breach of contract. X cannot obtain an order for specific performance against A as it is impossible for A to comply with it: see *Castle* v *Wilkinson* (1870). The only remedy that X would have as against A would be a claim for damages for breach of contract. If he cannot obtain the machine contracted for, or another machine, he might well be able to obtain damages for the loss of his crop, if such loss can be held to be within the reasonable contemplation of the parties.

    ii) X's rights against Z

X has no contractual rights against Z. The liability to provide the machine arises from a contract to which Z was not a party. To argue that the liability 'goes with' the machine would be a wholly unwarrantable extension of the decision in *Lord Strathcona Steamship Co* v *Dominion Coal Co* (1926) and, in any event, that decision of the Privy Council has been much criticised and never followed; see for example Diplock J in *Port Line Ltd* v *Ben Line Steamers Ltd* (1958) and Denning LJ in *Bendall* v *McWhirter* (1952).

Z, however, is aware of X's contractual rights. X may well therefore have an action in tort against Z for the wrong of interference with his contractual rights. The tort of inducing a breach of contract was established in *Lumley* v *Gye* (1853) and has been applied in many cases since and, indeed, extended to cover interference with contractual relations short of inducing a breach. A third party who, with knowledge of the contract, interferes with its performance, may be liable in tort: *British Motor Trade Association* v *Salvadori* (1949).

X would, therefore, have a claim in damages against Z for the commission of this tort. A further possibility is that X could seek an injunction against Z restraining him from interfering with his (X's) contractual rights. By this means he might obtain possession of the machine.

# 11 ILLEGALITY

## 11.1 Introduction

There are a number of different ways to categorise illegal contracts and readers of several text books will note that there is little agreement between the different writers.

Probably the simplest method is to split illegal contracts into those which in some way break the law, for example a contract to commit a crime or a tort and secondly, those contracts which by virtue of being contrary to public policy are considered illegal and thus void.

This is the classification which the authors Cheshire and Fifoot and Smith and Keenan use, but it is considered by other authorities to be oversimplified. Nevertheless, for convenience, the topic will be dealt with within this two-fold division.

Even having classified the type of illegality, further problems remain, notably the question of enforcement. Prima facie an illegal contract cannot be enforced in the courts. However, it will be seen that there are situations where, though the courts will not countenance enforcement, they will assist the injured party to recover money or goods.

## 11.2 Key points

It is important that the student understands the following:

a) *Contracts which break the law*

As well as contracts to commit a crime or tort, other possibilities include for example:

   i) cases where the contract itself is lawful, but the use to which the subject matter is to be put is illegal;

   ii) the way in which a legitimate contract is performed renders it illegal. This often includes administrative or procedural rules which have not been complied with;

   iii) a contract which purports to indemnify a party should he commit a crime, knowingly or otherwise (for example, an employer promising to indemnify a lorry driver against fines or other penalties for driving offences);

   iv) contracts which indemnify a party against committing a tort;

v)  contracts to waive rights conferred by statute, if this would undermine the purpose of the statute.

b)  *Contracts contrary to public policy*

Two things should be borne in mind here. Public policy is not the same as talking about fashions, though obviously changes in public morality do get reflected, eventually, in public policy. Secondly, the public policies of say, politics or morality are quite different from public policy as dictated by law. All the relevant law is initially dictated by the courts (though later, it may be incorporated into legislation) and for that reason most of the grounds of public policy on which a contract may be condemned as illegal, if not immutable are certainly very stringently applied and difficult to change. The whole area of public policy has a slightly 'dated' look.

The main grounds on which a contract may be declared void on the grounds of public policy are listed below. It should be noted that contracts in restraint of trade technically belong in this group, but they are of such importance that they are considered separately in Key point (c) below.

Contracts contrary to public policy include:

i)  contracts which pevert the course of justice, including concealing crimes, interfering with proceedings and agreements to prefer certain creditors over others in winding up and bankruptcy proceedings;

ii)  contracts which oust the jurisdiction of the courts; though it should be noted that to have a clause in a contract setting up arbitration is perfectly legal;

iii)  maintenance and champerty: instigation of or meddling in litigation by a person who has no interest at stake and a promise to finance proceedings in return for a share of any compensation, respectively;

iv)  contracts which promote sexual immorality – for example, contracts which have the effect of promoting prostitution;

v)  contracts relating to family – for example, contracts restraining marriage, or procuring marriage in return for consideration;

vi)  contracts which interfere either with the public affairs of this country or with foreign relations – for example, contracts to buy or sell public offices or public honours. Or contracts which, though quite legal in this country are illegal elsewhere, and would injure relationships between this country and another. Or, in times of war, contracts to trade with the enemy.

As will be seen, the list of contracts which might be declared void by the courts on the grounds of public policy is a long one. This is not, however, the complete list, nor is the list ever closed; there is always the possibility that some new type of contracts will be brought before the courts which they consider undesirable.

For recent cases on illegal contracts see *Euro-Diam* v *Bathurst* (1988); *Lemenda Trading* v *African Middle East Petroleum* (1988); and most recently *Edwin Hill & Partners* v *First National Finance Corporation* (1989) and *Picton Jones & Co* v *Arcadia Developments* (1989); *Howard* v *Shirlstar* (1990) and *City Index* v *Leslie* (1990).

131

c) *Contracts in restraint of trade*

As has been stated, this theoretically belongs in the group listed above; such contracts are prima facie void on the grounds of public policy. However, the whole topic has assumed such importance, especially in two fields – employment and sales of businesses – that it is more convenient to deal with such contracts separately.

Firstly, it should be noted that it is perhaps a misnomer to call these *contracts* in restraint of trade. More often they comprise one or more clauses, or covenants, in a much more complex contract, for example a contract of employment. While it is theoretically possible to have a whole contract devoted to restraint issues it is unlikely. Occasionally parties negotiating a major contract, say the sale of a business, may make restraint of trade competition the subject of a lesser, collateral contract.

Obviously if only a part of the overall contract is made up of the restraint covenant(s) the question of severance will arise. This is dealt with later in Key point (e), following. For definitions of restraint of trade the student should see the leading cases; starting with *Nordenfelt* v *Maxim Nordenfelt Guns and Ammunition Co* [1894] AC 535 up to cases like *Esso Petroleum Co* v *Harper's Garage (Stourport) Ltd* [1968] AC 269.

Space precludes listing all such relevant cases, many definitions have been attempted by the judiciary.

Although prima facie void, a covenant in restraint of trade will become enforceable if it can be proved that it is reasonable not only being in the interests of the parties (or at least the dominant party) but also that it is in the interests of the community as a whole.

The criteria for determining reasonableness will depend on which category the type of restraint falls into. For example, in a contract of employment, a court might consider the geographical limits, the time duration of the restricting imposed and so on. They might look at questions such as whether or not the employer has proprietary interests like secret trade processes to protect. When a covenant in restraint of trade occurs in a contract to sell a business, however, the criteria might be rather different. For one thing the parties are on a more equal footing and therefore it is not so difficult to prove restrictions to be reasonable. The courts might consider the sort of relationship with customers, for example, will the seller of the business be opening up elsewhere to draw trade away from the purchaser?

The student is recommended to read further on this topic; there is considerable case law and most textbooks devote rather more time and space to the main issues than can be spared here.

d) *Enforcement of illegal contracts*

When a contract is illegal, then it will be unenforceable and neither party can plead innocence or ignorance as an excuse.

Any attempts by the parties to enforce an illegal contract by indirect means will be declared invalid by the courts – for example, if an illegal contract provides for arbitration any such award will be declared null and set aside by the courts. The rules as to illegal contracts are extended to contracts which are legitimate in themselves, but the mode of performance is not. It is essential, however, that both parties be aware that the method of performance of the contract was illegal. When one party is innocent a slightly different situation will arise.

One party may be aware of the illegal aspect of the contract but the other be innocently unaware. In such cases the innocent party, while he will of course have no rights of enforcement, may have alternative means of redress. The main exceptions can be grouped as follows:

i)  Cases where the parties are not on an equal footing (in pari delicto) that is not equally in the wrong. The burden of proof will of course be on the weaker, less knowledgeable party to establish that he was unaware of the true situation and that the other party was in a better position than him to know all the facts.

ii)  Voluntary withdrawal from the contract. It needs to be established by the innocent party that this withdrawal or 'repentance' has occurred on learning the true nature of the contract and not merely because the illegal purpose of the contract has failed.

iii)  Rights independent of the contract. If a party can show that he has a right to property transferred under an illegal contract, quite separate from that contract. Obviously this will only apply when a party derives title to goods quite separately from the illegal contractual transaction and is unlikely to occur very often.

In all the above classifications, the courts will grant restitutionary remedies: they will help an innocent party recover money or goods already parted with. Otherwise the courts attitude to illegal contracts may be best summed up in the saying 'the loss lies where it falls'; the courts will not help to enforce illegal goods, nor will they assist the parties to recover money or goods handed over during performance of the contract.

e)  *Severance*

If a contract is only illegal in parts, then it may not be totally unenforceable. It may be possible to sever the unlawful sections and enforce the rest. Obviously the principles of severance are largely governed by sheer common sense. If the whole of the consideration for a contract is illegal, for example, the contract will be unenforceable and void.

The main difficulty is to disentangle the illegal sections of the contract and discard them, without rendering the remnants of the contract so vague and ambiguous as to be unenforceable. Hence the 'blue pencil test': the concept of striking out the offending words/phrases. The courts will not re-draft the illegal sections or add or substitute words. Essentially the contract should be just as the parties drafted it and as they intended, but without the illegal sections. The nature of the contract should remain unaltered.

Sometimes a contract will be so 'tainted with illegality' that severance is impossible.

## 11.3 Analysis of questions

Over the past twelve years of London University LLB examinations for external students there have been questions on illegality in most papers. Several of those have concentrated on restraint of trade!

Of the questions quoted below, three are general questions requiring a wide view of the law relating to illegality, the other requires a more specific knowledge of restraint of trade. Comparison of the questions over the years will show an abnormally high proportion of essay questions.

## 11.4 Questions

QUESTION ONE

'If a contract is tainted with illegality neither party can either enforce it or recover property which has passed to the other party under the contract.'

Explain and comment.

University of London LLB Examination
(for External Students) Elements of the Law of Contract June 1984 Q6

*Skeleton Solution*

• Definition of illegality.
• Knowledge of parties – both parties aware – one party innocent.
• Parties not in pari delicto.
• Property passing under contract usually irrecoverable – exceptions.
• No rights of enforcement.

*Suggested Solution*

There are two limbs to the proposition which will be discussed in turn, namely:

a) that neither party can enforce a contract tainted with illegality; and

b) that property which has passed under such a contract is irrecoverable.

First, limb (a). Although the attitude of English law to illegal contracts is generally summarised in the maxim ex turpi causa non oritur actis, it is submitted that the fact that a contract is tainted with illegality does not necessarily render the contract unenforceable by both parties. Such a simplistic formulation would ignore two important features to which the courts pay regard when considering the effect of illegality on a contract: (i) the nature of the illegality; and (ii) the state of the parties' knowledge.

The nature of the illegality is important because it is possible that the formation or performance of the contract may result in the commission of a statutory offence but that both parties (irrespective of their knowledge or otherwise of the illegality) will be able to enforce the contract. This will be so where, upon the true construction of the statute, the courts are of the view that it was the intention of Parliament to impose a penalty only in respect of the offence and not in addition to deprive the parties of their normal contractual rights arising out of the contract, of which leading examples are *St John Shipping Corporation* v *Joseph Rank Ltd* (1957) (overloading a cargo vessel) and *Shaw* v *Groom* (1970) (failure by a landlord to supply a tenant with a rent book).

There is an increasing tendency on the part of the courts to construe statutes in this way where the offence might perhaps be regarded as one of an administrative or technical nature, because of the drastic consequences of adopting the alternative construction as explained by Devlin J in the *St John Shipping* case (1957) and also in *Archbold's* v *S Spanglett* (1961).

The importance of the parties' knowledge is that in many cases if one party is unaware of and has not participated in the illegality, he may be able to maintain an action on the contract. Thus, in *Archbold*'s case (1961) a carrier who used an unlicensed vehicle for the carriage of goods was held liable in contract to the owner who did not know that the contract would be performed in an illegal manner. Conversely had the owner been aware of the illegality, the law would have regarded him as a participating party and deprived him of his normal contractual remedies, as was the case in *Ashmore, Benson, Pease & Co Ltd* v *A V Dawson Ltd* (1973). The *Ashmore* case concerned statutory illegality, the position is the same where the illegality is at common law: *Pierce* v *Brooks* (1866) (hire of a brougham to a prostitute). However, the ignorance relied on must be as to the facts constituting the illegality; it does not avail to say that one did not realise that the transaction contravened the law: *Miller* v *Karlinski* (1945) and *J M Allan (Merchandising) Ltd* v *Cloke* (1963).

By way of yet further qualification, there is one instance where the law regards guilt or innocence as being irrelevant. This is where the illegality is statutory and, upon its true construction, the statute or statutory instrument absolutely prohibits contracts of the type concluded by the parties. In such cases, neither can sue under any circumstances: *Re Mahmoud and Ispahani* (1921).

Thus, in conclusion on limb (a), one must qualify it by saying that both the nature of the illegality and the state of the parties' knowledge are frequently relevant in determining where either or both are prevented from suing on a contract tainted by illegality.

Next, limb (b). On the footing that illegality prevents one or other party pursuing his normal contractual remedies, does this also mean that property which has passed is irrecoverable?

The general rule is summed up in the maxim in pari delicto portior est conditio defendentis, the effect of which is that where both parties are implicated in the illegality, money paid or property transferred under the contract is irrecoverable: *Taylor* v *Chester* (1869) and *Parkinson* v *Royal College of Ambulance* (1925). This is not because the law regards the position of the person in possession as being less blameworthy, it is merely refusing its assistance to the transferor seeking recovery and is a further application of the maxim ex turpi causa non oritur actio. It is, however, a rule subject to a number of exceptions, as follows:

i)   The law allows a party to an illegal contract a locus poenitentiae or an opportunity of repentance. If he resiles from the transaction while it is still executory he will be able to recover property transferred or money paid, *Taylor* v *Bowers* (1876), but not once it has been partially performed, *Kearley* v *Thomson* (1890), nor where all that has happened is that for some reason or other the illegal objective has become impossible of performance: *Bigos* v *Boustead* (1951).

ii) The rule will not apply where the parties are not in pari delicto (ie equally in the wrong) in the following circumstances:

- where the offence is statutory and the statute is a class-protecting one, eg *Kiriri Cotton* v *Dewani* (1960) (illegal premium recoverable from a landlord by a tenant), but not *Green* v *Portsmouth Stadium* (1973) (statute not passed for the protection of bookmakers);
- where there has been fraud or oppression, eg *Atkinson* v *Denby* (1862) and *Reynell* v *Sprye* (1885);
- where there has been abuse of a fiduciary relationship, *Re Thomas* (1894).

iii) Property may be recoverable where all that was created under the illegal contract was a limited interest in that property, which interest will in the course of time be terminated or expire.

Illegality goes as to the enforceability of a contract: it renders it unenforceable but does not mean that the transaction is of no legal effect. Title to goods can pass under an illegal contract for the sale of goods, *Singh* v *Ali* (1960) and *Belvoir Finance Co Ltd* v *Stapleton* (1971) and an illegal lease vests a term of years in the tenant, *Feret* v *Hill* (1854). Thus, if the interest created under the contract pursuant to which possession of property passes is of a limited or temporary nature, on the determination of that interest the owner can recover possession. In so doing he would be relying not on the illegal contract but on his own legal right to possession. Thus, under an illegal contract of bailment, when the period of hire expires or is otherwise determined, the true owner can demand redelivery and claim damages for conversion if the goods are not returned, *Bowmakers Ltd* v *Barnet Instruments Ltd* (1945), and it is submitted, in the expiry of a term of years granted under an illegal lease, the landlord will be able to recover possession of the premises.

iv) Other minor exceptions are:

- where there has been a reasonable mistake of fact, *Oom* v *Bruce* (1810);
- where money has been paid under a marriage brokerage contract, *Hermann* v *Charlesworth* (1905); and
- where a statute expressly authorises recovery, eg illegal premiums are recoverable under ss119–125 of the Rent Act 1977.

Thus, although the general rule is that property which has passed under an illegal contract is irrecoverable, it is subject to a number of important exceptions.

QUESTION TWO

'The unsatisfactory nature of the doctrine of restraint of trade is due to the inherent contradiction between it and the idea of freedom of contract.'

Discuss.

University of London LLB Examination
(for External Students) Elements of the Law of Contract June 1989 Q6

*Skeleton Solution*

- Definition of covenant in restraint of trade.
- Concept of freedom of contract.
- Restraint of trade prima facie void – may be enforceable if reasonable – definition of reasonable.
- Areas where restraints used, eg employment, sales of businesses etc.
- Recent developments.

*Suggested Solution*

An agreement in restraint of trade has been judicially defined as 'one in which a party (the covenantor) agrees with any other party (the covenantee) to restrict his liberty in the future to carry on trade with other persons not parties to the contract in such manner as he chooses' – per Diplock LJ (as he then was) in *Petrofina (Great Britain) Ltd v Martin* (1966).

It must be conceded that there is a contradiction between the doctrine of restraint of trade and the idea of freedom of contract. The courts are required to balance the competing principles of freedom of contract and freedom of trade. A person is entitled to carry on any lawful trade or occupation that he chooses, but he should also be free to limit that right by a contract into which he freely enters. The doctrine has been justified in different ways. In the earliest cases the restriction on an individual's right to trade was regarded as being 'against the benefit of the Commonwealth': *Colgate v Bachelor* (1569). More recently, in *A Schroeder Music Publishing Co Ltd v Macaulay* (1974) the justification was said, in the House of Lords, to be that it protected the weaker party against the stronger.

The modern law on restraint of trade derives from the House of Lords' decision in *Nordenfelt v Maxim Nordenfelt Guns and Ammunition Co Ltd* (1894). The policy of the law was formulated by Lord Macnaughten in the following propositions:

a) all restraints of trade, if there is nothing more, are contrary to public policy, and therefore void;

b) but there are exceptions: restraints of trade may be justified by the special circumstances;

c) it is a sufficient justification, indeed it is the only justification, if the restriction is reasonable – reasonable in the interests of the parties and reasonable in the interests of the public.

It is for the party in whose interest the restriction is imposed (the covenantee) to show that it is in the interests of the parties; the onus of showing that it is against the public interest is on the party subject to the restriction (the covenantor).

For the restraint to be reasonable in the interests of the parties, the covenantee must show that he is protecting a legitimate interest, and that the restraint goes no further than is necessary for the protection of that interest. It has been said – and this is an expression of the inherent contradiction – that a restraint cannot be unreasonable if the parties have agreed to it: *North West Salt Co v Electrolytic Alkali Co Ltd* (1914).

But the courts, in their role of custodians of public policy and protectors of the weak against the strong, do make these findings.

It is not common for the courts to find that a restraint that is reasonable in the interests of the parties is nevertheless unreasonable in the interests of the public. In *Attorney-General for Australia* v *Adelaide Steamship Co* (1913) the Privy Council found that they were not aware of any such case. More recently, however, the importance of recognising the public interest has been recognised: *Esso Petroleum Co Ltd* v *Harper's Garage (Stourport) Ltd* (1968).

It is necessary to examine various types of contract in which the doctrine operates.

*Employment contracts*

In such contracts the employee covenants that he will restrict his work and trading activities after the termination of the contract. But the employer is not entitled to protect himself merely from competition: an employee must, as a matter of public policy, be allowed to use the skills and experience he has gained in the employment even if he then competes with his former employer: *Herbert Morris Ltd* v *Saxelby* (1916); *Faccenda Chicken Ltd* v *Fowler* (1986). The employer must show that he is protecting a legitimate interest; trade secrets or customer connections. Trade secrets consist of the knowledge of some secret process, formula or design. An employer is also entitled to protect his customer connections. But he must show that the employee had a direct influential relationship with the customers: in this regard the status of the employee will be an important feature; the more senior an employee the more likely it will be that he will have had this kind of relationship.

Having established that there is a legitimate interest to protect, the employer must then satisfy the court that the restraint goes no further than is necessary for the protection of that interest. This involves an examination of the area of the restraint, its duration and the activities which it covers. Much depends on the particular facts. In *Mason* v *Provident Clothing and Supply Co* (1913) a restraint which operated within 25 miles of London was held to be unreasonable, whereas in *Foster & Sons Ltd* v *Suggett* (1918) a restraint operating throughout the United Kingdom was upheld. In *M & S Drapers* v *Reynolds* (1957) a term of five years was held to be unreasonably long; in *Fitch* v *Dewes* (1921) a life-long restraint was upheld. See the recent case of *Spencer* v *Marchington* (1988) for a discussion of the extent to which an employer may protect himself. Note that in *Allied Dunbar* v *Frank Weisinger* (1987) (but only recently reported), the concept of proportionality as a test of validity in a restraint of trade covenant was held to be wrong. The proper test was held to be to consider whether the restraint is reasonably necessary to protect the interests of the employer.

*Contracts between the seller and purchaser of a business*

In these contracts it is legitimate for the purchaser to protect himself from competition from the former owner of the business. Without such protection the value of the goodwill he has purchased might be rendered nugatory. Whilst similar considerations apply with regard to the reasonableness of the restraint as will be invoked in employment contracts, the courts will subject it to much less scrutiny. The livelihood of the covenantor is not primarily in issue, and the parties will be regarded as being of equal bargaining strength. The courts here will have more regard to the concept of freedom of contract.

## Exclusive distributorship agreements

This is a comparatively recent development. The doctrine has been held to apply to an exclusive dealing agreement between a petrol company and a petrol station – a so-called solus agreement – whereby the petrol station undertakes to keep and supply only the company's products. In *Esso Petroleum Co Ltd* v *Harper's Garage (Stourport) Ltd* (1968) the House of Lords held that the doctrine applies where a person in occupation of land restricts his freedom to trade, it will not apply where a person who had no prior right of occupation acquires land subject to a restriction. This distinction has been adopted in, inter alia, *Cleveland Petroleum Co Ltd* v *Dartstone* (1969).

In *Pharmaceutical Society of Great Britain* v *Dickson* (1970) Lord Denning said that the doctrine of restraint of trade was not confined to particular kinds of contracts. Thus, it has been applied to the Football Association's player transfer system – *Eastham* v *Newcastle United FC* (1964); to the refusal of the Jockey Club to grant a woman trainer's licence – *Nagle* v *Fielden* (1966); and to a ban on cricketers who joined Mr Kerry Packer's 'circus' – *Greig* v *Insole* (1978).

QUESTION THREE

'Even if a person has entered into a contract which is unenforceable because of illegality the courts can provide him with redress so long as he comes with clean hands.'

Discuss.

University of London LLB Examination
(for External Students) Elements of the Law of Contract June 1990 Q5

## Skeleton Solution

- Pari delicto potior est conditio possidentis.
- Exceptions to this maxim.
- Parties not in pari delicto.
- Mistake as to an illegal contract.
- Repudiation (or repentence).
- Recovery without reliance on the illegal contract.

## Suggested Solution

This question requires discussion of the circumstances in which a party to an illegal contract, although he cannot enforce the contract, may be able to recover money or property passing under it.

The general rule is expressed in the maxim *in pari delicto potior est conditio possidentis.* This means that where the parties are equally culpable with regard to the illegality, recovery of money or property is not permitted, with the consequence that the person in possession is in the stronger position. However, there are exceptions to the rule. The broad principle behind the exceptions is that a court will decide whether or not to permit recovery depending on which option would give better effect to the prohibition of the contract.

The exceptions can be grouped under four headings: (i) where the parties are not in pari delicto; (ii) the contract has been entered into under a mistake; (iii) the person seeking recovery has repudiated the illegal contract; and (iv) where the plaintiff does not rely on the illegal contract to claim recovery. These will be considered in turn.

### Parties not in pari delicto

Where a statute has been enacted for the protection of a particular class of persons it is in the intersts of public policy that a plaintiff within that class should be permitted recovery. Thus in *Kiriri Cotton Co Ltd v Dewani* (1960) where the prohibition was against the payment of premiums exacted by landlords for the granting of a lease the tenant was allowed to recover the premium he had paid: see also *Kasumu v Bab-Egbe* (1956).

If a plaintiff has been coerced into entering into an illegal contract by duress recovery may be allowed: *Smith v Cuff* (1817).

Recovery will also be possible where the plaintiff enters into an illegal contract, being induced to do so by a fraudulent misrepresentation which concealed the illegality: *Hughes v Liverpool Victoria Legal Friendly Society* (1916).

### The contract entered into under a mistake

Where a party enters into an illegal contract under a mistake of fact he may not be without a remedy where he is innocent of the facts which render the contract illegal. Indeed the innocent party may in some circumstances be able to enforce the contract. Whether he is able to do so depends on the nature of the prohibition. If the statute prohibits both parties from concluding the contract neither the innocent nor the guilty party may enforce it: *Re Mahmoud and Ispahani* (1921). Where the prohibition is directed against one party, coupled with a sanction, the innocent party may be permitted to enforce the contract, depending on public policy considerations: *Archbold's (Freightage) v S Spanglett* (1961); *Phoenix General Insurance Co of Greece SA v Adas* (1987).

Even if the innocent party is not able to enforce the contract, which he entered into under a mistake of fact, he may be able to recover money or property: *Oom v Bruce* (1810). There can be no recovery where the mistake is one of law: *Harse v Pearl Assurance Co* (1904).

### Repudiation of the illegal contract

It is in the interests of public policy that people should be encouraged to repudiate illegal contracts into which they may have entered. A party is therefore afforded a *locus poenitentiae* and may withdraw from the illegal contract and recover his payment. But the repudiation must be in time. In *Kearley v Thomson* (1890) recovery of a payment was not allowed because the illegal purpose has been substantially carried out when the plaintiff sought to withdraw from the transaction. In contrast, where there was an illegal scheme to defraud creditors, the plaintiff had repudiated the scheme before the purpose had been carried out, and was permitted to recover the payment: *Taylor v Bowers* (1876).

Furthermore the repudiation must be voluntary. It will not avail a plaintiff if his repudiation of the illegal contract is occasioned by a third party or by the other party's breach of that contract: *Bigos* v *Bousted* (1951). A plaintiff cannot be said to have come with clean hands if the repudiation has been forced on him by external pressures.

## No reliance on the illegal contract

A plaintiff may be able to recover property (but not generally money) if he can establish a right to that property independent of the illegal contract. In *Bowmakers Ltd* v *Barnet Instruments Ltd* (1945) the plaintiffs delivered certain machine tools to the defendants under illegal hire-purchase agreements. The defendants, in breach of the agreements, failed to pay the due instalments, sold some of the machine tools and refused to return the remainder. The defendants, by virtue of their breaches of contract, no longer had any right to possess the goods. The plaintiffs were successful in an action for damages for the tort of conversion: they were able to establish their right to the goods without relying on the illegal transactions. See also *Belvoir Finance Co* v *Stapleton* (1970).

Recovery will not be permitted under this heading where the plaintiff is compelled to plead the illegality in order to found his claim: see *Taylor* v *Chester* (1869).

QUESTION FOUR

S was registered as a licensed plant and seed dealer under legislation which made it an offence to deal in such materials without an appropriate licence. Also, the relevant legislation required each delivery of seeds to be accompanied by a delivery note accurately describing the seeds.

In January, S agreed to deliver 20lbs of special spring cabbage seed to T for £200. By mistake the delivery note incorrectly described the seeds. T failed to pay for them but nevertheless went on to use them, which caused a failure in three fields causing losses of £44,000, since the seed delivered was ordinary spring cabbage seed.

In February, S delivered 3lbs of seed to U without any delivery note after U had said that 'Between friends we do not need to worry about such things.' U failed to pay.

In March, S provided rare plants to W to decorate her house. Unknown to S, W was notorious as a keeper of a well-known brothel and wanted the plants to create a more relaxing atmosphere for her customers. W failed to pay the £14,000 price for the plants.

In April, after S's licence had run out, he agreed to supply 39lbs of seed to V for which V had paid £1,250. When S discovered that his licence had expired, he refused to deliver the seed or return the money paid because, he alleged, it would be an offence to do so.

Advise S. What difference, if any, would it make to your advice if S knew, when the agreement with V was made, that the licence had expired?

University of London LLB Examination
(for External Students) Elements of the Law of Contract June 1991 Q4

*Skeleton Solution*

- Illegality in contracts.
- Enforceability.
- Recovery of money or property.
- Collateral contracts/warranties.

*Suggested Solution*

The general rule is that illegal contracts are not, as a matter of public policy, enforceable: this finds expression in the maxim ex turpi causa non oritur actio. Public policy also, as a general rule, prohibits the recovery of money or property passing under an illegal contract: this is reflected in the maxim in pari delicto potior est conditio defendentis. There are, however, exceptions to both these rules, or rather situations in which they do not apply. The relevant principles must now be applied to each of the contracts which S has concluded.

*The contract between S and T*

The illegality here lies in the incorrect description of the seeds in the delivery note. The contract is therefore illegal in its performance and not in its formation. The rights and liabilities of both parties must be considered in light of this.

S, having been responsible for the inaccurate delivery note, is the guilty party with regard to the illegality. Whilst the general rule is that the guilty party may not enforce a contract illegal in its formation: *Pearce* v *Brooks* (1866), the law adopts a more flexible attitude where the illegality relates merely to its performance. The question that will then be considered is whether the legislation intended to prohibit the contract or merely to penalise conduct: *St John Shipping Corp* v *Joseph Rank Ltd* (1957). It is clear that the legislation prohibits dealing in the relevant materials without the appropriate licence, but the requirement with regard to the *accuracy* of the delivery note may relate only to conduct in the performance of the contract and the legislation may provide an adequate penalty for failure to comply with this requirement. In this event S would be entitled to enforce the contract and claim the purchase price of £200. This is subject to any claim T may have against him.

T is the innocent party in the transaction. *Archbold's (Freightage)* v *S Spanglett* (1961) is authority for the proposition that the innocent party may bring an action on the contract in the event of breach. However, it is not entirely clear whether or not S has been in breach of contract. The problem presented does not make explicit whether particular cabbage was agreed upon and delivered, though incorrectly described in the delivery note, or whether the contract was for the seed described in the delivery note, which was not in fact delivered. In the latter event S was in breach of contract and T would be entitled to bring an action for the loss he has sustained.

*The contract between S and U*

In this situation the parties agree to contravene the requirement of the delivery note. Where the parties collude in the method of performance which they both know is illegal then both parties are denied enforcement: *Ashmore, Benson, Pease & Co Ltd* v *AV Dawson Ltd* (1973). It follows that S cannot recover the purchase price.

## The contract between S and W

In this situation there does not appear to have been any infringement of the legislation relating to dealing in the relevant materials. The illegality relates to the use to which W put the materials. It is clear that, if S had provided the plants knowing that they were to used for an immoral purpose, he would be denied enforcement: *Pearce* v *Brooks* (above). However S is innocent of W's intention and there is no public policy rule that would prevent recovery of the purchase price.

## The contract between S and V

When S entered into the agreement to sell the seeds to V he had no authority to do so. The position of the innocent party in this situation is not without difficulty. The leading case of *Re Mahmoud and Ispahani* (1921) held that where a statute prohibits both parties from concluding a contract, when one or either of them has no authority to do so, the contract is impliedly prohibited. But it does not follow that because it is an offence for one party to enter into a contract, the contract itself is void: *Bloxsome* v *Williams* (1824); and see the analysis of these two cases by Pearce LJ in the *Archbold's* case (above). 'Whether or not the statute has this effect depends on considerations of public policy in the light of the mischief which the statute is designed to prevent, its language scope and purpose, the consequences for the innocent party, and any other relevant considerations' (per Kerr LJ in *Phoenix General Insurance Co of Greece SA* v *Adas* (1987)).

On the present information it is not possible to say with certainty whether considerations of public policy would allow enforcement of the contract by V, who is an innocent party. Arguably the decision in the *Phoenix Insurance* case would prohibit such enforcement. In this event no claim would lie against S by V for the failure to deliver the seed or return the money.

V might not be without a remedy, however, if S knew that the licence had expired at the time the agreement was made. He may be able to rely on an implied collateral warranty that S had the requisite licence: *Strongman (1945) Ltd* v *Sincock* (1955) – though the warranty was express in that case. V might also be able to recover damages for misrepresentation: *Shelley* v *Paddock* (1980) and he might be able to rescind the contract. A further possibility is that V could recover the money he has paid in reliance on S's fraudulent misrepresentation that the contract was legal: *Hughes* v *Liverpool Victoria Legal Friendly Society* (1916).

QUESTION FIVE

a) 'Contracts illegal as formed and illegal as performed are treated differently but there is no reason why they should be.'

Discuss.

b) P was a registered supplier of electrical goods. The Supply of Electronic Goods Act 1992 which set up a registration system required all designated goods to be supplied by a registered supplier and accompanied by a statutory note of delivery.

Q received 200 designated goods without a statutory note after Q had persuaded P that as they knew each other well it was unnecessary.

R ordered a massage machine for R's brothel from P. The statutory note was provided.

P supplied 100 designated goods to S when unknown to P his statutory registration had expired because he had failed to renew it.

P has not been paid for any of these goods.

Advise P.

University of London LLB Examination
(for External Students) Elements of the Law of Contract June 1993 Q6

*Skeleton Solution*

a) • The position of the guilty party: contracts illegal as formed and illegal in the performance; the difference of treatment by the courts and the rationale for that difference.

• The position of the innocent party with regard to enforcement of an illegal contract: when he may enforce and when he may not.

b) • The contract with Q; illegal as formed or merely as performed.

• The contract with R; whether P is to be regarded as an innocent party.

• The contract with S; whether P's ignorance allows him to enforce.

*Suggested Solution*

a) The different treatment of contracts illegal as formed and illegal as performed is in respect of the right to enforce such contracts. It is convenient, in discussing this question, to look in turn at the positions of the guilty party and the innocent party.

*The position of the guilty party*

The guilty party cannot enforce a contract which is concluded for an illegal purpose. A landlord who drew up a lease in a manner designed to deceive the local authority in respect of rates could not sue for the rent: *Alexander v Rayson* (1936). The owner of a brougham who knowingly let it to a prostitute for the purpose of her profession could not sue for the hire: *Pearce v Brooks* (1866).

The courts take a different view, however, where the illegality is merely in the method of performance. In *St John Shipping Corp v Joseph Rank Ltd* (1957) the shipowner was held entitled to his freight even though he had overloaded his ship, in contravention of the statute. Devlin J found that, the offender having been deprived of the fruits of his crime by the penalty imposed by the statute, it would be curious if he were also to be deprived of his freight charges. In *Howard v Shirlstar Container Transport Ltd* (1990) the illegality was in the performance of the contract. The offender was engaged to remove an aircraft from Nigeria, and did so in breach of Nigerian air traffic control regulations. His criminal conduct was designed to free himself from danger. The Court of Appeal held that this was an instance where it would not be an affront to the public conscience to permit enforcement of the contract.

## The position of the innocent party

'Innocent' in this context means that the party is mistaken as to the law or as to the facts. Mistake as to the law does not generally give the innocent party the right to enforce a contract affected by illegality: *Nash* v *Stevenson Transport Ltd* (1936).

Where he is mistaken as to the facts, the innocent party *may* be able to enforce the contract, depending on the nature of the prohibition which engenders the illegality: contrasting cases are: *Archbolds (Freightage) Ltd* v *S Spanglett Ltd* (1961) and *Re Mahmoud and Ispahani* (1921). The distinction between these cases, and the position with regard to the statutory prohibition on contracts, was analysed by Kerr LJ in *Phoenix General Insurance Co of Greece SA* v *Adas* (1987). This may be summarised as follows:

i)   Where a statute prohibits both parties from concluding or performing a contract, the contract is prohibited and neither party can enforce it – as in *Re Mahmoud and Ispahani*.

ii)  But where a statute merely prohibits one party from entering into a contract and/or imposes a sanction on him if he does so, this does not necessarily render the contract unenforceable: (the unilateral prohibition in *Archbolds (Freightage) Ltd* on the carrier did not debar his innocent customer from bringing an action on the contract). Whether or not the statute has this effect depends on considerations of public policy.

A party to an illegal contract is not 'innocent' if he enters into a contract with the intention that the other party should perform an illegal act: *Ashmore, Benson, Pease & Co Ltd* v *A V Dawson Ltd* (1973).

It appears that, with regard to both the guilty and the innocent party, the paramount question is one of public policy. In the case of the guilty party the court will not assist him to gain the fruits of his crime, but if the illegality is merely in the performance of the contract, and there is a criminal sanction attached to the illegal performance, public policy does not necessarily require the further imposition of a civil penalty. As far as the innocent party is concerned the effect of a statutory prohibition is construed in the light of the mischief which the statute was designed to prevent.

b)   This part of the question involves an application of the principles discussed above to the three contracts into which P has entered. These contracts will be dealt with in turn.

## The contract with Q

Here the illegality consists in the failure to provide the required statutory note. If that were all it might well be that P could enforce payment as in the *St John Shipping case* (above). But in that case Devlin J said that '... a contract which is entered into with the object of committing an illegal act is unenforceable.' Where an intention that one party should do an unlawful act exists at the time of contracting neither party can enforce the contract: *Ashmore, Benson* (above). There appears to have been such intention here; accordingly P cannot enforce payment.

### The contract with R

The statute is not relevant to this contract. It is not stated whether or not the massage machine is one of the 'designated goods' so it is not clear if the statute applies. In any event P has complied with the statutory requirements. The illegality lies in the fact that the machine has been ordered for an immoral purpose.

If P knew the purpose for which the machine was intended, it is clear that he could not enforce payment: *Pearce* v *Brooks* (above). If P knew neither the purpose for which the machine was intended, nor that R kept a brothel, it is equally clear that he could enforce payment. What is less certain is the situation – possibly unlikely – if he knew that R kept a brothel, but did not know that R intended to use the machine in the brothel. There is authority which supports the view that this limited knowledge would not deprive P of enforcement: *Appleton* v *Campbell* (1826).

As P's state of knowledge is not known it is not possible to give a more definite answer for this particular contract.

### The contract with S

The position here is that P is no longer a 'registered supplier' but that P is ignorant of this. What has to be investigated is the purpose of the statute. Does it intend merely to impose an obligation on suppliers of designated goods, possibly coupled with a penalty for non-compliance, or does it mean to prohibit the contract? In *St John Shipping* (referred to previously) Devlin J gave this example:

' … a person is forbidden by statute from using an unlicensed vehicle on the highway. If one asks oneself whether there is in such an enactment an implied prohibition of all contracts for the use of unlicensed vehicles, the answer may well be that there is, …'.

Applying that example to the present facts it seems that there is an implied prohibition on the supply of designated goods by unregistered suppliers, and that the contract with S falls within the prohibition. P cannot therefore enforce payment.

# 12 FRUSTRATION

## 12.1 Introduction

The original rule in common law was that no matter how harsh it might appear, once a party had bound himself to a contract he was obliged to fulfil the obligations under that contract regardless of the fact that he was deriving no benefit from the contract. Thus, under the original, basic rule, if a person hired a cottage for a year, and it burned down just before he moved in, he would still be liable to pay the rent on it.

The turning point came in 1863 with the case of *Taylor* v *Caldwell* (1863) 3 B & S 826. Up to that point, the courts had resolutely refused to accept that there were any circumstances at all in which a party might be relieved of his obligations under a contract which subsequently became impossible to perform; unless, that is, the parties had anticipated events and made express provision in the contract for them. *Taylor* v *Caldwell* was the archetypal frustration case: a music hall, hired by Taylor for four concerts, burned down before any of the concerts could be held. The courts decided that, since the contract was subject to the implied condition that the music hall would continue to exist, because the hall no longer existed, the contract was impossible to fulfil and the parties were to be relieved of their obligations.

It should be borne in mind that contrasted with, for example, contracts void ab initio for mistake; frustration is concerned with contracts which are quite valid when made, but where subsequent events change the nature of the contract, or make it physically impossible to perform.

When a contract becomes completely impossible to perform because of some physical change in circumstances, it is unlikely that anyone, least of all the courts would quibble with the description of the contract as frustrated. However, when subsequent events after the formation of the contract, while not rendering it totally impossible to perform, remove the whole purpose of the contract and make it pointless to continue – *then* it might be more difficult to decide whether the contract is truly frustrated.

## 12.2 Key points

It is important the the student understands the following:

a)  *The tests for frustration*

There are, basically, two tests to determine whether a contract is frustrated. Each test has its supporters and its critics; while there are also those, for example,

Lord Wilberforce (in *National Carriers* v *Panalpina (Northern) Ltd* [1981] AC 675, who believe that the two tests merge into one and the choice depends on what 'seems most appropriate to the contract under consideration'.

While this is probably true, it has been suggested that there are borderline cases where the use of one test or another might give a different result.

The two tests are:

i)   The 'radical change in obligation' test

In the case of *Davis Contractors Ltd* v *Fareham UDC* [1956] AC 696 the majority of the Lords adopted this test. It has recently been supported by other judicial decisions. The student should consult a text book for more details. In the *Davis* case, the Lords decided that the application of this test was a three-fold process:

- to construe the contractual terms in the light both of the contract and surrounding circumstances at the time of its creation;
- to examine new circumstances and decide what would happen if the existing terms were applied in the light of those circumstances;
- to compare the two sets of contractual obligations and see whether there has been a radical or fundamental change.

Thus, on reading these guidelines it is apparent that it is the nature of the *obligation* that must have changed, not just the surrounding circumstances.

ii)   The implied term theory

This was always the more heavily criticised of the two tests. It seems likely that it can now, to all intents and purposes be regarded as abandoned by the courts. The main feature of the test was the argument that implied terms could be incorporated into certain contracts that would, if not complied with and a particular state of affairs not continue, release the parties from their obligations. It was the artificiality of this concept – the 'conjuring up' of an implied term to deal with a situation which the parties probably never envisaged, that was its greatest weakness and the cause of most of the criticism.

b)  *Examples of frustration*

There are a number of possible ways in which a contract can become frustrated and a number of those possibilities are listed below. However, this list is by no means exhaustive. Most of this list has developed from cases and the student should read a textbook for more detailed information on relevant case law.

i)   Destruction of the specific object essential for the performance of the contract.

ii)   Illness or other personal incapacity where the personality of one of the parties is crucial to the effective performance of the contract, eg in show business contracts.

iii)   The non-occurrence of a specified event.

iv)   Interference by the government, eg wartime restrictions.

v)  Supervening illegality.

vi) Inordinate and unexpected delay.

vii) The frustration of leases: for a long time thought to be impossible to frustrate, the House of Lords decided in the *Panalpina* case that in principle a lease *could* be frustrated when there was only one purpose fixed for the property/land leased; of which the lessor was aware and this purpose became impossible.

c) *Limitations on the doctrine of frustration*

There are a number of rules which tend to restrict the application of the doctrine. For example, the parties may anticipate the frustrating event and make express provision for it; in which case the contract will not be frustrated.

The fact that supervening events made the contract more onerous than anticipated does not frustrate it. The *Davis Contractors* case has already been mentioned; it was held that merely because bad weather, together with labour shortages meant the work took longer and cost more, did not mean the contract could be considered frustrated. Similarly, on the closure of the Suez Canal in 1956; there were a flurry of shipping cases, all of which revolved round the question as to whether, since the ships were forced to go 'the long way round' the contracts were frustrated.

It was held that the change in circumstances was not sufficiently fundamental; although costing more and taking longer, the contracts could in most cases still be performed.

It should be noted that frustration should not be self-induced. That is, the party relying on frustration should be able to prove that the events leading to frustration are externally caused. If there is a suggestion of self-inducement, the burden of proof switches to the party who alleges it.

In other words the frustration should be caused by some extraneous event or change, and this should be quite without any fault or blame attributable to either party. If there is any suggestion that one party was instrumental in *causing* the extraneous factor, then there may be self-induced frustration.

See, for example, the cases of *F C Shepherd* v *Jerrom* (1986) and, more recently, *Lauritzen AS* v *Wijsmuller BV* (1989) both of which examine the question of self-induced frustration in more detail than is possible here.

d) *The effects of frustration*

Unlike breach of contract when the injured party may elect to repudiate the contract or to affirm it; frustration ends the contract automatically.

Since the contract was valid until the frustrating events rights and liabilities incurred up to that point remain, only obligations still to be discharged are cancelled. Prior to 1943, the attitude of the courts was harsh, there was no provision for pre-frustration restitution and no possibility of suing for breach, because that required total failure of consideration which had not occurred.

In 1943 the Law Reform (Frustrated Contracts) Act was introduced to remedy the defects of the common law.

Its main provisions are contained in s1(2) which states:

'All sums paid or payable to any party in pursuance of the contract before the time when the parties were so discharged, shall, in the case of sums so paid be recoverable from him as money received by him for the use of the party by whom the sums were paid and in the case of sums so payable, cease to be payable.'

Section 1 goes on to provide, inter alia, for a party to recover such expenses as the court thinks just for expenditure already incurred to the point of frustration. Similarly it makes the proviso that if one party has obtained a valuable benefit (for example, work done) before the frustrating event occurs he must be made to pay a reasonable sum for it.

Thus, there are really three basic rules:

i) all sums actually paid at the time of frustration can be recovered;

ii) sums still to be paid, cease to be payable;

iii) a party who has incurred expenses in performing the contract prior to frustration may recover expenses and a party who has derived any valuable benefit from the contract as performed, must pay for it.

The Act is very flexible and designed to ensure justice as between the parties. It is not concerned with detailed apportionment between the parties or specific restitution for particular items – more with obtaining an overall balance in the parties' position without unjust enrichment on either side.

Note that the Act does not apply to:

i) voyage charterparties;

ii) contract for carriage of goods by sea;

iii) insurance contracts;

iv) contracts for sale of specific goods which perish.

## 12.3 Analysis of questions

Of the twelve years of London University's Elements of the Law of Contract papers available; there has been a question or part question on frustration in each paper, except, most recently, 1994.

As might be expected, when a topic crops up every year, there is a considerable degree of overlap between the questions. The format of the questions seems to be almost equally divided between problems and essays with one or two which are half and half.

The two most likely issues are firstly whether if a contract is frustrated the parties can salvage anything by way of restitution; and secondly, the actual tests imposed by the courts to decide whether frustration has occurred. Though the questions quoted below cover a lot of common ground, it will be seen that the first, earlier question is concerned to a greater degree with the question of restitution than the second question. The third question is primarily concerned with the origins and basis for the theory of frustration, while the final question is confined to a very narrow aspect of the doctrine.

## 12.4 Questions

QUESTION ONE

Tom agrees to give Ellen private tuition for her Law of Contract examination to be held in eight months' time. The fee is £300, of which Ellen pays £25, with the balance to be paid on completion of the tuition. Tom spends £50 in the preparation of some printed tuition notes. After two months Tom goes to Spain for a week long holiday at Christmas. Whilst on holiday he is arrested, having been mistaken for Tim, and detained for two months. On his return he discovers that Ellen has engaged another tutor and is demanding the return of her £25. Tom sues for the balance of the £300.

Discuss. How would your answer differ, if at all, if Tom had been detained for careless driving?

University of London LLB Examination
(for External Students) Elements of the Law of Contract June 1983 Q7

*Skeleton Solution*

• Statement of doctrine of frustration.
• Test for frustration as laid down in *Davis Contractors* (1956).
• Rights and liabilities of parties.
• Law Reform (Frustrated Contracts) Act 1943.
• Valuable benefits derived under contract prior to frustration.
• Self-induced frustration.

*Suggested Solution*

First one must consider whether Tom's arrest and consequent detention for two months frustrated the contract between him and Ellen. Secondly, if it did, one must look at the parties' respective rights and liabilities as a result of the frustration.

The now generally accepted test for frustration is that laid down by the House of Lords in *Davis Contractors Ltd v Fareham UDC* (1956) in particular the speech of Viscount Radcliffe, recently approved in two decisions of the Lords *National Carriers Ltd v Panalpina Ltd* (1981) and *Pioneer Shipping Ltd v BTP Tioxide Ltd* (1982), namely have events subsequent to the conclusion of the contract rendered the contractual obligation undertaken by one or other of the parties radically different to that contemplated at the time the contract was made? It is submitted that the answer is plainly yes. Ellen has engaged Tom as a tutor for eight months, but for two of those months he has been detained in Spain. One quarter of the period during which tuition was to be given is a substantial time, and on Tom's being detained Ellen would be justified in treating the contract as discharged. Reported cases show that the personal incapacity of one party preventing him from performing, eg in *Horlock v Beal* (1916) (detention as an enemy alien) and *Condor v The Barron Knights Ltd* (1966) (illness) will frustrate a contract.

151

On behalf of Tom it might be said that the contract was still possible of performance on his return, there will being four months' before Ellen's examination. However, on Tom's being detained Ellen has no means of knowing how long it will last and is therefore justified in making alternative tuition arrangements. In the *Pioneer Shipping* case (1982) a vessel being strikebound for an apparently indefinite period of time was held to frustrate a charterparty, and the same will be the case with Tom and Ellen's contract. The detention being due to a mistake and not Tom's fault, there is no question of the frustrations being self-induced.

What then are the parties' respective rights and liabilities? The contract having been frustrated. Tom's action for the £300 will fail. The effect of frustration is to discharge the contract from the date of the frustrating event and thereafter both parties are excused from further performance. This common law principle has, however, been partly qualified by the Law Reform (Frustrated Contracts) Act 1943.

Under s1(2) of the 1943 Act, sums paid in pursuance of a frustrated contract before the frustrated event are recoverable by the payer, subject to the proviso that if the payee has incurred expense in or for the purpose of the performance of the contract prior to the discharge, the payee may retain all or part of such sums as the court considers just up to the amount of the expenses incurred. Thus, prima facie Ellen can recover the £25 paid to Tom subject to his being able to retain all or part of it in respect of the £50 he spent on preparing tuition notes. The likelihood is that Tom will be allowed to retain the full £25, it representing one-half of his expenditure: such a solution would in effect apportion the loss equally.

Next one must consider s1(3) of the 1943 Act, which may allow Tom to recover a just sum from Ellen if she has obtained a valuable benefit under the contract prior to its being frustrated. It seems likely that she has done so, in that she has had the benefit of two months' tuition. The relevant principles for calculating an award under s1(3) are to be found in the judgment of Robert Goff J (as he then was) in *BP Exploration Co (Libya) Ltd v Hunt (No 2)* (1983). Although that case went on appeal, the Court of Appeal seemingly approved the learned judge's approach to s1(3) and the matter was not argued in the Lords; accordingly one must look to and apply the judgment at first instance.

First, Robert Goff J said, one must identify the benefit conferred and value it. The learned judge emphasised that the benefit must be distinguished from the service produced, ie it is the value of the benefit in the Defendant's hands, not the cost to the plaintiff of conferring it. The judge said this followed from s1(3) which distinguishes between the two, and also from s1(3)(b) which requires the court to have regard to the effect on the benefit of the frustrating event; the latter may mean, in some cases, that the benefit is reduced to nil. As already stated, Ellen's benefit is the tuition she received in the two months before he went to Spain.

Next, Robert Goff J held, one must consider what would be a just sum to award under s1(3) having regard to the underlying principle of the Act, which is the prevention of unjust enrichment. The learned judge said that the Act was 'surprisingly silent' as to how a just sum was to be calculated, but that normally the best guide is the contracted rate of remuneration. It would not normally be just to award that, or a rateable part of it. Further s1(3)(a) requires one to take into account any advance payment made by Ellen to Tom and retained by Tom under s1(2), ie the £25 discussed above. On the facts there seems no reason why Tom should have to give credit for the £25 and it is submitted that a just sum will be the full contract remuneration for two months' tuition.

Finally, Robert Goff J held, having (a) valued the benefit and (b) assessed a just sum, the plaintiff should recover the lesser of the two. The value of the benefit is the ceiling for an award under s1(3), ie the plaintiff will recover the just sum or, if less, the value of the benefit. Here it seems likely the two would be the same, ie two months' remuneration for tuition rendered.

If Tom's detention were due to his having been detained for careless driving, it is submitted that the above conclusions would still apply. Whereas at first sight it might appear that the frustrating event was 'self-induced', there is no clear authority in English law that a mere negligent act constitutes self-induced frustration. In *Joseph Constantine SS Line Ltd* v *Imperial Smelting Corporation Ltd* (1942) the House of Lords left the issue open, and although as a matter of principle negligence ought to be capable of being self-induced frustration, cases on similar facts involving employees unable to perform due to their serving sentences of imprisonment have been held to be within the doctrine of frustration: *Hare* v *Murphy Bros Ltd* (1974) and *Chakki* v *United Yeast Co Ltd* (1982). Those two cases concerned offences of criminal intent; Tom's offence being one of negligence only, the case would be a fortiori and the doctrine would apply.

QUESTION TWO

Alban is a baker and confectioner. One of his most famous specialities is a 'golden sun cake' which he makes according to a secret recipe known to him alone. A vital ingredient for the cake is a liquer produced only in Ruritania. In March this year Alban concluded a contract with Tessbury plc, a supermarket chain, under which he agreed to supply 5,000 golden sun cakes a week for a period of three years commencing on 1 June at a price of £2 each. Alban told Tessbury that the cakes contained Ruritanian liquer, so that this could be stated on the packets. Tessbury paid Alban £2,000 on the signing of the contract and agreed to pay monthly in arrears for cakes delivered. During April and May Alban spent £8,000 extending his bakery premises and installing new ovens in order to ensure that he could produce enough cakes to fulfil the Tessbury order.

On 2 June, when Alban tried to obtain fresh supplies of the Ruritanian liqueur, he discovered that the failure of the spring rains had brought production of the liqueur to a standstill and that it would be unobtainable until June 1990 at the earliest. When Tessbury heard this they wrote to Alban cancelling the contract and demanding the return of the £2,000.

Advise Alban.

Would your answer be different if the Ruritanian liqueur was still available but the price had risen to such an extent that it would now cost Alban £3 to make each cake?

University of London LLB Examination
(for External Students) Elements of the Law of Contract June 1989 Q2

*Skeleton Solution*

- Statement of doctrine of frustration.
- Development of doctrine, tests for frustration.
- Limitations on doctrine.
- Contract which becomes more onerous may not be frustrated.
- Effects of frustration.
- Law Reform (Frustrated Contracts) Act 1943.

*Suggested Solution*

What is at issue here is whether the contract between Alban and Tessbury has been frustrated.

The doctrine of frustration applies when a change of circumstances renders a contract physically or commercially impossible to perform or the circumstances transform the performance into something radically different from that which the parties undertook when they entered into the contract.

Prior to 1863 contractual obligations were regarded as absolute: *Paradine* v *Jane* (1647). The doctrine was first recognised in English law in *Taylor* v *Caldwell* (1863) where the subject matter of the contract – a music hall – was destroyed by fire. Blackburn J held that the effect of the destruction of the subject matter was to discharge the parties from their further obligations under the contract. The basis of the doctrine of frustration in that case was the implied term theory: the parties had contracted on the basis of the continued existence of the subject matter.

The implied term theory has now been largely rejected by the courts and has been superseded by the 'radical change in obligations' test. This was first formulated by Lord Radcliffe in *Davis Contractors Ltd* v *Fareham Urban District Council* (1956) in the following words:

'... frustration occurs whenever the law recognises that without default of either party a contractual obligation has become incapable of being performed because the circumstances in which performance is called for would render it a thing radically different from that which was undertaken by the contract. *Non haec in foedera veni.* It was not this that I promised to do.'

In two subsequent decisions of the House of Lords this test has been approved and adopted: *National Carriers Ltd* v *Panalpina (Northern) Ltd* (1981); *Pioneer Shipping* v *BTP Tioxide, The Nema* (1981).

However, the doctrine of frustration will only apply in limited circumstances. The mere fact that the contract has become more expensive or onerous to perform will be be sufficient for the doctrine to be invoked. In *Davis* the particular circumstances caused considerable delay in the performance and caused the contractors considerable additional expense but this was held to be a long way from a case of frustration. In *Ocean Tramp Tankers Corporation* v *V O Sovfracht, The Eugenia* (1964) the unforeseen circumstances again caused delay and extra expense in the performance of the contract but this did not warrant finding that the contract had been frustrated. See also *Tsakiroglou & Co Ltd* v *Noblee Thorl GmbH* (1962).

In the present problem an event has occurred without the fault of either party and which was not provided for in the contract. This will cause a delay of at least a year in the performance of the contract which is of three years' duration. It has been recognised that a delay can be so long as to put an end in a commercial sense to the venture entered upon by the parties: *Jackson* v *Union Marine Insurance Co* (1874). It is submitted that, in the present context, the delay of a year does have this effect, and does make the contract 'a radically different thing' from that which the parties entered into. Thus, the contract has been frustrated.

What must now be considered is the effect of this. At common law, as has been noted, the effect of frustration is to discharge the parties from their further obligations. With regard to the commitments of Alban and Tessbury prior to the frustrating event one must turn to the provisions of the Law Reform (Frustrated Contracts) Act 1943.

Section 1(2) of the Act provides that the £2,000 paid by Tessbury is recoverable. There is, however, a proviso to this. Where a party who has received a payment has incurred expenses for the purpose of performing the contract the court has the discretion to allow him to retain the whole or part of the sums paid, not being an amount in excess of the expenses incurred. Alban has incurred expenses of £8,000 but this recovery for this expenditure is limited by the amount paid or payable before the frustrating event. Tessbury had paid £2,000, but no further sums were payable when the contract was frustrated. It would appear, therefore, that the court might well allow Alban to retain the £2,000, but the loss of the additional expenditure will fall on him.

Under s1(3) of the Act provision is made for the award of a 'just sum' where one party has obtained a valuable benefit before the contract was discharged. The benefit must be valued at the date of the frustration: *BP Exploration Co (Libya) Ltd* v *Hunt* (1979). In this problem no benefit has been obtained by either party at the date of frustration, so s1(3) does not apply.

Alban is therefore advised that the contract with Tessbury has been discharged by frustration, but that he should resist the demand for the return of the £2,000, relying on the proviso to s1(2) of the Act.

It remains to consider what the position would be if the Ruritanian liqueur was still available, but the cost had now risen to the extent stated.

As set out above the fact that a contract has become more expensive to perform is not a sufficient indication of frustration. Treitel quotes authorities in the United States to the effect that a 'marked increase in cost' or a price increase 'well beyond the normal range' might constitute a frustrating event. But the tendency in the United States has been to widen the scope of the doctrine of frustration. In contrast the House of Lords held in *British Movietone News Ltd* v *London and District Cinemas* (1952) that 'a wholly abnormal rise or fall in prices' would not affect the bargain.

In view of the restrictive attitude of our courts to the doctrine of frustration it seems that Alban would be held to the contract despite the substantial increase in price of the liqueur. As this would involve him in having to carry out the contract at a considerable loss it may be that a court would hold that this entailed a radical change in the obligations. But Alban could not be advised with confidence that a court would take this view.

QUESTION THREE

'Unless performance of the contract has become actually impossible, the fact that unforeseen events have made performance more burdensome is usually regarded as no more than one of life's misfortunes which the defendant has to bear.'

Discuss.

University of London LLB Examination
(for External Students) Elements of the Law of Contract June 1985 Q8

*Skeleton Solution*

• Frustration.

• Basis of the doctrine.

• Criteria for frustration to occur.

• Strict impossibility as against a more onerous contract.

*Suggested Solution*

The doctrine referred to in the question is known as frustration, which is the term used to describe a situation where, owing to a change of circumstances occurring after the conclusion of the contract, both parties are discharged from their outstanding obligations by operation of law; in such a case the contract is said to be frustrated.

The question requires a discussion of the circumstances in which the doctrine of frustration will be held to apply, and in particular whether actual impossibility of performance is required or whether something less might suffice.

The case which first introduced the doctrine of frustration in 1863, *Taylor* v *Caldwell* (1863), was a case of physical impossibility. Prior to that date English law had always regarded contractual obligations as being absolute and as continuing to bind the parties irrespective of the effect of extraneous events, as in *Paradine* v *Jane* (1647). In *Taylor* (1863) it was held that a licence to use a music hall was frustrated when the building was destroyed by a fire for which neither party was responsible. The Court of Queen's Bench said that it was an implied condition of the contract that the building should continue to exist and, on its destruction, both parties were discharged from further peformance.

The law has moved on from *Taylor* (1863) in two significant respects. First, the theory that frustration depends upon an implied term to that effect forming a part of the contract can no longer be regarded as good law, and secondly, it is possible for a contract still to be physically possible of performance but frustrated in law because the commercial purpose or adventure is no longer possible of performance. These two developments in the law will be discussed in turn.

As to the theory that frustration depended upon there being an implied term in the contract, it has been seen that the doctrine owes its very existence to the court in *Taylor* (1863) finding such a term and, further, this view commanded a good deal of support for a considerable number of years: *F A Tamplin SS Co Ltd* v *Anglo-Mexican Petroleum Products Co Ltd* (1916) and *Bank Line Ltd* v *Arthur Capel Ltd* (1919) are charterparty cases in which the House of Lords applied the implied term approach.

Judicially, however, the implied term theory was not found to be satisfactory, in that there was no rational legal basis for implying or not implying the necessary term. Its implication could not be justified by any subjective test, since if the parties had foreseen the frustrating event they would almost certainly have made provision for it. Alternatively, to imply its objectivity involves much artificiality as it involves attributing to the parties an intention which they never had in relation to an event which, on hypothesis, they did not foresee.

It was for this reason that the courts subsequently discarded the implied term approach in favour of, as it is now known, the radical change in the obligation test, which derives from the decision of the House of Lords, and in particular the speech of Viscount Radcliffe in *Davis Contractors Ltd* v *Fareham UDC* (1956). His Lordship stated that frustration occurs whenever the law recognises that, without default in either party, a contractual obligation has become incapable of being performed because the circumstances in which performance is called for would render it a thing radically different from that which was undertaken by the contract: 'Non haec in foedera veni. It was not this that I promised to do'.

This statement of principle has recently been approved in two further decisions of their Lordships' House, *National Carriers Ltd* v *Panalpina (Northern) Ltd* (1981) and *The Nema* (1982), and can accordingly now be regarded as settled law. Other judicial analyses as to the judicial basis of the doctrine, eg the just and reasonable solution (per Denning LJ in *British Movietone News Ltd* v *London and District Cinemas* (1951)) and the disappearance of the foundation of the contract theories (per Goddard J in *Tatem Ltd* v *Gamboa* (1939) can now be discarded.

*Davis* v *Fareham* (1956) is also of interest in that it is a good illustration of the principle that merely because a contract has become more onerous or expensive for one side to perform does not justify a finding of frustration: delay caused by bad weather and shortages of skilled labour which rendered the contract unprofitable for the appellants did not discharge the contract. Thus it is correct to say that where the unforeseen events simply make performance more burdensome, frustration does not apply.

Nevertheless, turning to the second point above mentioned, it may be doubted whether actual impossibility is a necessary requirement for the application of the doctrine. Although Viscount Radcliffe's speech in *Davis* v *Fareham* (1956) does refer to a contract obligation being 'incapable of performance' and, as such, would appear to support a test of physical impossibility only, it is submitted that read as a whole, his Lordship's speech does not support such a proposition. In particular his Lordship contemplated that the contract might still be capable (ie not impossible) of performance but frustrated because the changed circumstances mean that the obligation, if performed, would be a different thing from that contracted for. Further, it is submitted that this is borne out in any number of reported frustration cases.

One might point to cases such as *Jackson* v *Union Marine Insurance Co Ltd* (1874) where a ship under charter ran aground and required repairs which took some eight months, and *Krell* v *Henry* (1903), where a contract to hire rooms to view the coronation procession of King Edward VII was held to be frustrated when the event was cancelled, were cases in which physical performance was still possible, but the supervening events had rendered the nature of the contractual obligation fundamentally different. Moreover the recent recognition by the House of Lords in the *National Carriers* case (1981) that leases may, albeit only in exceptional circumstances, be frustrated also lends support to this view. Once a lease is executed, the legal estate vests in the tenant irrespective of what might happen thereafter, so in that sense, there is no impossibility, yet the lease is, as the House of Lords held, capable of being frustrated.

However, one must add the caveat that although strict impossibility is not always required, the court will almost certainly require something falling not far short of it before allowing the doctrine of frustration to be invoked. The courts are reluctant to allow parties to escape their contractual obligations except in the very clearest of cases. The Suez cases concerning charterparties and contracts for the sale of goods which became more expensive of performance as a result of the closure of the Suez Canal, *The Eugenia* (1964) and *Tsakiroglou & Co Ltd* v *Noblee Thorl* (1962) being good examples of this.

In conclusion, therefore, one would say certainly that where the unforseen events merely render performance more burdensome, the contract is not frustrated, but that strict physical impossibility is not always necessary.

QUESTION FOUR

'The doctrine of frustration cannot properly be used to help a party out of a difficulty which he could have foreseen, but the Courts have not always been consistent in this respect.'

Discuss.

University of London LLB Examination
(for External Students) Elements of the Law of Contract June 1991 Q6

*Skeleton Solution*

• Doctrine of frustration.
• Foreseen and foreseeable events.
• Exclusion of doctrine.

*Suggested Solution*

The doctrine of frustration has had an uneven development with regard to the question of foreseen and foreseeable events. At one time supervening or unforeseen events were not regarded as an excuse for non-performance, because the parties could provide for such accidents in their contracts: *Paradine* v *Jane* (1647). This approach was relaxed in *Taylor* v *Caldwell* (1863) and in following cases such as *Jackson* v *Union Marine Insurance Co Ltd* (1874) and *Krell* v *Henry* (1903), which made it considerably easier to invoke the doctrine of frustration. These cases were based on the implied term theory now largely abandoned in favour of the 'radical change in the obligations' test enunciated by Lord Radcliffe in *Davis Contractors Ltd* v *Fareham UDC* (1956), a test adopted by the House of Lords in *National Carriers Ltd* v *Panalpina (Northern) Ltd* (1981) and in *Pioneer Shipping Ltd* v *BTP Tioxide Ltd, The Nema* (1982). In these three decisions the House of Lords reverted to a more restrictive approach, expressed by Lord Roskill in *The Nema* when his lordship said that the doctrine of frustration was 'not lightly to be invoked to relieve contracting parties of the normal consequences of imprudent commercial bargains'.

In the modern law, then, a frustrating event is a supervening, unforeseen event, which the courts will only recognise in exceptional circumstances as significantly changing the nature of the obligations. It should follow that an event which was foreseen or foreseeable should not permit the doctrine to be invoked. In *Walton Harvey Ltd* v *Walker & Homfrays Ltd* (1931) the defendants granted the plaintiffs the right to display an advertising sign on the defendants' hotel for seven years. Within this period the hotel was compulsorily acquired and demolished by the local authority. The contract was not frustrated because the defendants knew of the risk of compulsory acquisition. There are dicta in support of the view that an event which is foreseen or foreseeable cannot frustrate a contract (eg in *Krell* v *Henry* and in *Davis Contractors*) and in principle this seems correct. But this principle has not been consistently applied.

In *Ertel Bieber & Co* v *Rio Tinto Co Ltd* (1918) a contract was held to be frustrated by a war-time prohibition against trading with the enemy, even though the war was a foreseeable event. In *W J Tatem Ltd* v *Gamboa* (1939) a ship which had been chartered by the defendant as agent for the Republicans during the Spanish civil war was detained by the Nationalists. Whilst such an event was foreseeable, the contract was held to be frustrated; the basis of the decision appears to be that it was not foreseeable that the ship would be detained for the period involved. But Goddard J also expressed the view, obiter, that the contract would have been frustrated even if that had been foreseen. He said that:

'If the true foundation of the doctrine (of frustration) is that once the subject-matter of the contract is destroyed or the existence of a state of facts has come to an end, the contract is at an end, that result follows whether or not the event causing it was contemplated by the parties.'

In *Ocean Tramp Tankers Corporation* v *VO Sovfracht, The Eugenia* (1964) Lord Denning MR stated, also obiter, that:

'It has frequently been said that the doctrine of frustration only applies when the new situation is "unforeseen" or "unexpected" or "uncontemplated", as if that were an essential feature. But it is not so. The only thing that is essential is that the parties should have made no provision for it in their contract.'

The exact status of these dicta is not clear. The usual inference is that the parties contracted with reference to the particular event and so took the risk of it occurring, thus precluding the operation of the doctrine of frustration. Treitel (*Law of Contract*) argues that this inference can only be drawn if the event was actually foreseen or if the degree of foreseeability was a very high one. 'To support the inference of risk-assumption, the event must be one which any person of ordinary intelligence would regard as likely to occur.'

It should also be noted that this inference can be excluded by the evidence of a contrary intention. In *Bank Line Ltd* v *Arthur Capel Ltd* (1919) the parties appeared to have foreseen the risk but had possibly not thought about its effect. If this were so the contract could be held to be frustrated. The normal inference was displaced by the special terms of the contract.

# 13 DISCHARGE OF THE CONTRACT: PERFORMANCE, AGREEMENT AND BREACH

13.1 Introduction

13.2 Key points

13.3 Analysis of questions

13.4 Questions

## 13.1 Introduction

In the last chapter we looked at how the parties might be discharged from their obligations by frustration and in the next two chapters we shall look at remedies for breach. In most cases, however, a contractual obligation is discharged by actually performing the contract, according to the terms negotiated.

More rarely the parties may agree to end, or to vary, or substitute another contract rather than perform the existing agreement as it stands.

This chapter is mainly concerned with two issues: what constitutes performance and secondly, the consequences of a party failing to perform his obligations under the contract.

## 13.2 Key points

It is important that the student understands the following:

a) *Performance – the general rule*

Essentially, a party must perform *precisely* all the terms of the contract.

The harshness of this strict rule is offset by a number of modifications to the general rule.

i) Divisible contracts

Some contracts are 'entire', that is, complete performance by one party is a condition precedent to contractual liability being incurred by the other. Others are 'divisible' when contracts are performed in stages – each party honouring their liabilities at that point before proceeding to the next. Thus, if in a contract A agrees to build a house for B, to be paid for in stages, £10,000 per storey with extra sums for interior work; if A defaults after the first storey is complete and does no further work, he will still, because the contract is divisible, be entitled to £10,000.

ii) Acceptance of part performance

When some part of the contract has been performed by one party and the other derives valuable benefit, the party gaining from this work must pay a reasonable sum. In many cases, however, it will be apparent that the parties have, by their behaviour, effectively varied the existing contract, or substituted a completely new contract.

iii) Completion of performance prevented by the promisee

Where an entire contract cannot be completed because the willing party is prevented by the promisee from carrying out his obligations in full; the willing party will be entitled to claim a *'quantum meruit'* (see Chapter 16) payment for that part of the contract that he has completed.

iv) Substantial performance

The doctrine of substantial performance dates back to the eighteenth century. The main problem is one of definition. Certainly the common law talks of performing a contract fully save for minor differences but there is no way of telling what will be construed as a minor difference. It will be a question of looking at the individual circumstances of each case.

Where the doctrine of substantial performance *does* apply the party concerned will be entitled to recover the contract price, adjusted according to the minimal differences in performance.

v)  Tender of performance

When one party makes an offer to complete his side of the contract, and this is for some reason rejected by the other party then the contract will be regarded as completed, given certain conditions. Firstly, it must be a contract of the sort where one party requires the co-operation of the other party: to take delivery for example. If the contract could be completed quite effectively without the other party's co-operation, then the rule will not apply. Secondly, the tender must be correct: if goods are tendered, they must be as specified in the contract in quality and quantity, if money, then it must be legal tender or other acceptable form such as a cheque.

When goods are correctly tendered and rejected, the tendering party is absolved from further liability, but when money is involved, although there is no obligation to repeatedly tender the money, the debt remains and must be paid when demanded by the creditor.

b) *Stipulations as to time*

The rule at common law used to be, that in the absence of any express provision the performance of the contract within the proper time was essential. The Law of Property Act 1925, however, gave priority to the rules of equity as to time.

Equity does not regard time as being 'of the essence' unless certain conditions apply. The two main provisos are either: that the parties must expressly stipulate time of performance to be of the essence – or words to that effect – or that one party may give notice during the period of the contract that the contract must be performed within a reasonable time, thus rendering time of the essence.

If neither of these circumstances apply, then even if there are stipulations as to time in the contract, if they can be disregarded (or at least not followed very stringently), without causing undue hardship or causing either party to lose the benefit of the contract; this is the approach equity will take.

Thus, since the changes of the LPA in 1925, equitable rules prevail unless the parties expressly provide otherwise, either at the time of making the contract or later, during the actual performance of the contract. If time is not of the essence, then late performance does not give the right to terminate but will give rights to damages. Look in particular at the two recent cases *Alghussein Establishment* v *Eton College* (1988) and *British & Commonwealth Holdings* v *Quadrex Holdings* (1989).

c) *Agreements*

There is a saying that what has been created by agreement may be extinguished by agreement.

Bear in mind that such an agreement is in itself a binding contract and can take several forms.

Firstly, there may be discharge by one or both parties in a deed, under seal. Strictly speaking this will be enforceable by the party in whose favour the deed operates, without proof of consideration.

Secondly, there may be a unilateral discharge which is not under seal. This takes place when one party, having completed his obligations under the contract and having power to compel the other party to perform this side of the bargain, does not do so, but instead releases the other party from the remainder of the contract. The main problem here, is that when the discharge is not under seal it needs consideration to be furnished (other then performance or partial performance of existing contractual duties) in return for the unilateral promise. In most cases this additional consideration is simply not present and therefore a unilateral discharge not under seal has little chance of being enforceable in the courts.

Thirdly, there is bi-lateral discharge. This occurs when both parties have still to complete all, or part of their contractual obligations.

The parties may agree mutually to discharge the contract in one of several ways:

i) Accord and satisfaction

This is the purchase of relief from a contractual obligation by means of offering some valuable consideration, though not the performance of the contract itself.

A mutual agreement for release from existing contractual obligations is considered to be sufficient to amount to valuable consideration.

ii) Rescission

The parties may intend to rescind the original agreement and to create another to take its place. This is different from variation (see below) because the substituted contract is new in all respects. The very fact of agreeing the substitution of a new contract implies automatically that the parties intend the original to be considered discharged.

iii) Novation

This applies only in particular debtor-creditor situations. If, for example, A owes £100 to B and C owes £100 to A if a new contract whereby C pays £100 directly to B this is novation.

Each party furnishes consideration and all three of them are parties to the new contract which replaces those discharged.

iv) Variation

This is where the parties alter or modify an existing contract. It should be distinguished from cases where the parties merely clarify certain points on the original contract, or fill in more detail.

v) Waiver

When one party voluntarily relinquishes his rights under a contract, he may be held to have waived his right to performance by the other party. This is not to say that he does not anticipate some degree of performance by the other party and herein lies the difficulty. Waiver maybe written, oral, or inferred from conduct and particularly in the latter case each interpretation depends on individual circumstances. A party may merely be waiving his right to have the contract performed in a particular manner; though he still requires substantial performance, it may not be in quite the manner contemplated by the parties. Alternatively he may be waiving all his rights under the contract completely.

vi) Provision in the contract itself

It may be that the contract will make express provision for discharge on the happening of certain stated events. A common example is in partnership agreements where provision is made more or less automatically, for the partnership to end on the happening of specific occurrences.

d) *Breach*

It is perhaps a misnomer to call breach a form of discharge. For a start it is quite unlike the usual forms which are all situations when the parties have performed the contract (more or less) in a way which is mutually acceptable. Also not every breach automatically brings a contract to an end.

Having said that it is true, that if the breach if sufficiently serious, the innocent party will be able to repudiate the contract and consider it at an end. The innocent party will then be relieved of all further obligations under the contract. Obviously, however, though the contract is treated as being at an end, there will still be repercussions (see the various chapters on remedies, following).

A breach may arise at any point in the contract. Sometimes one party will have performed all his obligations under the contract before it becomes apparent that the other is in breach of his side of the bargain.

Alternatively one party may show expressly or otherwise from a very early stage that he does not intend to honour his contractual obligations – this is known as anticipatory breach. In cases of anticipatory breach the innocent party does not have to wait until time of performance, he may immediately treat the contract as being at an end and sue for damages. However, it should be stressed that repudiation is an *option* for the innocent party, it is not forced on him; he may equally well choose to affirm the contract and treat it as still in force.

The main difficulty with anticipatory breach lies in assessing whether the conduct of the party at fault does actually amount to an anticipatory breach, or repudiation of the contract.

The House of Lords examined the problem in detail in *Woodar Investment* v *Wimpey Construction* [1980] 1 WLR 277 and the student should refer to a textbook for further details on this and other relevant case law. See, for example, the recent cases of *H B Raylor* v *Henry Lewis & Co* (1987) and *Fercometal Sarl* v *Mediterranean Shipping Co SA* (1988).

## 13.3 Analysis of questions

Since this is a topic that lends itself to being coupled with remedies, it is perhaps not surprising that it has been the sole subject of a question in only one of London University's past papers. That question is quoted below.

The student will find, however, that in looking at questions and solutions on remedies (Chapters 14 and 15 following) that quite frequently as a preliminary stage in the question the answer requires some discussion as to the nature of breach. The student should remember also that in Chapter 4 on contents of a contract the question of conditions, warranties and fundamental breach was discussed.

Question 3 on the 1986 paper and Question 3 in 1987, are both perfect examples of the way breach of contract can be combined with the subject of contents of a contract. Both questions are quoted in Chapter 4 and the student should refer back to them. Look also at Q3 on the 1993 paper (Question 2, below), which is largely concerned with part performance.

## 13.4 Questions

QUESTION ONE

Fab Five Freddy is a disc jockey. He agreed to work last Wednesday night at the Red Lion Club. The Club agreed to provide Freddy with all the necessary equipment for his show including a selection of fifty records. The Club also agreed to pay Freddy £60 for his performance on Wednesday and to pay Bill, Freddy's mate, £20 for Bill's work in setting up the equipment before Freddy went on stage and taking it down afterwards. Bill was not a party to the contract between the Club and Freddy.

On Wednesday Bill arrived at the Red Lion early and set up the equipment for Freddy. However, when Freddy arrived he found that there was only a selection of thirty records available. He thereupon informed Richard, the manager of the Red Lion, that he refused to perform and left.

Richard was furious, he told Bill to leave the equipment set up and began telephoning around to find another disc jockey for the evening. He eventually contacted a disc jockey called Super Sally who agreed to perform at the Red Lion that evening for £100. Richard agreed to pay for this fee but when she arrived at the Club Richard found that Bill had taken down the disc jockey equipment and gone home. Richard was forced to pay two local boys £35 each to set up the equipment for Sally. Sally then performed that evening and was very successful.

Freddy and Bill are demanding their fees of £60 and £20 from the Red Lion Club. Richard has refused to pay them and is threatening legal action by the Red Lion Club (which is a limited company) against Freddy for breach of contract.

Discuss.

University of London LLB Examination
(for External Students) Elements of the Law of Contract June 1988 Q5

*Skeleton Solution*

• Conditions and warranties.

• Nature of breach.

• Anticipatory breach: response repudiation/affirmation.

• Two contracts:
  – Red Lion Club and Freddy;
  – Red Lion Club and Bill.

• Damages, assessment, *Hadley* v *Baxendale* rules.

*Suggested Solution*

This question involves a discussion of breach of contract, in particular what amounts to a repudiatory breach and damages. It will be convenient to discuss these matters in connection with the two contracts:

a) The contract between the Club and Freddie;

b) The contract between the Club and Bill.

a) *The contract between the Red Lion Club and Freddie*

The relevant term in this contract is the undertaking by the Club to provide a selection of 50 records. They appear to have been in breach of that term, by only providing a selection of 30 records. The question is: was the breach of that term a repudiatory breach? The answer to that depends on whether the term is considered a condition or a warranty.

Traditionally contractual terms were divided into conditions and warranties. A condition was regarded as an essential term of the contract, the breach of which entitled an innocent party to treat the contract as repudiated; to terminate it and claim damages. For a breach of warranty the innocent party was not entitled to treat the contract as repudiated; his remedy was limited to a claim in damages. Certain terms do not readily fit into the conventional classification of conditions and warranties. Although the concept was not new the first case to use the expression 'innominate term' was the Court of Appeal decision in *Hongkong Fir Shipping Co Ltd* v *Kawasaki Kisen Kaisha Ltd* (1962). In the case of an innominate term the consequences of the breach depend on whether or not the innocent party has been deprived of the substantial benefit of the transaction. In *Bunge Corporation, New York* v *Tradax Export SA Panama* (1980) Lord Scarman said that:

'Unless the contract makes it clear, either by express provision or necessary implication arising from its nature, purpose and circumstances ... that a particular stipulation is a condition or only a warranty, it is an innominate term, the remedy for a breach of which depends on the nature, consequences and effect of the breach.'

It is difficult to say whether the relevant term here should be treated as a condition or only as a warranty. It is submitted that it is difficult to argue that the term would be considered a condition. The breach does not appear to deprive Freddie of the substantial benefit of the transaction.

Even if the term is considered a condition, Freddie in order to succeed in his claim would have to establish that the failure to provide the required number of records constitutes a repudiation by the Club of the contract. In *Woodar Investment Development Ltd* v *Wimpey Construction (UK) Ltd* (1980) Lord Wilberforce said that:

' ... in considering whether there has been a repudiation by one party, it is necessary to look at his conduct as a whole. Does this indicate an intention to abandon and refuse performance of the contract?'

Freddie then has to establish that the Club has committed an anticipatory breach of contract. If there has been an anticipatory breach of contract by the Club, Freddie is entitled to elect between accepting the breach or holding the Club to the contract: *Frost* v *Knight* (1872); *Hochster* v *De la Tour* (1853); *White & Carter (Councils) Ltd* v *McGregor* (1962). By refusing to perform, and leaving Freddie would appear to have accepted the breach and be entitled to the amount of his fees as damages.

It is submitted, however, that on the present facts it is unlikely that the court would find that there has been an anticipatory breach of contract by the Club.

If that submission is correct, and the Club has not committed an anticipatory breach of contract, it is Freddie who has committed such a breach by refusing to perform and leaving. In the event of Freddie's anticipatory breach it is the Club who is entitled to elect between accepting the breach and affirming the contract.

The Club appears to have accepted the breach. There is nothing to indicate that they have affirmed the contract, on the contrary their conduct in engaging a substitute clearly manifests the intention to accept the breach. On acceptance of the breach the Club is entitled to claim damages – see the cases in connection with acceptance of the breach cited above.

The further question then is for what damages would Freddie be liable? It seems clear that the Club has acted reasonably in mitigating its loss by going on to the market and engaging Super Sally as a substitute performer. The measure of damages would be the difference between the contract price agreed with Freddie and the fee that the Club was obliged to pay the substitute. Such damages appear to fit within the first limb of *Hadley* v *Baxendale* (1854) as arising naturally, that is from the ordinary course of things from the breach.

What is more arguable is whether Freddie can be also held liable for the additional costs incurred by the Company in having to hire the local boys to set up the equipment. The additional loss was caused by the intervening act of a third party, Bill. In accordance with the principles of *Victoria Laundry (Windsor) Ltd* v *Newman Industries Ltd* (1949) and *The Heron II* (1969) Freddie will be liable for Bill's intervening act if that was reasonably foreseeable, or within Freddie's reasonable contemplation. It can be argued that as Bill was Freddie's mate, Bill's action in removing the equipment was something that was 'liable to result'. In that event Freddie will also be liable for these additional costs.

b) *The contract between the Club and Bill*

Bill was not a party to the contract between the Club and Freddie, consequently the rights and obligations of that contract cannot be conferred or imposed on him: *Dunlop Pneumatic Tyre Co Ltd* v *Selfridge & Co Ltd* (1915).

Under his contract with the Club, Bill is required to set up the equipment and to remove that equipment after the end of the performance. He in fact removes the equipment before the performance has commenced. He appears therefore to be in breach of an express term of the contract. It can be argued, in the alternative, that there was an implied term in the contract that the equipment was to remain until the conclusion of the performance in accordance with the principles of *The Moorcock* (1889) and *Shirlaw* v *Southern Foundries Ltd* (1939). As Bill is in breach of contract he is clearly not entitled to demand his fees from the Club. Moreover, he would be liable in damages for the increased costs incurred by the Club in having the equipment reinstated, but the Club does not appear to be contemplating such a claim against him.

Finally, we are informed that the Red Lion Club is a limited company. The relevance of this is that the contractual capacity of a limited liability company is limited by the ultra vires doctrine. Under this doctrine an act which is not authorised by the objects clause of the company is void in law: *Ashbury Railway Carriage & Iron Co* v *Riche* (1875). By statute a third party may be able to sue limited companies on ultra vires contracts – s35 Companies Act 1985. Whether a company can itself sue on an ultra vires contract remains uncertain (see *Bell Houses Ltd* v *City Wall Properties Ltd* (1966).

There is, however, nothing to indicate that the transactions concerned are ultra vires the company.

QUESTION TWO

a) 'A party who does not perform the whole of the contract is not entitled to any payment.'

Discuss.

b) E, an architect, was engaged to design building premises for F for F's business. E was to be paid a fee of £2,000 a month plus 'reasonable expenses'. E worked on the design for six months during which time E received only his fee payments from F. F then wrote to E saying that because of financial difficulties he was postponing E's contract. In fact, F did not like the design which E had produced and used the financial difficulties as an excuse for terminating E's contract. F refused to pay the expenses which E had incurred, arguing that they were not reasonable.

In the letter accepting appointment E had enclosed his 'Standard terms' which stated,

'18. It is agreed that in matters of judgment E's decision shall be final and in the event of any dispute there shall be no resort to the courts.

'19. In the event of a client not paying expenses when due, that client shall pay double the amount due as expenses.'

Advise E.

University of London LLB Examination
(for External Students) Elements of the Law of Contract June 1993 Q3

*Skeleton Solution*

a) • Entire and divisible obligations.
   • The general rule – entire obligations.
   • Divisible obligations.
   • Partial performance of an entire obligation.
   • Performance accepted, prevented or tendered.

b) • Performance of the contract, the termination by F.
   • E's rights if he is prevented from performance, or if F is in breach.
   • The possible illegality of clause 18.
   • Clause 19 and the prohibition against penalty clauses.

*Suggested Solution*

a) An obligation is 'entire' when a party is required to perform that obligation in its entirety before being entitled to demand payment from the other party, or to enforce that other party's counter-performance. The harsh effect that this rule may have is reflected in the case of *Cutter* v *Powell* (1795), where a seaman contracted to serve on a ship sailing from Jamaica to Liverpool. He was to be paid the sum of 30 guineas provided that he continued the performance of his services until the ship reached Liverpool. He died about three weeks before the ship reached its port of destination. It was held that his administratrix could not recover for his work before his death, as the contract meant that no payment was to be made unless and until he had completed the voyage.

Where the rule applies, it does so even if the other party suffers little or no inconvenience as a result of the shortfall in the performance. This is illustrated by *Arcos* v *Ronassen* (1933), and more particularly by *Re Moore & Landauer* (1921): the latter decision has been criticised as being 'excessively technical' by Lord Wilberforce in *Reardon Smith Line Ltd* v *Hansen-Tangen* (1976).

The rule is, however, subject to modification. The contract itself may provide that the obligations under it are divisible (or severable). A divisible contract is one where payment becomes due as and when the several parts of the obligation are performed. A normal contract of employment is one such contract; the employer, in effect, makes a payment in respect of services rendered by the employee during the preceding month. Building contracts usually provide for progress payments, that is for payment to be made on the completion of specified portions of the building work.

The distinction between divisible and entire contracts may be illustrated by a comparison of *Ritchie* v *Atkinson* (1808) with *Vlierboom* v *Chapman* (1844). In the former case a shipowner contracted to carry a cargo at a stipulated rate per ton. He carried only part of the cargo and was entitled to a proportionate part of the freight. In the latter case the contract provided that the freight became due on the arrival of the cargo at a specified port. The shipowner was not entitled to payment of the freight, or any portion of it, when he was compelled to abandon the voyage due to circumstances beyond his control.

Where the obligation is an entire one, then partial performance of it will be insufficient to found a claim for payment. This is exemplified in the Court of Appeal in *Sumpter* v *Hedges* (1898), where the plaintiff builder abandoned the building work when it was some two-thirds completed. As the obligation was entire, he was not *contractually* entitled to payment for the work that had been done; nor was there room for a claim based on quantum meruit: see also *Appleby* v *Myers* (1867) and the more recent decision in *Bolton* v *Mahadeva* (1972).

The rigour of the rule relating to entire obligations has been mitigated by the courts in finding that the party concerned, though not having completed his task, has *substantially* performed the obligation required of him: *Dakin & Co Ltd* v *Lee* (1916); *Hoenig* v *Isaacs* (1952). In the latter case the plaintiff contracted to redecorate the defendant's flat for the sum of £750. There were minor defects in the work which could be rectified at a cost of £55. The Court of Appeal held that the plaintiff was entitled to the full contract price less the cost of remedying the defects.

It remains to note that the rule does not apply where: (i) partial performance has been accepted, as in *Christy* v *Row* (1808); (ii) completion has been prevented by the promisee, as in *Planche* v *Colburn* (1831); or when the promisor has duly tendered performance – *Startup* v *M'Donald* (1843).

b) It appears that E had worked on the design for six months and had received payment of his fees for that period: there is no suggestion that E was in any way in breach of contract in the work that he did: the only question is that of E's entitlement to the expenses.

In informing E that he was postponing his contract F might well be considered as having prevented E from completing the performance of his (E's) obligations. A wrongful refusal to allow a party to complete allows that party to claim damages for breach of contract; or alternatively to claim a quantum meruit for the work done: *Planche* v *Colburn* (above). It seems that F's intention was to terminate the contract, in which event he is guilty of a repudiatory breach. The election open to E is between affirming the contract, or accepting the breach: *Hochster* v *De La Tour* (1853). If E affirms, he can claim the expenses under the contract, but must be willing to perform his own obligations: if he accepts the breach, he can claim the expenses as damages for breach of contract.

Whether or not the expenses are reasonable depends on the facts, the evidence that can be adduced. E has sought to avoid a judicial determination of this issue by providing, in clause 18, that his judgment shall prevail. The clause provides further that in the event of any dispute there shall be no resort to the courts. This clause purports to deprive the courts of a jurisdiction which they would otherwise have, and is contrary to public policy and therefore unenforceable: *Anctil* v *Manufacturers' Life Insurance Co* (1889).

E cannot therefore rely on this clause.

Clause 19 provides for the payment of double the amount in the event of F not paying the expenses when due. What falls for decision here is whether this clause is a liquidated damages clause or a penalty. The essence of liquidated damages is a genuine agreed pre-estimate of damage; the essence of a penalty is a payment of money stipulated as in terrorem of the offending party: *Clydebank Engineering and Shipbuilding Co* v *Don Jose Ramos Yzquierdo y Castaneda* (1905).

In *Dunlop Pneumatic Tyre Co Ltd* v *New Garage and Motor Co Ltd* (1915) Lord Dunedin dealt with the various tests that had been suggested to determine whether the sum stipulated is a penalty or liquidated damages. The two tests which are relevant to this problem are:

i) It will be held to be a penalty if the sum stipulated for is extravagant and unconscionable in amount in comparison with the greatest loss that could conceivably be proved to have followed from the breach.

ii) It will be held to be a penalty if the breach consists only in not paying a sum of money, and the sum stipulated is a sum greater than the sum which ought to have been paid.

By these tests it is submitted that clause 19 is clearly a penalty.

In conclusion E is advised that he has a claim for his expenses, provided they are shown to be reasonable, but that he cannot rely on either of the clauses that have been mentioned.

# 14 REMEDIES FOR BREACH OF CONTRACT: DAMAGES

14.1 Introduction

14.2 Key points

14.3 Analysis of questions

14.4 Questions

## 14.1 Introduction

As noted earlier, a breach of contract may be so severe that the injured party is entitled to treat the contract as being at an end and repudiate it. In such a case the normal remedy of the injured party will be to obtain damages for the breach. Alternatively in less serious cases of breach, there may be a right to damages, but no right to repudiate the contract.

Damages are not always a satisfactory remedy and equity has over the years supplemented the common law with a number of additional or alternative remedies; these will be dealt with in the next chapter. The normal approach to contract damages is to put the plaintiff in the position, financially, that he would have been in, had the contract been performed, he will be compensated for this expectancy. It should be remembered, however, that damages are meant to be compensation, not a punishment of the defendant. Therefore it will not be fair to include in the assessment for compensation a loss which would have been suffered anyway had the contract been performed properly. Thus a sudden change in the market which would have meant a loss to the plaintiff cannot be shifted to the defendant, as it is a loss which would have been suffered anyway by the plaintiff even had the contract been performed. This has only recently been made clear in two cases: *C & P Haulage* v *Middleton* [1983] 3 All ER 94 and *CCC Films* v *Impact Quadrant Films* [1985] QB 16.

No injured party should make a profit from damages and it must be established that there is loss to the plaintiff in actual consequence of the breach.

## 14.2 Key points

It is important that the student understands the following:

a) *Compensation for the plaintiff's loss*

There are several ways in which the plaintiff can be compensated for loss, usually the plaintiff may choose whichever head of compensation he feels most appropriate to the circumstances; or he may combine certain forms of compensation as appropriate.

The most common modes of claim are:

i) Loss of bargain

Damages assessed to put the plaintiff as nearly as possible in the same position as if the contract had been performed.

ii) Reliance loss

Damages to put the plaintiff in the position he would have been, if the contract had never been made, by compensating him for abortive expenditure.

iii) Restitution

When a bargain is made, the price paid, but the goods are never delivered, the plaintiff is entitled to recover the price paid plus interest.

iv) Incidental and consequential losses

Incidental losses are losses incurred by the plaintiff after the breach has come to his attention. They include the cost of, for example hiring substitutes, sending back defective goods and so on.

Consequential losses are those incurred as a result of the breach, such as personal injury or damage to property. For example the sale of a defective car, in itself a breach of contract, might have further repercussions such as injury to the plaintiff or others.

As already stated, the plaintiff may choose whichever head of claim seems most appropriate, but his choice is limited to the extent that the onus of proof is on the plaintiff to establish that the claim is a suitable one in the circumstances – for example, if claiming restitution he must prove total failure of consideration.

On occasion more than one form of claim will be available, the plaintiff may then combine his claims as he wishes. Bear in mind, however, that no one may make a profit or claim for the same loss twice over.

b) *Remoteness of damage*

*Hadley* v *Baxendale* (1854) 9 Exch 341 is, of course, the main starting point here. Every student should be familiar with the case and the two 'rules' that stem from it.

If the loss falls into either of the categories below:

i) damages which may fairly and reasonably be considered as arising naturally from the breach; or

ii) damages which may reasonably be supposed to have been in the contemplation of the parties at the time of the contract;

then damages will be recoverable.

The first limb or rule covered loss which any reasonable person would expect to result in the usual way from that type of breach of contract. The second limb will only operate when special circumstances apply to the contract and the information about these special circumstances is expressly communicated to the defendant by the plaintiff. In the case of *Victoria Laundry* v *Newman Industries* [1949] 2 KB 528 the Court of Appeal took the opportunity to review the development of the law since *Hadley* v *Baxendale*. Asquith J found that there were six basic propositions which emerged from the case law to that date:

i) General purpose of damages is to put the injured party, so far as money can do so, in the same position as if the contract had been properly performed.

ii) Injured party is entitled to recover such loss as was, at the time of the contract reasonably foreseeable to be liable to result from the breach.

iii) What was reasonably foreseeable depends on the knowledge possessed at that time by the parties.

iv) 'Possessed' here can mean imputed or actual. Every reasonable person is assumed to be aware of certain things, and to be able to forecast the likely consequences of breach if these things apply. This is imputed knowledge. Additionally a person may have specialist information which is outside the ordinary course of things. This is actual knowledge of some special state of affairs. Every person will be possessed of common 'imputed' knowledge under the first limb of *Hadley* and some may be possessed of actual special knowledge to which the second limb applies.

v) It is not important that the parties did not actually contemplate all the consequences of breach and the loss arising therefrom. It is sufficient that, had the question been considered, a reasonable person would have concluded that the loss in question was a natural consequence.

vi) Nor need it be proved that the parties must have believed that a breach would inevitably result in a particular form of loss – it is enough if a reasonable person could forsee it as a likely, though not essential, consequence of breach.

The principles thus set out were further considered and refined by the House of Lords in *The Heron II* [1969] 1 AC 350. In particular they were unhappy with the terms 'foreseeable' or 'reasonably foreseeable' as used in the *Victoria Laundry* case. In *Heron II*, however, the Lords could not achieve unanimity – and no general formula for defining the terms was agreed. Note that the test of remoteness determines only whether the plaintiff is entitled to damages and not the amount. The test does not mean that the defendant is liable for all loss once liability has been founded. Whether or not a plaintiff may recover damages depends substantially on what loss the courts are prepared to identify as being within the contemplation of the parties. The defendant's knowledge of special circumstances under the second limb, for example, is not in itself sufficient to make him liable. There must be knowledge and acceptance by the defendant of the purpose and intention of the plaintiff in stressing the importance of the special circumstances.

c) *Causation*

To prove causation exists the plaintiff must establish that the state of affairs which he alleges caused his loss was a direct consequence of the breach. The fact that the contract was breached is not in itself necessarily indicative that the ultimate loss was sustained because of the breach. Note two points in particular:

i) When there are two causes of loss, one arising from breach and one not, the one will be sufficient to sustain an action. Thus, in *Smith, Hogg & Co v Black Sea Insurance* [1940] AC 997 cargo was lost, partly because of bad weather, partly because the ship was unseaworthy. This latter, a clear breach of contract, was held sufficient to support a claim for damages.

ii) An intervening act of a third party which causes additional loss, or aggravates the existing situation, will not relieve the defendant from liability if that intervening act was reasonably foreseeable.

d) *Type of damages recoverable*

It is important always to remember that damages for breach of contract are for compensation only.

There are certain instances in which damages are *not* recoverable:

i)   for injury to reputation;

ii)  for injury to feelings;

iii) for failure to show title to land (save in cases of fraud).

In the first two cases there are in any event suitable remedies provided for in tort for an aggrieved party.

Although damages in breach of contract were never intended to be punitive, there are cases in which exemplary damages are recoverable presumably because the law seeks to discourage the type of breach concerned.

Two examples are:

i)   Dishonoured cheques: a trader on whose account a cheque has been wrongfully dishonoured is entitled to substantial damages, without pleading and proving actual damage. This would seem to be confined purely to traders.

ii)  Wrongful eviction: a landlord who fails to give the appropriate notice to his tenant under the Rent Act 1977 and then proceeds, contrary to the Protection from Eviction Act 1977, to try to wrongfully evict him must pay exemplary damages to his tenant.

The three main bases of quantifying damages have already been discussed, for example:

| | | |
|---|---|---|
| reliance loss | – | cost to the plaintiff of reliance on the contract; |
| restitution | – | benefits obtained by defendant under the contract; |
| loss of bargain | – | plaintiff's claim to be put in the same position as if the contract had been performed. |

Other types of damage include:

i)   Damage to commercial reputation

Dishonour of cheques has already been discussed and it has been noted that damages are not available in the ordinary way for loss of reputation; it being the basis for an action in tort only. *Commercial* reputation is, however, treated separately and may be protected. See: *Anglo-Continental Holidays* v *Typaldos Lines* [1967] 2 Lloyd's Rep 61.

ii) Discomfort, vexation, disappointment

There is a limit to damages for distressed feelings. It is noted in two recent cases that the award should be confined to cases where the contract itself 'was to provide peace of mind or freedom from distress': *Bliss* v *S E Thames Regional Health Authority* [1987] ICR 700, while in *Hayes* v *James & Charles Dodd* (1988) The Times 14 July, it was noted that the class of cases might be somewhat wider than that postulated in *Bliss*. Certainly simple commercial contracts with profit as a sole motive are unlikely to attract such awards.

iii) Inconvenience

This is closely linked to distressed feelings and awards for inconvenience probably apply to the same type of case.

iv) Diminution of future prospects

Wrongful breach of contract can have other damaging consequences on a person's life. For example, to be wrongfully expelled from a trade union may cause the injured party to lose his job and that in turn may damage his future prospects for employment: *Edwards* v *SOGAT* [1971] Ch 354.

v) Speculative damages

This is the most difficult category of all to quantity. It is often very much a last resort since if a person could prove a particular loss he would presumably claim for the specific value of that loss. All that can be said is that if, as a result of breach of contract, a plaintiff loses the chance of doing something and this contingency was outside the parties' control then if he loses a chance, he should be compensated for the value that chance might represent.

Quantification requires an assessment of the prospective benefit and the plaintiff's chance of succeeding. Thus, if the last chance was the opportunity to enter a beauty competition, the plaintiff can *only* recover for the lost chance, not the full prize on the assumption the plaintiff would have won.

e) *Mitigation of damages*

No plaintiff should make a profit. Therefore it will be a duty of the plaintiff to show that so far as was possible he mitigated his loss. Essentially there are three rules:

i) The plaintiff cannot recover for loss, if that loss could have been avoided by taking reasonable steps. He is not, however, expected to take risks to mitigate losses; the test is what is 'reasonable'.

ii) The plaintiff cannot recover for any loss he has avoided, even if he did rather more than was necessary for compliance with rule (i) above. Thus, if a plaintiff obtains any benefits as a result of his efforts to mitigate, these must be taken into account.

iii) The plaintiff may recover loss incurred in taking reasonable steps in mitigation, even though, ultimately he was unsuccessful.

Note that the duty to mitigate does not compel an innocent party to accept an anticipatory breach of contract, even though, by continuing to affirm the contract, this will increase the defendant's loss.

## f) *Liquidated damages*

This form of damages consists in claims for specific amounts, supported by proof from the plaintiff as to actual loss sustained. Thus, the assessment of damages to be claimed is the responsibility of the plaintiff rather than the court.

Sometimes both parties, in an effort to cater for things that might go wrong, pre-estimate likely losses and incorporate them into the contract.

A liquidated damages clause in a contract will be effective in the event of a breach of contract and no action for unliquidated damages will be permitted, *provided* the so called 'liquidated damages clause' is a genuine attempt to pre-assess damages and not a penalty clause.

Penalty clauses are not valid, in an action for breach of contract they are disregarded.

Penalties are intended as a punishment, imposed '*in terrorem*', to frighten a party into completing a contract; they are not genuine attempts to pre-estimate damages. Terminology is not necessarily conclusive; the mere fact that a clause is described as a 'penalty' (or the reverse) is not decisive.

In *Dunlop Pneumatic Tyre Co v New Garage and Motor Co Ltd* [1915] AC 79 Lord Dunedin formulated a number of rules concerning penalty clauses. For more details of this and other case law, the student should consult a textbook. See, for example, the recent case of *Jobson v Johnson* (1989).

In *Dunlop* Lord Dunedin also mentioned four tests which would prove helpful in deciding if the clause was a penalty or not.

i) If the sum(s) stipulated is extravagant and unconscionable in amount in comparison to the greatest loss that might be sustained, it will be a penalty.

ii) If the breach consists in not paying money and the sum(s) stipulated is far greater (eg to make a debtor pay £1,000, if he fails to repay £100 by the due date) then it will be a penalty.

iii) When a whole series of potential breaches, some serious, some not are to be 'compensated' by the payment of a single lump sum, then it is a strong presumption that this must be a penalty.

iv) Even if it is almost impossible to pre-estimate financial consequences of breach to any degree of preciseness, it will not be a penalty, provided there really is a genuine attempt by the parties to pre-assess likely damages, even if their attempt is not accurate.

If the clause is decided by the courts to be a penalty it will be disregarded and the courts will award general or unliquidated damages. If the clause is a genuine liquidated damages clause, then even if it underestimates damages, whether by bad assessment or because of inflation or whatever, then the courts will give effect to the clause and damages will be limited to the amount stipulated in the contract.

Note that there is a distinction between liquidated damages clauses which provide for payment on the event of breach and the type of contract which provides for payment of a sum of money on the happening of a certain event which is not a breach. These clauses are not liquidated damages, and the rules relating to distinction between liquidated damages and penalties, inapplicable. Thus, in *Alder* v *Moore* [1961] 2 QB 57, the defendant, a footballer having been injured, received £500 from an insurance company. He signed an agreement that he would not return to professional football and that if he did, he must pay the £500 back. When he did return, the courts held that this was neither liquidated damages, nor penalty clause, simply a contract for the (re)payment of a certain sum on a certain event. Since the event had occurred, the sum was payable. It was not a sum payable on breach. It should be noted also, that where the contract requires that a purchaser makes a part payment, or deposit in advance, then this will be recoverable by the plaintiff. Essentially, though deposit is payable before the breach, not after, there is little real difference between retaining a deposit and enforcing a penalty. The courts will countenance neither.

## 14.3 Analysis of questions

In most years, London University has a question on remedies in the Elements of the Law of Contract papers. In some of the other questions also, the problem type especially, the student may have, very briefly, to consider whether in a given set of circumstances relating to say, mistake or misrepresentation, the plaintiff is entitled to a remedy and if so, which seems most appropriate. So, in one form or another it seems a good bet that the question of remedies will crop up somewhere, even if there is not a full question devoted to it. The problems are almost equally divided between straight essay questions or problems, with a couple of years when the question falls into two sections, essay and problem together. Almost all the questions are concerned in some way with the measure of damages so obviously there is a lot of overlap between them. Occasionally, however, there is some degree of difference in the amount of detail required and the questions quoted below reflect that.

## 14.4 Questions

QUESTION ONE

a) 'Damages cannot, in principle, be recovered in a contractual action for hurt feelings, disappointment or injury to reputation.'

Discuss.

b) A Ltd employ B Ltd to build a multi-purpose sports complex. B Ltd engage sub-contractors, C Ltd, who use cement which turns out to be highly unsuitable for the purpose for which it is used. Soon after completion and occupation of the building cracks begin to appear. The complex has to close for expensive repairs and a lot of revenue is lost. A Ltd had also put in a bid, which has to be withdrawn, to host the World Badminton Championships which would have produced large amounts of revenue.

Advise A Ltd.

University of London LLB Examination
(for External Students) Elements of the Law of Contract June 1987 Q8

*Skeleton Solution*

a) • Development of law on damages for hurt feelings – originally only for physical inconvenience – early 1970s broadly based claims like *Jarvis* v *Swan's Tours* (1973) – mid 1980s type of case to which applicable begins to narrow – relevant case law.

   • Injury to reputation – usually any damages result from action in tort – damages not generally available in breach of contract – three specific exceptions.

b) • Main contract between A and B; sub-contractors employed by B – no contractual link between A and C.

   • Two limbs of *Hadley* v *Baxendale* (1854).

   • Cost of repairs, loss of revenue within first limb.

   • Loss of revenue from hosting world championships within second limb? Were special circumstances known.

   • Relevant case law.

*Suggested Solution*

a) The proposition which falls to be discussed contains, it is submitted, two distinct areas:

   i)   damages for hurt feelings or disappointment;

   ii)  damages for injury to reputation.

   Until relatively recently, it could be stated with confidence that whilst damages could be awarded for physical inconvenience (eg *Hobbs* v *L & S W Railway* (1875)), the decision of the House of Lords in *Addis* v *Gramophone* (1909) was conclusive that in contrast damages were not available in respect of mental distress suffered as a result of a breach of contract. A succession of cases starting in 1973 has, however, made substantial inroads into their principle.

   First came *Jarvis* v *Swan's Tours* (1973) and *Jackson* v *Horizon Holidays* (1975) in which damages were awarded for distress and disappointment suffered as a result of package holidays falling below the standard promised by the tour operators. In both cases the judgment of the Court of Appeal were on a sufficiently broad basis to warrant the conclusion that henceforth damages could be awarded for distress providing that was something that could reasonably have been contemplated as being a probable consequence of the breach.

   These cases were followed and applied in *Cox* v *Phillips* (1976) in which an employee suffered distress as a result of being wrongfully demoted (*Addis* was distinguished as dealing with wrongful dismissal only), in *Heywood* v *Wellers* (1976) where a firm of solicitors failed to start the necessary proceedings to prevent the plaintiff from being molested by an ex-boyfriend, and in *Perry* v *Sidney Phillips* (1982) where a surveyor negligently failed to observe major structural faults in a dwelling house.

   It appeared that the courts were assuming a general jurisdiction to award damages for distress until two recent discussions which represent something of a retreat from these advances. In *Shove* v *Downs Surgical* (1984) Sheen J applied *Addis* and held that damages were not available for distress in a wrongful dismissal case. Then in *Bliss* v *S E Thames Health Authority* (1985) the Court of Appeal overruled *Cox* v *Phillips* (1976) and held that damages were not generally available for distress in contract, saying that the *Jarvis* line of cases concerned contracts which were either for the provision of pleasure or the alleviation of suffering from which (exceptionally) damages for distress were available. This undoubtedly is a considerable narrowing of the broad statements which are to be found in cases such as *Jarvis* and *Jackson*.

As to injury to reputation, in a specific area of law – defamation – provides the appropriate procedures and remedies. Accordingly contract damages are not generally available for injury to reputation consequent upon a breach of contract: *Addis* v *Gramophone* (1909). The only exceptions to this are:

i)   where a banker wrongfully dishonours a trader's cheque, *Gibbons* v *Westminster Bank* (1939);

ii)  where an actor suffers loss of publicity and the chance to enhance his reputation, *Clayton* v *Oliver* (1930);

iii) where an apprentice is wrongfully dismissed before the end of his apprenticeship, *Dunk* v *Waller* (1970).

b)  In advising A Ltd one must consider whether it can recover damages in respect of (i) the cost of repairs; (ii) loss of revenue while the complex is closed; and (iii) loss of revenue from hosting the world championships.

First, two preliminary points must be made. The contract for the construction of the complex was made between A Ltd and B Ltd. It was the latter who employed the sub-contractors, C Ltd, who used the unsuitable cement. No contractual relationship existed between A Ltd and C Ltd. C Ltd therefore cannot have incurred any liability in contract to A Ltd since priority of contract did not exist between them. On the other hand it matters not that B Ltd may have acted reasonably in engaging C Ltd and may have believed them to be competent sub-contractors. Liability in contract is strict and if B Ltd have not built or caused the complex to be built in a proper manner, they are in breach of their contract with A Ltd.

Turning now to the items of loss listed (i) to (iii) above, item (i) causes little difficulty. If a building (be it a sports complex or anything else) is incorrectly constructed, it is plain and obvious that the owner is going to incur expense in correcting the fault. Such a head of loss is within the first limb of the rule in *Hadley* v *Baxendale* (1854) – loss occurring in the usual course of things – and A Ltd can therefore recover the cost of repair from B Ltd.

Item (ii) is also relatively straightforward. B Ltd must have known that A Ltd wishes to have the complex built in order to use it. So long as it is undergoing repairs, it will clearly be out of commission and incapable of being used. The loss of revenue which results is again within the first limb of the rule in *Hadley* v *Baxendale* (1854). Indeed, their head of claim is very similar to the general loss of profits claim which succeeded in *Victoria Laundry* v *Newman Industries* (1949), where knowledge of the likely use of the subject matter of the contract to earn revenue was imputed to the contract breaker. Alternatively, adopting the test used by the majority of the Court of Appeal in *Parsons* v *Uttley, Ingham & Co* (1978), loss of revenue during repair was a serious possibility if the complex was not properly built.

It is the third head of loss, the loss of revenue from possibly holding the world badminton championships, which raises most difficulties.

In this regard first it should be noted that although there was no certainty that the complex would play host to the championships, that of itself is no bar to A Ltd recovering damages. Where possible, the courts will put a value on the loss of a chance: *Chaplin* v *Hicks* (1911).

The problem regarding this item is that of remoteness. Hosting a world sports championship is something far out of the ordinary for any sports complex. There is a real danger the court would regard this head of loss as being too remote.

*Hadley* v *Baxendale* (1854) is the source of the modern law of remoteness. Clearly this head of loss is not within the first limb of the rule, so is it within the second limb viz something the parties could have contemplated as being the probable result of the breach? As explained in *Victoria Laundry* v *Newman Industries* (1949) (a part of the case approved by the House of Lords in *The Heron II* (1969)), remoteness depends on knowledge and the second limb of the rule is concerned with actual knowledge of special circumstances which make additional loss (over and above loss arising in the ordinary course of things) likely.

It is submitted that the possibility of A Ltd hosting the world championships was so unlikely that unless B Ltd had actual knowledge of this possibility, the lost revenue is irrecoverable (by analogy with the lucrative dyeing contracts in *Victoria Laundry* v *Newman Industries* (1949)). Alternatively, to apply the test of Orr and Scarman LJJ in *Parsons* v *Uttley, Ingham* (1978), it was not something both parties could have contemplated at the time the contract was concluded as being a serious possibility in the event that B Ltd was in breach. This third head of loss is, therefore, irrecoverable.

QUESTION TWO

'The rules on remoteness of damage and mitigation in contract are simply instruments which courts use in their attempt to legitimise the arbitrary damages awards that they make'.

Discuss.

University of London LLB Examination
(for External Students) Elements of the Law of Contract June 1989 Q4

*Skeleton Solution*

- The basic rule in *Hadley* v *Baxendale* (1854).
- Reformulated into a series of tests or propositions in *Victoria Laundry* (1949).
- Considered by Lords in *The Heron II* (1969) 'reasonable foreseeability' test changed to 'reasonable contemplation'.
- Divergence between tortious and breach of contract actions.
- Duty to mitigate
- Consideration of statement under discussion in the light of these aspects.

*Suggested Solution*

The proposition contained in this quotation would not gain universal acceptance. It can be argued that damages awards appear to be arbitrary because the courts attempt to achieve a balance between two objectives. On the one hand they seek to compensate the plaintiff for the loss he has suffered, on the other hand they seek to avoid visiting the defendant with liability for loss that he could not have contemplated or loss that could, with reasonable prudence, have been avoided.

'The rule of the common law is that where a party sustains a loss by breach of contract, he is, so far as money can do it, to be placed in the same position as if the contract had been performed.' (*Robinson* v *Harman* (1848)). This is an expression of the first objective. It must be noted that the courts will, in awarding damages, avoid placing the plaintiff in a better position than he would have been in if the contract had been fully performed: *C & P Haulage* v *Middleton* (1983).

The rule that the plaintiff should be put in the position he would have been in if the contract had been performed would, if logically pursued, afford the plaintiff a complete indemnity for all loss resulting from a breach, however improbable or unpredictable. In order, therefore, to meet the second objective the rule is subject to the limitation that the damages must not be too remote. Accordingly the courts have developed a further rule to limit the liability of the defendant to loss which the law regards as sufficiently proximate.

This further rule found expression in the judgment of Alderson B in *Hadley* v *Baxendale* (1854) where it was said to consist of two limbs. To be recoverable the damages should be such as may fairly and reasonably be considered as either arising naturally, that is according to the usual course of things, from such breach of contract itself, or such as may reasonably be supposed to have been in the contemplation of both parties, at the time they made the contract, as the probable result of the breach of it.

In *Victoria Laundry (Windsor) Ltd* v *Newman Industries Ltd* (1949) Asquith LJ re-formulated the rule in *Hadley* v *Baxendale* (1854) in the following propositions:

i)   the plaintiff is only entitled to recover loss which was at the time of the contract reasonably foreseeable as liable to result from the breach;

ii)  what was reasonably foreseeable depends on the knowledge then possessed by the parties;

iii) knowledge is of two types, imputed and actual. Imputed knowledge is the knowledge that everything, as a reasonable person, is taken to have of the ordinary course of things. Actual knowledge is knowledge which the contract-breaker actually possesses of special circumstances outside the ordinary course of things, which make additional loss liable to result;

iv)  the contract-breaker need not have actually asked himself what loss was liable to result, it is sufficient that as a reasonable man he would have done so;

v)   the plaintiff need not prove that it would be foreseen that the loss would necessarily result from the breach, it was sufficient that it was a 'serious possibility' or a 'real danger'. This could be expressed as 'liable to result'.

These propositions were considered by the House of Lords in *The Heron II* (1969). Their Lordships approved them in general terms, but they held that the test was not one of 'reasonable foreseeability' – which was the test in tort – but one of 'reasonable contemplation' which term denoted a higher degree of probability. The distinction between tests in contract and in tort might be regarded as arbitrary. In *H Parsons (Livestock) Ltd* v *Uttley, Ingham & Co Ltd* (1978) both Lord Denning MR and Scarman LJ (as he then was) expressed the view that it was absurd that the test for remoteness of damage should differ according to the legal classification of the cause of action. Lord Denning was also of the opinion that different tests applied to physical damage (damage to person or property) and economic (deprivation of profit) loss. But Scarman and Orr LJJ rejected this distinction.

In this case the Court of Appeal re-affirmed the principle that, if physical injury or damage is within the contemplation of the parties, recovery is not limited because the degree of such damage could not have been anticipated. In *Wroth* v *Tyler* (1974) Megarry J applied a similar principle with respect to economic loss.

It could be suggested that somewhat arbitrary limits have been defined as to the damage recoverable. In *Addis* v *Gramophone Co Ltd* (1909) the House of Lords held that damages could be recovered for loss of reputation or injury to feelings. This limitation has more recently been re-affirmed by the Court of Appeal in *Bliss* v *S E Thames Regional Health Authority* (1985). It appears, however, that in certain types of contract damages may be awarded for distress occasioned by the breach of contract: *Jarvis* v *Swan's Tours Ltd* (1973); *Jackson* v *Horizon Holidays Ltd* (1975). But there is a limit to damages for distress. In *Bliss* v *S E Thames Regional Health Authority* (1985) Dillon LJ said that such damages should be confined to cases where the contract which has been broken was itself a contract to provide peace of mind or freedom from distress.

The plaintiff's recovery of damages might also be limited by the duty imposed on him by the common law to mitigate his loss. He must take reasonable steps to minimise his loss; furthermore, he must refrain from taking unreasonable steps that increase his loss.

If the plaintiff fails to take reasonable steps to minimise his loss he cannot recover anything for the extra loss arising from his failure. What is usually required of the plaintiff is that he should seek a substitute contract. If a seller fails to deliver the goods the buyer has the duty to go into the market and purchase substitute goods. The plaintiff is required only to take *reasonable steps*. Where there are two reasonable courses of action open to the plaintiff either will be sufficient to comply with his duty to mitigate: *Gebruder Metelmann GmbH & Co* v *NBR (London) Ltd* (1984). The plaintiff is not required to take risks in order to mitigate his loss: *Pilkington* v *Wood* (1953). An employee who is wrongfully dismissed is under the duty to seek alternative employment. Again only reasonable steps are required of the employee. He need not accept an offer of a job at a reduced status: *Yetton* v *Eastwoods Froy Ltd* (1967).

The plaintiff must avoid taking unreasonable steps in attempting to mitigate which would actually increase his loss. Thus, he should not incur expense in attempting to tender performance after it has become clear that the defendant will reject it.

The benefits a plaintiff obtains as a result of his mitigation must be taken into account in assessing his damages, even if he acquires these benefits as a result of steps which he was not required to take: *British Westinghouse Co* v *Underground Electric Rys Co of London* (1912).

In conclusion it is submitted that whilst there are possibly arbitrary distinctions drawn and anomalous limits set in the rules relating to remoteness of damage and mitigation, it is not justifiable to characterise these rules as merely instruments to justify the awards that the courts make.

QUESTION THREE

In 1990 the S Club engaged T's services as a professional squash coach for five years at a salary of £22,000 a year. In March 1991 the Club appointed a new manager to run the club house and friction developed between the manager and T. Six weeks ago, the Committee of the Club wrote to T terminating his engagement with immediate effect. Since that time, T has been unable to find work other than one or two painting and decorating jobs. T is 32. He believes that he will never again be employed as a squash coach because of his age and because the Club refuses to supply him with a reference. T has made one attempt at suicide and is in a state of deep depression. In addition to his salary, T has lost gratuities from club members of approximately £5,000 a year.

Advise T.

University of London LLB Examination
(for External Students) Elements of the Law of Contract June 1991 Q7

*Skeleton Solution*

• Breach of contract.

• Damages.

• Remoteness.

• Special circumstances.

• Measure of damages.

*Suggested Solution*

T was engaged on a fixed term contract for five years commencing in 1990. He was summarily dismissed in 1991. There is nothing to indicate that this dismissal was justified, so T has been wrongfully dismissed and the S Club are in breach of contract. (It is assumed that the S Club have the requisite legal capacity to enable an action to be brought against them.)

The general rule regarding damages for breach of contract is that the plaintiff is entitled to be put in the position he would have been in if the contract had been performed. But in contract there is a limitation on the award of damages. The plaintiff is entitled to recover for all the loss he suffered as a result of the breach, provided, however, that the loss is not too remote. The justification for this limitation is that it would be unfair to impose liability on the defendant for all the loss resulting from the breach, however extreme or unforeseeable.

The rule as to remoteness has its origin in *Hadley* v *Baxendale* (1854), in which two principles were established: (a) the injured party is entitled to the damages which may fairly and reasonably be considered as arising naturally, ie according to the usual course of things, from such breach of contract itself; (b) the injured party is also entitled to such damages as may be reasonably supposed to have been in the contemplation of the parties at the time they made the contract as the probable result of the breach.

This rule was amplified by Asquith LJ in *Victoria Laundry (Windsor) Ltd* v *Newman Industries Ltd* (1949) in a series of propositions. The effect of these propositions was to state that the injured party was only entitled to recover for such loss as was reasonably foreseeable. What was reasonably foreseeable depended on the state of knowledge of the parties. Knowledge was of two kinds; imputed and actual. Knowledge is imputed as to the 'ordinary course of things'; everyone, as a reasonable person, is assumed to know what loss is liable to result from that ordinary course. In addition there may be special circumstances beyond the ordinary course of things which caused more loss. Actual knowledge of those special circumstances would be required to make that loss recoverable.

The propositions of Asquith LJ were considered, and largely approved, by the House of Lords in *Koufos* v *C Czarnikow Ltd, The Heron II* (1969). Their lordships held, however, that the test for remoteness was not reasonable foreseeability, but what was within the reasonable contemplation of the parties: this denoted a higher degree of probability. This degree of probability was conveyed by expressions such as 'liable to result', 'not unlikely to occur', 'a real danger', or 'a serious possibility'.

It should be further noted that a defendant will be liable if the *kind* of damage is within reasonable contemplation, even if the *extent* of such damage is not: *H Parsons (Livestock) Ltd* v *Uttley, Ingham & Co Ltd* (1978); *Wroth* v *Tyler* (1974).

It is necessary to apply these principles to the facts of the problem.

As T is on a fixed term contract he is, prima facie, entitled to his salary for the remainder of the contract. The loss he has sustained falls within the category of damages arising 'according to the usual course of things'. This is subject to T's duty to mitigate his loss. This duty requires him to seek alternative employment. But he is only required to take reasonable steps to mitigate his loss. He is not require to to accept employment which involves a significant reduction in his previous status: *Yetton* v *Eastwoods Froy Ltd* (1967). It appears that he has not been able to obtain suitable alternative employment. His duty to mitigate is impeded by the failure of the club to provide him with a reference.

T has also lost gratuities from club members in the amount of approximately £5,000 per year. But this is not a contractual entitlement; it cannot, therefore be regarded as falling within the first limb of *Hadley* v *Baxendale*. Whether it is recoverable at all is extremely doubtful. In order to fix the S Club with liability for this loss it would have to be shown that the circumstances were within their actual knowledge. Moreover these gratuities would appear to depend on the whim of the club members.

The further information is that T is in a state of deep depression and has made an attempt at suicide. It is clear that the depression which the dismissal has caused T cannot be compensated for in a contractual claim. This was established by the House of Lords in *Addis* v *Gramophone Co Ltd* (1909) and re-affirmed by the Court of Appeal more recently in *Bliss* v *South East Thames Regional Health Authority* (1987).

Damages for distress have been awarded in particular kinds of contracts, such as that for a holiday in *Jarvis* v *Swan's Tours Ltd* (1973), but such an award is limited to cases where the object of the contract is the provision of comfort or pleasure or the relief of discomfort: *Hayes* v *James and Charles Dodd* (1990).

T's suicide attempt is not an event within 'reasonable contemplation', nor is there a causal connection in law between that attempt and his dismissal.

T is advised, therefore, that only his claim for his loss of salary is likely to prove successful.

# 15 REMEDIES FOR BREACH OF CONTRACT: EQUITABLE REMEDIES

15.1    Introduction

15.2    Key points

15.3    Analysis of questions

15.4    Question

## 15.1 Introduction

In the last chapter, the remedy of damages was discussed. Undoubtedly this is the most likely and most useful remedy, but there are cases when damages, although they might be obtainable for breach, are inadequate as a remedy, because mere money will not compensate the plaintiff properly.

Equity has provided other remedies, notably specific performance and injunction, to supplement the common law system of monetary compensation. Because of their equitable history this sort of remedy is, unlike damages in common law, not available 'as of right'. Usually it is for the plaintiff to show cause why damages would not be sufficient remedy and the courts have a discretion to order an equitable remedy where it would seem fair and just to do so.

## 15.2 Key points

It is important that the student understands the following:

a) *Specific performance*

Damages will probably be inadequate in the following cases and therefore specific performance might be awarded:

i)  Where the plaintiff cannot get a satisfactory substitute; for example when the subject matter of a contract is land, or antiques or irreplaceable paintings and so on.

ii) When the plaintiff has contracted for services of a personal nature from the defendant – however note restrictions on specific performance in this respect (see below: key point (b)).

iii) When damages are difficult to assess, for example specific performance will be ordered on a contract to pay an annuity.

iv) Section 52 Sale of Goods Act 1979, the courts have a discretion to order specific performance in the case of specific or ascertained goods.

186

## b) *Factors relevant in awarding specific performance*

The courts will take into account the following factors, as applicable, before they order an award of specific performance.

i) Mutuality: the plaintiff will only be successful if the contract could also be enforced by the defendant. Thus, if there still exist some unperformed obligations which will now never be enforceable, the contract will be lacking in mutuality.

Note that the date of the hearing is the crucial time for assessing mutuality. In: *Sutton* v *Sutton* [1984] 1 All ER 168, the court held that while lack of mutuality might have been a good defence while the contract was still executory, by the time the contract came before the court to be considered the plaintiff had performed her side of the contract and it was too late to plead lack of mutuality.

ii) Hardship: This is more a ground for refusing specific performance than a basis for awarding it. Thus specific performance will not be awarded if it would cause the defendant undue hardship.

iii) Unfairness: If the plaintiff has acted unfairly or dishonestly he will be refused the remedy. 'He who comes to equity must come with clean hands'.

iv) Plaintiff's failure to perform a particular promise, which induced the defendant to contract, will render the remedy not available to the plaintiff.

v) Impossibility: Since 'equity does nothing in vain' it will never be the case that specific performance is ordered of a contract impossible to perform.

vi) Supervision: A court will rarely if ever grant specific performance of a contract that would need to be constantly supervised. While supervision is not an absolute bar, it is a factor the courts will take into account.

vii) Uncertainty. The agreement must be one sufficiently definite to allow the court to formulate an award of specific performance.

viii) Delay. While there is no specific time limit the longer a party waits before applying for specific performance, the more likely it is that the equitable doctrine of *Laches* may operate to bar his claim.

All or some of these factors will be taken into account by the courts in deciding whether to grant specific performance. Certain types of contract create particular problems:

i) Contracts for personal service

The courts will not normally order performance of this type of contract; in part due to problems of supervision. It should be noted that the Employment Protection (Consolidation) Act 1978 permits orders of reinstatement or re-engagement which are a statutory equivalent of specific performance; but, of course this Act applies only to contracts of employment.

ii) Building contracts

A court will usually refuse specific performance on three main grounds:

• Damages may be an adequate remedy as the plaintiff can engage another builder.

- The contract may be too vague and not describe the work required sufficiently precisely.
- There may be difficulties of supervision.

However it has been known for the courts to effectively ignore the third item if the other two reasons do not apply and go ahead and order specific performance.

iii) Entire or severable contracts

If the contract is entire and cannot be severed the courts will not award specific performance of certain aspects of the contract. If the contract is to be performed in instalments or stages and each part is severable, specific performance may be granted separately for each stage or instalment.

b) *Injunction*

There are three main types of injunction:

i) Interlocutory: granted to regulate the conduct of the parties, pending a hearing.

ii) Prohibitory injunction: orders something not to be done by the defendant.

iii) Mandatory injunction: orders the defendant to do something positive, to refrain from doing something he had promised not to do.

The choice of injunction depends on specific circumstances. For example an interlocutory injunction, if applied for quickly enough, might be used to prevent a breach of contract even before it occurs. It should be noted that an injunction will not be granted if it would be an indirect form of specific performance, when the plaintiff would have no right to specific performance. A contract, particularly an employment contract, may have certain negative obligations expressly included and it may be able to frame an injunction in such a way that the negative aspects of the contract can be enforced without compelling the plaintiff to work or infringing the rule that an injunction will not be available where the plaintiff could not have obtained specific performance.

c) *Damages in lieu of specific performance or an injunction*

By virtue of Chancery Amendment Act 1858 (now incorporated into s50 Supreme Court Act 1981) the rule that damages could only be awarded at common law was amended. When a court has the power to grant specific performance or an injunction, it may make an award of damages in addition to or instead of such an order.

Since it will be recalled that the main reason for applying for an equitable remedy is because damages would not be adequate compensation, there would at first sight seem little advantage to such a change in the law. Two instances arise when it will be beneficial to invoke the Supreme Court Act:

i) When there is no completed cause of action. In such cases it would not be possible to get damages at common law.

ii) When the plaintiff wishes to have the time of assessment of damages fixed at some other date than is usual at common law.

Damages at common law are assessed as of the date the breach occurred. In equity, by virtue of the SCA, the courts may fix such other date as seems appropriate for assessment, if it would be more beneficial for the plaintiff, and generally more fair and equitable.

## 15.3 Analysis of questions

Although common law damages has formed the basis of several questions in past London University papers, the topic of equitable remedies has never yet arisen as a complete question.

The issue of remedies can be combined with virtually any other topic though, since it is common to set a question on some form of breach of contract and, as well as an analysis of that breach, require the student briefly to consider what remedies might be available. For example, there is an increasing trend (see Q2 on the 1993 paper (Chapter 20)) to link the doctrine of mistake with equity and equitable remedies.

Question 8 in the University of London 1983 External LLB Examination, Elements of the Law of Contract paper, which is mainly concerned with privity of contract, requires some mention of specific performance.

Similarly in a number of questions on restraint of trade, the question of enforcement by use of an injunction crops up.

Since there is no specific past question to quote, the one below should be fairly typical of any likely to be asked on the topic of equitable remedies.

## 15.4 Question

a) In what circumstances might a court grant an injunction in relation to a contract for personal services?

b) With reference to decided cases, explain the extent to which the intervention of equity may be restricted when the remedy of specific performance is being considered.

Written by Editor

*Skeleton Solution*

a) • Injunctions not normally granted in contracts for personal service, because it would be an evasion of the rule barring specific performance.
   • May be available if negative part of contract is limited.
   • If negative part is too wide, can be severed and enforced only in part.
   • Must leave defendant with a true choice.

b) • Circumstances of specific performance – the nature of the remedy.
   • Availability, times when it will not be awarded.
   • Types of contract where there are likely to be problems.

*Suggested Solution*

a) The two permanent forms of injunction, prohibitory and mandatory, will not be granted if the effect is directly or indirectly to compel the defendant to do acts for which a plaintiff could not obtain specific performance.

Also, unlike specific performance, a defendant cannot resist an injunction on the grounds that it is burdensome to him. However since this is an equitable remedy it will be available only at the court's discretion, when it seems fair and equitable to make such an award.

Injunctions are often seen by the courts as an attempt by the plaintiff to evade the rules under which specific performance might be barred and may be refused for that reason.

However certain service contracts lend themselves to enforcement in this way, because express negative obligations can be entered without actually compelling a defendant to work often by enforcing such negative aspects as not allowing a party to work for any other party; it will indirectly force the defendant back to work: *Lumley* v *Wagner* (1852), *Warner Bros* v *Nelson* (1937). Although in theory, the defendant is free to refuse to perform his contract, so long as he fulfils the terms of the injunction and does not work for anyone else, nevertheless there is such a degree of economic pressure on the defendant, such an injunction is often tantamount to ordering specific performance anyway. The law now seems to be moving away from the sort of situation that arose in *Warner Bros* v *Nelson* (1937) and it seems that an injunction will not now be granted unless it leaves the defendant with some viable alternative means to earn a living (*Page One Records* v *Britton* (1968)).

The courts will not grant an injunction when the clause in the contract is too wide to enforce fairly. They may however construe the negative clause in question to see what was intended and award an injunction to give effect to this clause, as they construe it (*The Littlewoods Organisation* v *Harris* (1977)). If severance is feasible they will apply the 'blue pencil test' and use an injunction to enforce the (severed) negative aspect of the contract which seems reasonable. In *Evening Standard* v *Henderson* (1986) the defendants' employers successfully obtained an injunction to prevent him working for a rival newspaper even after he had (wrongfully) left their employment.

b) In cases where damages seem an inadequate remedy, specific performance may be a suitable alternative. Like all equitable remedies however, it is at the court's discretion and there are a number of circumstances when it will not be available. There must be mutuality of performance and this is assessed as of the time of judgment (*Price* v *Strange* (1978), *Sutton* v *Sutton* (1984)). If hardship would be caused, the award may be refused by the courts (*Denne* v *Light* (1858), *Patel* v *Ali* (1984)).

If the courts feel the plaintiff has acted unfairly or dishonestly he will be refused the remedy (*Walters* v *Morgan* (1861)).

The courts will be reluctant to grant an award where constant supervision is needed (*Ryan* v *Mutual Tontine Westminster Chambers Association* (1893)) though it is not an insuperable bar (*Posner* v *Scott Lewis* (1987)). The courts attach more importance to the protection of the plaintiff's interests than to problems of supervision (*Luganda* v *Service Hotels* (1969)).

The contract must not be ambiguous in any way, lack of certainty may make it impossible to make an award sufficiently definite as to be enforceable (*Joseph* v *National Magazine* (1959)). Any undue delay in seeking specific performance may lose the plaintiff the right to an award, though a lot depends on the type of contract, and whether the parties envisage past performance of it (*Lazard Bros* v *Fairfield Properties* (1977)).

As well as these general guidelines, the courts have also formulated more specific rules to deal with particular types of contract. For example they will rarely if ever grant specific performance to enforce a contract for personal services (*Chinnock* v *Sainsbury* (1861), *England* v *Curling* (1844)), but see also *Hill* v *C A Parsons Ltd* (1972) where specific performance to make an employer retain an employee he had dismissed was effectively granted, through the medium of an interim injunction.

In the case of building contracts, the general rule is that such a contract will not be specifically enforced. However it would seem from cases like *Wolverhampton Corporation* v *Emmons* (1901) that where the building obligations are defined precisely by plans and the plaintiff could not get the work done by another contractor as the defendant had possession of the site, this rule might be relaxed.

# 16 QUASI-CONTRACT

## 16.1 Introduction

The remedies we have looked at in Chapters 14 and 15 are effectively indirect attempts to enforce the contract, or at least redress the damage caused by breach. There are, however, instances when benefits have been transferred from one party to another before breach occurs and the law of quasi-contract is concerned with the restoration of such transferred benefits.

The law of quasi-contract, also called the law of restitution, is traditionally viewed as a part of the law of contract.

In a leading text: *The Law of Restitution* by Goff and Jones the authors analyse the rationale of quasi-contract as pre-supposing three things:

i)    that the defendant has been enriched by the receipt of a benefit;

ii)    that he has been so enriched at the plaintiff's expense;

iii)    and that it would be unjust to allow him to retain the benefit.

Thus, quasi-contract is an area of law which deals with unjust or unfair enrichment and assists the plaintiff in recovering fair restitution. The term 'quasi' stems from the fact that it is not necessary for a contract to exist. The availability of remedies by way of restitution do not depend on a contractual relationship.

There are three main quasi-contractual actions:

i)    an action for money had and received;

ii)    an action for money paid;

iii)    a quantum meruit claim;

which will be briefly dealt with below.

## 16.2 Key points

It is important that the student understand the following:

a) *Action for money had and received*

   This was an old common law remedy, not unlike the equitable trust remedy. It has been gradually expanded to cover the following types of case:

i) Money paid under a mistake of fact

When money is paid to another under the mistaken belief that a fact or state of affairs exists which if true, would make the person paying liable to pay money

Note that the person paying will have no right of recovery if he knew that the payment was not due, but paid it anyway.

It was once thought that the plaintiff had to be under the belief that the payment was legally obligatory, but cases like *Laines* v *LCC* [1949] 2 KB 683, show that if the plaintiff believes payment to be morally required (provided the belief is genuine), this will be sufficient.

The nature of the mistake is important. It must be one of fact, not law. The mistake must not be made recklessly or negligently, though it is apparent that the severity of mistake is assessed less stringently than in ordinary law of contract. The mistake should not relate to any illegal contract. Finally, the mistake of fact on which the plaintiff relies need not have arisen in connection with a contract at all.

ii) Money paid in pursuance of an ineffective contract

The term ineffective contract can have a number of connotations. In this context there must be a total failure of consideration. Partial failure is not enough to sustain an action for money had and received. Thus goods which are supplied which are defective, or items supplied in insufficient quantity will not be a total failure of consideration. However 'total' needs to be considered with care. In *Butterworth* v *Kingsway Motors* [1954] 1 WLR 1286, a car was 'sold' to the plaintiff by a party with no title. The 'purchaser' had the use of the car for nearly a year, but it was still held that failure to pass title amounted to total failure of consideration.

iii) Benefits different in kind

If a plaintiff receives a benefit, very different from that for which he bargained, then even though he may have derived some benefit, total failure of consideration will be presumed and he will be entitled to recover his money.

b) *Action for money paid*

This covers cases where the plaintiff pays money to a third party for the use and benefit of the defendant.

To succeed in his claim the plaintiff must prove:

i) that he was constrained to pay the money by some reasonable fear or anticipation of legal proceedings being brought or to be brought against him.

At one time voluntary payments were, therefore, outside the ambit of this action; but more recently it has seemed that the courts are prepared to extend the rules and permit the recovery of voluntary payments.

ii) The plaintiff must establish that he has paid money to the use of the defendant, which the defendant had a liability to pay.

At one time the payment had to be at the express request of the defendant, but the courts are now willing to imply such a request from the circumstances of the case.

c) *Quantum meruit*

A *quantum meruit* is sought where a plaintiff sues for reasonable payment for work done to date, rather than seeking either a precise sum, or general damages for a breach of contract.

A *quantum meruit* may be sought when either

i)  the contract is terminated by breach

ii) the contract is void

To this extent it cuts across the traditional divisions in contractual and quasi-contractual remedies; it sometimes operates as a legitimate remedy in contract and sometimes as a form of restitution a quasi-contractual remedy.

## 16.3 Analysis of questions

Over the past twelve years the University of London examiners have not featured questions on quasi-contract in their Elements of the Law of Contract papers. To some extent, this is not really surprising: the 'true' contractual topics list is long enough and there are doubts as to how the subject of quasi-contract may best be examined or even whether it belongs in a contract paper at all.

Should a question ever occur on the subject it might look something like the one quoted below.

## 16.4 Question

Restitutionary or quasi-contractual remedies do not, strictly, fall into the usual category of contractual remedies. Such remedies are nevertheless available to those faced with a partial or total failure of consideration and may if sought put the plaintiff in a better position than if he sought the orthodox remedy of damages.

Discuss.

Written by Editor

*Skeleton Solution*

• Definition of quasi-contract. Extent – application.
• Total failure of consideration.
• Partial failure of consideration.
• Restitution versus damages.
• Possible reforms.

*Suggested Solution*

The law of restitution or quasi-contract covers a much broader field than contract extending in particular to the law of tort. Goff and Jones (*The Law of Restitution*) suggest that the whole area should be reclassified as a separate topic in its own right, not just a 'fringe' or twilight area on the edges on contract and tort. This would bring English common law more in line with Roman classifications in law, the latter having a very strong and well identified law of restitution.

The law as it stands at present was defined by Lord Wright in *Fibrosa Spolka Akcynja v Fairburn Lawson Combe Barbour Ltd* (1943) as follows:

'It is clear that in any civilised system, law is bound to provide remedies for what has been called unjust enrichment or unjust benefit, that is to prevent a man from retaining money of, or some benefit derived of, another which it is against his conscience he should keep. Such remedies in English Law are generally different from remedies in contract or in tort, and are now recognised to fall within a third category of the common law which has been called quasi-contract or restitution.'

Quasi-contractual remedies' availability is not solely dependent on the existence of a breach of contract, but where there *has* been a breach the innocent party may have to decide whether an action for damages in the normal way, or a quasi-contractual remedy would place him in a better position.

When there has been a total failure of consideration, the normal response to such a breach of contract would presumably be to sue for damages. Indeed since the party will wish to cover loss of expectation if the contract is an advantageous one, the expectation measure of damages will almost certainly be more attractive than seeking restitution. If the bargain proves a bad one however – if the innocent party would have made a loss had the contract been properly performed – then he may prefer to seek restitution to retrieve the money or other consideration he gave in pursuance of his side of the contract.

*Fibrosa Spolka Akcynja v Fairburn Lawson Combe Barbour Ltd* (1943) is a classic example of the law of restitution in action. Here the seller was prevented from completing the contract by outbreak of war. The buyer, who was situated in enemy occupied territory, had paid a part of the purchase price. Since there had been a total failure of consideration it was held the buyer was entitled to recovery of money paid over to date.

*Fibrosa* is a true case of total failure of consideration, but the term 'total' should be defined with care. See cases such as *Butterworth v Kingsway Motors* (1954) and *Rowland v Divall* (1923) for a further examination of the term.

Partial failure of consideration on the other hand will as a general rule not entitle the injured party to restitution (*Baldry v Marshall* (1925), *Hunt v Silk* (1804)).

The reasoning given for this rule is usually that in cases of partial performance it is impossible to apportion consideration between performed and unperformed sections of the contract.

It may, however, be possible to get around this rule either by the innocent party returning any benefit received from such of the contract that has so far been performed thereby converting partial into total failure of consideration. Or in cases where the contract is of a type easily divisible into sections (the consideration can be easily apportioned among the different parts of the divided contract), recovery of part of any money parted with will be permitted for those parts of the contract not performed (*Ebrahim Dawood v Heath* (1961)).

The distinction between total and partial failure of consideration is thus a rather artificial and arbitrary distinction. Indeed in 1975 (Working Paper No 65) the Law Commission was in favour of permitting restitution, even when failure of consideration was not total. It had however, by the time it presented its final report (Working Paper No 121), changed its mind, seemingly on the grounds that this would often involve putting the plaintiff in a better position than if the contract had been performed. This can in any event happen when the failure of consideration is total.

The courts have consistently been reluctant to extend the doctrine of quasi-contract. In *Meates* v *Westpac* (1990), a New Zealand case, the government of New Zealand with a view to encouraging new industries, had issued a number of formal documents. The appellants claimed that these documents, together with certain conversations, press statements and so on had been regarded by them as an indication that the government was prepared to indemnify them. They had incurred great expense, but the project had never got under way. The court held that implied undertakings made verbally will not give rise to a quasi-contractual obligation. There seems little doubt that any expansion of the law of quasi-contract seems unlikely.

# 17 AGENCY

## 17.1 Introduction

It will be remembered that the topic of agency has already been under discussion earlier in Chapter 10, in the context of the doctrine of privity of contract.

An agent is merely a tool used by the principal to negotiate the contract; under normal circumstances, the agent having completed the contractual negotiations and concluded the contract, drops out; he is not a party to the contract. The principal, however, is a party and although he may not have played any part in making the actual arrangements for the contract, all the usual rules as to contractual capacity and intention to create legal relationships and so on apply to the principal. Very occasionally it may be found that things go wrong and the agent becomes personally liable on the contract.

There are different ways of classifying agents, either according to the type of agreement they are appointed to negotiate, or according to the way they are appointed. A number of these categories overlap, thus for example an agent may be a special agent – appointed for one particular purpose – and also an agent appointed expressly.

In 1994, the Commercial Agents (Council Directive) Regulations 1993 were implemented. These regulations cover only commercial agents and there are already difficulties as to the exact definition of this term.

The regulations represent an attempt to standardise the law relating to agency in EC Member States, prior to the advent of the Single Market. For this country the main significance lies in the fact that, where applicable, agency relationships will be governed by statute, rather than contractual common law. The regulations cover, inter alia, the rights and obligations of the commercial agent and his principal, remuneration and the rights and duties of the agent, especially on termination.

But it should be stressed that the regulations are facing teething problems: they are taking much longer than anticipated to phase in; as stated, there are problems of definition, and it seems likely that further amending regulations will be required.

Whilst the student should read the Key Points that follow below with the regulations in mind, it should be appreciated that they do not apply to all forms of agency anyway, and that their precise impact on existing common law as it applies to commercial agents remains so far untested in the courts.

## 17.2 Key points

It is important that the student understands the following:

a) *Appointment of agents*

An agent might be:

i) a universal agent – appointed to act in unlimited ways, with no curb on his power – such an agent is usually appointed by power of attorney; or

ii) a general agent – appointed to act in a particular group of transactions, for example a banker or an estate agent; or

iii) a special agent – appointed for one particular purpose.

Usually, but not always, an agent is created by virtue of a contract between him and the principal. Although an agent need have no capacity to contract on behalf of his principal, he must if this other contract between him and the principal is to be enforceable have full contractual capacity.

The agency relationship may arise initially without any contractual agreement between agent and principal; as for example with ratification – a form of retrospective adoption by the principal of the agent and recognition (belatedly) of his powers to negotiate on the principal's behalf.

The main ways in which an agent may be appointed include:

i) Express

This may be in any form, written or oral. If the agent is to be authorised to make contracts under seal, his appointment must be by deed, in the form known as power of attorney. Though note that the Law of Property (Miscellaneous Provisions) Act 1989 does *not* require an agent to be appointed by deed in order to execute a deed involving disposition or creation of interests in land.

ii) Implied

This often applies as an extension of express appointment, and covers acts which are either in the ordinary course of the agent's business (though not specifically authorised) and, similarly, acts which become necessary for the efficient performance of an express agency.

iii) Ratification

This is, as has been noted, a form of retrospective recognition of agency. To operate, it requires certain fairly strict conditions to apply:

• agent must have acted for a named principal;

• principal must have contractual capacity both at the time of making the contract and the time of ratification;

• ratification must be of the whole contract;

• It must take place within a reasonable time;

• principal must ratify in full knowledge of all material terms.

iv) By operation of law

This mode of creation of agency (also known as agent of necessity) arises without prior agreement when a person is compelled in an emergency to act as agent. It is usually the case that such a form of agency arises when goods belonging to the principal are in the possession of the person driven to act as agent.

Such agency can only operate where there is a definite emergency, a definite commercial need to act and it is truly impossible for the agent to obtain instructions from the principal. With today's instantaneous communications it is rare for agency of necessity to arise.

v)  By estoppel (or 'holding out')

If a principal makes some sort of representation to a third party to the effect that A has been appointed agent, the principal will be estopped from later denying the effect of such a representation. Thus if the third party, on the strength of the principal's remarks negotiates a contract with A, believing him to be an agent acting for the principal, the principal cannot later retract or deny his representation.

b)  *Authority of agent*

Obviously a great deal depends on whether the agent has been appointed to do one specific thing, or to negotiate contracts of one particular type, or whether he is a universal agent with extensive powers. The main forms of authority an agent might have are:

i)  Actual authority

The agent has authority to do any act expressly or impliedly authorised by the principal

ii) Ostensible (or apparent) authority

This is the power of the agent to bind his principal by any act in the ordinary course of the agent's business. For a recent examination of the concept of ostensible authority see *United Bank of Kuwait* v *Hammond* (1988).

Since a third party is not in a position to know the exact terms of an agent's appointment, if the act would appear to be within the ostensible authority of this type of agency, the principal will be bound, even if he has specifically forbidden that very thing. Thus protection is afforded to a third party when an agent is in breach of his arrangement with his principal. The principal will of course have a potential course of action against his agent.

In the case of ostensible/apparent authority there must be three main factors:

• a representation that the agent has authority;
• reliance on that representation;
• alteration of position by the person relying on the representation.

The representation cannot be relied on if the person to whom it was made had actual or constructive knowledge of the truth. (Note particularly the Companies Act 1989 on this point.)

iii) Usual authority

This is authority possessed by an agent in consequence of his involvement with a certain trade or profession.

Provided acts are in character with the type of agency and the third party has no cause to be aware of any restriction on the agent's activities, the principal will be bound by the acts of his agent even if he has restricted the agent's conduct in some way.

Obviously, what is *usual* depends largely on factual rather than legal criteria.

c) *Relationship between principal and agent*

i) Duties of agent to principal

These include:

- duty to carry out the terms of the agency;
- to account for all money and property received for the principal and to keep proper accounts;
- not to make a secret profit, or take bribes.

ii) Rights of agent against principal

These include:

- to be remunerated;
- to be indemnified;
- to a lien on goods belonging to the principal in his possession when the principal owes the agent money;
- to stop goods in transit, for the same reason.

d) *Principal, agent and third parties*

An agent may negotiate a contract, revealing from the first the fact that he is an agent and for whom he is acting. Alternatively, he may disclose the fact of agency but not name the principal. In some cases the fact of agency is concealed altogether, revealing the principal only when the contract is concluded. The consequences to a third party will depend on the fact of disclosure or lack of it.

i) Disclosed principal

If an agent indicates he is acting on behalf of a principal, whether he names him or not the contract is between principal and third party. The agent will normally have no liability. However there are a number of exceptions to this rule:

- if the agent expressly or impliedly assumes liability on the contract;
- if he signs a written contract in his own name;
- by trade usage or custom;
- on a bill of exchange;
- if he is actually contracting on his own behalf;

• if he signs a deed in his own name (unless he has power of attorney);

• if he refuses to identify his principal.

In all such cases the agent will become personally liable on the contract.

ii) Undisclosed principal

When the fact of agency is concealed until the last minute the third party can hold the principal liable on the contract when he discovers his existence and identity. Or he can hold the agent personally liable, even though he now knows he was acting on behalf of another. However, this is an option; having exercised a choice, the third party is then bound by it.

iii) Unauthorised acts of the agent

It is always possible, as had already been noted, for an agent to be doing something unauthorised, even specifically forbidden and still be within his ostensible authority. In such a case the principal will be bound and liable on the contract to a third party. If the agent is outside both his actual and his ostensible authority, the principal will not be liable on the contract as such but the agent will be liable to the third party for breach of warranty of authority. This is the case, even where the agent acted in good faith.

e) *Termination of agency*

i) The act of the parties

Termination may occur on some act of one or both the parties.

Thus when:

• there is mutual agreement to end the agency; or

• the agent renounces his appointment; or

• the principal revokes the agent's appointment (save where the agency is of the irrevocable type),

all these are conscious acts of the parties, voluntarily made, which end the contract of agency. The simplest possibility of all in this category is however that both parties perform their obligations and the transaction is completed.

ii) Operation of law

There are three main possibilities here:

• when the principal dies, becomes bankrupt or becomes insane (but note that there are special rules as to insanity); or

• supervening illegality or impossibility frustrates the contract; or

• by lapse of time.

A number of cases on agency have come before the courts recently. See in particular: *The Choko Star* (1990); *Foalquest* v *Roberts* (1990).

## 17.3 Analysis of questions

There has been no full question on agency in any of London University's Elements of the Law of Contract papers.

In one or two questions on privity of contract, it has rated a brief mention as an apparent exception to that doctrine, but nothing more.

The questions quoted below are from London University's *Commercial Law* papers; and any student seeking enlightenment on the range of topics possible in the field of agency is recommended to have a look at past papers from this examination. Bear in mind, however that the two syllabuses are such that an examiner in Contract Law would not expect to see such detail as that commonly found in Commercial Law. To that end, the questions below have been specifically selected to reflect a very general approach to the subject and the solutions show that the examiner does not require great depth of analysis or detail. It is just feasible that the advent of the Commercial Agents (Council Directive) Regulations 1993 might prompt a question on the changing face of the law of agency in the next round of papers, but in view of the extensive syllabus and the examiners' previous reluctance to examine on the topic this seems unlikely.

## 17.4 Questions

QUESTION ONE

'In some circumstances an agent is personally liable on the contract made with a third party'. Discuss.

University of London LLB Examination
(for External Students) Commercial Law June 1984 Q1

*Skeleton Solution*

• Normally, once contract negotiated agent drops out, not liable on contract
• Agent may have personal liability in a number of cases.
• Agent undertakes personal liability.
• Undiscovered principal.
• Agent makes contract under seal in his own name.
• Other possible exceptions to normal rule.

*Suggested Solution*

The origins of the concept of agency are to be found in the idea of commercial necessity. Without an all-embracing law of agency, modern commerce would not exist; the idea behind agency is that a principal can bind himself in contract to a third party by the use of an agent. The most important type of principal for practical purposes is a limited company which is of course a distinct legal (although purely artificial) person. Without a law of agency a company would never be bound nor have any rights in a contract because of the doctrine of privity, that is, that a stranger can never benefit nor be obliged under a contract.

The idea of agency is that a relationship will exist between a principal and an agent whereby the agent, if he is acting within his authority, can bind the principal in contract with a third party. Because of the nature of the relationship, the agent is merely acting as a go-between and thus the general rule evolved that he was not to take any advantages nor disadvantages from the principal's contract with the third party. In other words the agent cannot sue on the contract or be sued upon it. This rule was again a matter of commercial necessity, for if the agent was liable on the contract there would be no need for a distinct and separate principal and also few men would be willing to act as agent if they knew that they would incur personal liability.

Thus the important point that appears from the cases is that the contract entered into with the third party is the contract of the principal *not* of the agent. *Montgomerie v UK Mutual SS Association* (1891). When an agent makes a contract with a third party he is generally said to 'drop out' of the transaction and does not become a party to it. However, as was stated in the *Montgomerie* case, in a number of circumstances an agent will become liable on the contract with the third party.

The first and probably the most important exception to the general rule is where the agent undertakes personal liability. This can be done in a number of ways; firstly, he can expressly undertake personal liability, in which case both the principal and agent will be liable on the contract; *The Swan* (1968); or he may impliedly undertake liability where, for example, there is a custom in the particular trade to that effect: *Hutchinson* v *Tatham* (1873).

Whether an agent has undertaken personal liability or not will depend on a construction of the agreement entered into. If, for example, he enters into an agreement on behalf of an undisclosed principal then he will be liable to the third party because the third party is unaware of the existence of a principal. It may be that his liability will end when the principal intervenes but in these cases where the principal cannot intervene, the agent will remain liable. In *Humble* v *Hunter* (1848) the agent had described himself on the charterparty as 'CJ Humble Esq owner' of the ship. The principal sought to sue on the contract and it was held that he could not as his existence was impliedly excluded by the agent describing himself as 'owner' of the ship. The only person liable was the agent in such circumstances. In *UK Mutual SS Association* v *Newin* (1887) the rules of the Association were such that only members of it could insure their ships under the association's policies. A co-owner of a ship, who was a member of the association, entered into an insurance contract with the association who later tried to sue another co-owner who was not a member. It was held that they could not do so by the terms of their own association. Again, only the 'agent' would be liable here.

It may be in certain circumstances that an agent will be liable on the contract even though on the face of it, this is not a likely result. For example, if an 'agent' contracts on behalf of a fictitious or non-existent principal, the courts are ready to hold an agent liable if on a true construction of the contract it is possible to reach this result. *Kelner* v *Baxter* (1866) and s9(2) European Communities Act 1972. See particularly s36(4) Companies Act 1985 as to contracts purported to be made on behalf of a company not yet legally formed. Further, if an agent is in fact the principal he is clearly liable even though he describes himself as an agent. In *Schmalz* v *Avery* (1851) a party who was described in a charterparty as an 'agent for the freighters' was held liable when it was proven that he was the freighter.

If an agent makes a contract under seal in his own name, it has been held that he will be personally liable on it even though he describes himself on the document as acting on behalf of a principal: *Hancock* v *Hodgson* (1827). A similar rule applies in the case of negotiable instruments, for under s26(1) of the Bills of Exchange Act 1882 an agent who signs an instrument will be liable on it unless he makes it quite clear that he signed the bill solely in a representative capacity.

A further example of an agent being personally liable was where the agent was acting on behalf of a foreign principal. In such a case there was a presumption that he would be liable but since *Teheran-Europe Co Ltd* v *Belton (Tractors) Ltd* (1968) it has been held that the presumption no longer applies and the normal rules apply.

It can be seen from the above that there are many instances when an agent will be liable on the contract between the principal and third party. In those cases where the agent is not liable on the contract, his liability is not at an end for it may be the case that he is liable to the third party for a breach of his warranty of authority. If he claims to have an authority which he does not possess a third party who relies on that representation can sue on the warranty: *Collen* v *Wright* (1857).

QUESTION TWO

On January 3, 1984, Smith, the owner of Hill View Garage, sold it to Grey, who kept the same name and appointed Smith as the manager under a contract which stated that:

i)   Smith was appointed for three years as from 5 January, 1984;

ii)  he was not to buy any tyres except new ones; and

iii) he was to be paid a commission on all sales of petrol in excess of the figures for the year ending 31 December, 1983.

Grey seeks your legal advice and says:

'I have just sold the garage to Northern Garages and have terminated Smith's employment. I find that Smith let out my spare breakdown vehicle to Cook on hire-purchase terms. It was defective and Cook was injured. He has now discovered my existence and is suing me for the return of his instalments and in respect of his injuries. Smith bought 5,000 retread tyres from Safety Tyres Ltd but the price has not been paid. He was given a birthday present by them and received a trade discount which he did not disclose to me. He employed Go-Ahead Builders Ltd to build two new inspection pits at the garage at a cost of £4,000, but nothing has yet been paid. The petrol sales in 1984 were well up on those of 1983.'

University of London LLB Examination
(for External Students) Commercial Law June 1985 Q3

*Skeleton Solution*

* Breakdown vehicle – authority of agent – remedy against agent – remedy against Cook.
* Re-tread tyres – authority of agent – scope of usual authority – bribe/gift – secret profit – remedy against agent.
* Inspection pits – agent's authority – scope of usual authority – ratification – liability of principal to third party.
* Agent's position – breach of contract – dismissal – remuneration.

*Suggested Solution*

a) *Breakdown vehicles*

We are told that Smith let the spare breakdown vehicle on HP to Cook, who now wishes to take action against Grey. Such an action could only succeed if the disposition by Smith was within his actual or apparent authority. Clearly Smith was an agent of Grey, in that he was expressly appointed to manage the garage. The terms of the agency contract given do not mention anything about dispositions of Grey's property; therefore we must see whether the disposition was within his implied authority. There is no evidence to suggest that it is necessarily incidental to the running of a garage to let out spare machinery on hire purchase. It must be concluded that this was not within Smith's incidental authority. The precise scope of usual authority is far from clear (see Fridman's *Law of Agency*), but Bowstead stresses the position of the managerial agent as giving rise to the right to do all acts usual for a manager of that type. He deals with professional agents separately and the argument that usual authority arises in all cases of managers is compelling. Usual authority can arise whether the act done was specifically prohibited by the principal or was simply not mentioned by the parties. In this case there was no mention by Smith that he was acting as agent and since he was the owner before Grey and Cook has 'now discovered' Grey's existence it seems that in the eyes of Cook Smith acted as principal. This makes no difference because in so far as usual authority is part of actual authority acts within the agent's usual authority always bind the undisclosed principal *(Thomson v Davenport* (1829)). Therefore the only question is whether the disposition was within Smith's usual authority (s21(1) Consumer Credit Act 1974). It is submitted, in any event, the disposition of property on credit terms would not be within the usual authority of a manager of a garage. The owner of the garage may have to be licensed under the Consumer Credit Act 1974 if credit terms are to be given and it is by no means clear that such a disposition of goods would normally fall within the authority of a garage manager. Therefore the evidence does not suggest that the disposition was within Smith's usual authority. We are given no evidence of trade authority and, further, there is nothing to suggest that any special circumstances apply giving rise to implied authority. Therefore it is submitted that the disposition of the breakdown truck was not within Smith's actual authority.

The result of this is that there has been an unauthorised disposition by the agent of the principal's property. It is necessary to consider therefore what remedy Grey may have against Smith or Cook. As regards Smith the unauthorised disposition was a conversion, which entitles Grey to sue Smith for damages (s2 Torts (Interference with Goods) Act 1977), but this is complicated by the fact that money may have been paid to Grey for the breakdown truck. We are told that Cook has demanded a refund of instalments, but have not been told what happened to the instalments once received by Smith. If they have been paid to Grey then he must give credit for the amount already paid when claiming damages. The reason for this is that the payment of damages acts as a transfer of Grey's rights to the breakdown vehicle to Smith, and therefore validates the HP contract, and the value of Grey's interest is the value of the vehicle minus the amount he has already received in payment for it (s5 Torts (Interference with

Goods) Act 1977). On the other hand, if Grey has not received the instalments he can claim the full value of the truck at the time of the conversion. Alternatively Grey may claim repossession of the truck from Cook, who has also committed a conversion (s3 Torts (Interference with Goods) Act 1977), but it will be a matter within the court's discretion to order Cook to pay damages rather than give up possession. Whichever remedy is given against Cook it will be subject to a set-off in so far as Grey has received any instalments. If action is taken against Cook then he in turn will have an action against Smith for breach of contract (ss8 and 10 Supply of Goods (Implied Terms) Act 1973), but that does not involve Grey.

In conclusion then, the disposition of the truck was unauthorised and Grey has an action against either Smith or Cook in conversion. The taking of such an action will not be a ratification of the wrongful disposition, because Smith acted as principal and ratification is only possible when the act was done as agent *(Keighley, Maxted v Durant* (1901)). In addition the conversion by Smith was a breach of contract in that he was a bailee for reward under a contract of agency. The damages payable would be the same as those in conversion (under the first head of *Hadley v Baxendale* (1854)), therefore nothing more will be said about the breach until the question of Smith's right to remuneration is discussed.

b) *Purchase of retread tyres*

The purchase of these tyres raises two issues, firstly whether there is a binding contract between Grey and Safety Tyres Ltd and secondly whether any action can be taken against Smith for making a contract he was specifically told not to make.

The purchase of remould tyres was outside Smith's express actual authority, but it binds Grey if it was within his implied actual authority. It has been explained above how implied actual authority can arise and the question in this transaction is whether the purchase was within Smith's usual authority. The rationale behind the doctrine of usual authority is that the principal will be bound by acts done by his agent if it appears to a reasonable third party that the agent has authority, even if in fact the agent is directed not to make the contract concerned. The third party will not know of the limitation on authority and should not be prejudiced by the agreement between principal and agent. The facts here are similar to those in the leading case of *Watteau v Fenwick* (1893), but that case has been criticised. In order to consider whether it would be applied here it is necessary to examine whether the fact of Smith's agency was disclosed. If the agency was disclosed, then the rationale mentioned above is clearly applicable and, indeed, there is authority to apply the doctrine of usual authority to such cases *(Edmunds v Bushell & Jones* (1865)), so *Watteau v Fenwick* (1893) need not be relied on. If, though the fact of agency was not disclosed to Safety Tyres Ltd, then *Watteau v Fenwick* (1893) is directly to point. The problem with *Watteau v Fenwick* (1893) is that it binds a principal to unauthorised acts of the agent despite the fact that the third party does not believe the agent to be an agent. There can be no estoppel based on the principle having represented the authority of the agent, because he is unknown to the third party and has made no representation. The only way to justify the case is to say that the principal should be bound where he has put his agent in a position where he has been able to represent himself as principal (Conant, 'The Objective Theory of Agency' (1968) 47 Neb LR 678).

But, such an estoppel would go far beyond normal equitable doctrine. It must be conceded that in the most influential study of the applicability of rules of equity to such cases, *Watteau* v *Fenwick* (1893) was said to be perfectly justifiable (Higgins, 'The Equity of the Undisclosed Principal' (1965) 28 MLR 167, 173), but the study concerned approached the case as one of disclosed agency and the rationale of usual authority stated above is applicable to disclosed agency, but not to undisclosed agency. Therefore, it is submitted that a distinction should be drawn between disclosed and undisclosed agency, such that the agent who deals as agent will bind his principal despite the express limitation on his authority, because there is nothing to suggest to the third party that there is such a limitation and the contract may well be made in reliance on the existence of the principal. But, there is little justification in holding a principal liable because of usual authority where the third party cannot have relied on his existence. The general principal is that an undisclosed principal is only bound by acts within the actual authority of the agent, but for these purposes actual authority normally means express and necessarily incidental authority (Bowstead). There is no significant judicial support for *Watteau* v *Fenwick* (1893) and, indeed, it has not been followed in Canada (*McLaughlin* v *Gentles* (1919)) and Australia (*International Paper Co* v *Spicer* (1906)). For these reasons it is submitted that *Watteau* v *Fenwick* would not be followed today. So, if the agency here was not disclosed to Safety Tyres Ltd, Grey is advised that he is not liable to pay the price.

There are two other matters which would affect this contract, one of which affects the extent to which Grey may be bound. It has been stated above that Grey is only bound by the contract if the fact of agency was disclosed. Even so, the principal is always entitled to repudiate the contract if the third party bribed the agent. Distinction must be drawn between a bribe and a bona fide gift. A bribe is a payment which induces the contract; a gift is a payment without corrupt motive and which does not induce the contract. We are not told whether the 'birthday present' was given before or after the making of the contract. It can be said, though, that if given before the contract there is a presumption of bribery (*Hovenden* v *Milhoff* (1900)). The effect of a bribe is to allow the principal to repudiate the contract, which acts as rescission *ab initio* (*Panama & S Pacific Telegraph* v *India Rubber* (1875)). Furthermore, the amount of the bribe can be recovered from either the agent or the third party (*Reading* v *Attorney-General* (1951)). If Grey can prove any other loss caused by the acceptance of the bribe, then he can recover damages from either the agent or third party, but he would not be able to recover the bribe as well if that would amount to double recovery (*Mahesan* v *Malaysian Government* (1979)). If the payment was made without corrupt motive and did not induce the contract then although it would not be a ground for rescinding the sale contract, the agent would nevertheless have to account to Grey for the amount of the gift (*Boardman* v *Phipps* (1967)). As regards the trade discount, there is a duty on an agent to make full disclosure of all profits made of which the rules on bribes and gifts just mentioned is the most obvious manifestation. The trade discount here appears to be either a bribe or a secret profit made by the agent without the third party being privy to the secrecy of the profit. If it was a bribe, then the consequences already mentioned arise. If the trade discount was a bona fide transaction so far as Safety Tyres Ltd were concerned but was not disclosed because of Smith's decision not to disclose, then that is a breach of his fiduciary duty of disclosure, but does not render the contract voidable. In such circumstances Smith would have to account for any profit he made from the discount.

c) *New inspection pits*

As with the contract relating to the breakdown truck, nothing was said in the agency contract about Smith's right to make such a contract, therefore, Grey will only be bound if it was within Smith's implied actual authority to employ a builder. The position is that if Go-Ahead Builders Ltd knew that Smith was an agent then we have to ask if the contract was within his usual authority; if they contracted with him as principal, however, the doctrine of usual authority will not assist and we must ask whether it was necessarily incidental for the management of the garage. To dispose of the latter point first, the authorities on incidental authority are cases where the act done was an inevitable part of carrying out a specific task; for example the express authority in *Rosenbaum* v *Belson* (1900) was to sell the house and the incidental authority was to sign a memorandum of agreement; the incidental authority was incidental to a closely defined express authority. The other cases found in the books are similar – incidental authority is always necessarily incidental to a closely defined express authority. That is not the case here. The express authority was to manage the garage, it was not necessarily incidental to that task to employ a builder to build new inspection pits and therefore the contract was outside incidental authority. So, the problem is limited to one issue – whether it was within Smith's usual authority to make this contract. For reasons given earlier the doctrine of usual authority does not apply where the fact of agency is not known to the third party.

Assuming that Go-Ahead knew Smith was an agent it seems that Grey would be bound by the contract. Usual authority arises where the third party is led to believe that there is authority simply because the agent is employed in a role which normally carries with it the power to make contracts of the type in question. Although it could be argued that the building of new inspection pits would be a decision to be taken by the owner of the garage and not the manager, there is at least equal force in the argument that it would be the manager who would make the arrangements after the owner has authorised the building. Therefore the builder would, it is submitted, normally deal with the manager and for that reason the contract here would be within Smith's usual authority.

If the above argument is incorrect and Smith's usual authority did not extend to this contract, then Grey will still be bound if he ratified the contract made on his behalf. The difficult point is in considering whether the mere receipt of the benefit of the contract amounts to ratification. Ratification is often said to be a voluntary acceptance of the contract made on the principal's behalf by the unauthorised agent (Fridman). It must be said though that acceptance by acquiescence is not always voluntary (Fridman). Ratification does need an acceptance of the act done in such a way as shows either that the principal has voluntarily approved of the act or has acted in such a way that it is now unfair for him to decline to be bound by the act. The mere acceptance of a benefit is not ratification (*Forman* v *Liddesdale* (1900)), particularly when the principal has had the benefit forced upon him. Therefore if the making of this contract was outside Smith's usual authority then Grey will not be bound because he has not ratified. Grey would not be liable to pay Go-Ahead on principles of quasi-contract (*Munro* v *Butt* (1858)) or restitution (Jones, 'Restitutionary Claims for Services Rendered' (1977) 93 LQR 273) since he does not have any alternative but to take the benefit.

d) *Smith's position*

We have seen so far that Smith made three contracts. On the assumption that Smith did not disclose the fact of his agency, each was unauthorised. We have already seen that the disposition of the breakdown vehicle on HP leaves Smith liable in damages for conversion. As regards the tyres and the new inspection pits there would be a breach of the contract of agency for such contracts if they were unauthorised. In fact no loss would be incurred by Grey in that if the contracts were unauthorised they would not bind him. Therefore nothing revolves around these breaches except that misconduct by an agent is a ground for dismissal. This right to dismiss Smith for misconduct means that the termination of his agency by selling to Northern Garages (if indeed the agency was terminated, we are not given enough information to be able to say) was justified and will not give Smith any remedy against Grey (*Boston Deep Sea Fishing* v *Ansell* (1888)). Furthermore the making of a secret profit by Smith is a breach of his fiduciary duty and is equally a ground for dismissal. See the recent case of *Anangel Atlas Compania Naviera SA* v *Ishikawajima-Harima Heavy Industries* (1990) for a detailed examination of the terms 'bribe' and 'secret profit' in the context of agency.

The contract of agency provided that Smith would receive a commission on petrol sales if they exceeded those of 1983. In fact the sales for 1984 did exceed those of 1983. Therefore, prima facie, Smith is entitled to the commission. It is often stated that an agent cannot receive commission if he is guilty of misconduct (Fridman) but this must be understood in context. In order to receive commission the agent must be able to prove that he earned it, in other words that he was the cause of the event which gave rise to the right to remuneration. He will not be allowed to recover the commission, however if the means used to bring about the event (in this case the increase in turnover of petrol) were wrongful. This does not prevent the earning of commission where there is misconduct which does not directly relate to the earning of commission (*Hippisley* v *Knee* (1905)). Any breaches there may have been in this case did not relate, as far as we can tell, to the turnover of petrol and, therefore, they do not prevent Smith recovering his commission.

# 18 SALE OF GOODS, CONSUMER CREDIT AND SUPPLY OF GOODS AND SERVICES

18.1   Introduction

18.2   Key points

18.3   Analysis of questions

18.4   Questions

## 18.1 Introduction

This is an area more properly related to commercial law for, while most contractual dealings are governed by common law – certain types of contract are now regulated by legislation in such a way as to override common law.

The three relevant statutes are, respectively: the Sale of Goods Act 1979 (recently amended by the Sale and Supply of Goods Act 1994), the Consumer Credit Act 1974 and the Supply of Goods and Services Act 1982. There are however a number of other statutes which have an important effect on this area of law, probably the most important being the Unfair Contract Terms Act 1977.

This is an area of contract law where, quite frequently, the parties are most definitely *not* on an equal footing and to pretend otherwise would place one party, the individual consumer, at a grave disadvantage. Thus the usual common law assumptions as to equality of bargaining power and the allegiance of common law to the doctrine of freedom of contract have had to be replaced by a clear set of rules governing such transactions and giving more protection to the weaker party than would otherwise exist.

The title of each statute is indicative of the type of contract it regulates. It would be a grave mistake to conclude that these statutes have replaced the ordinary laws of contract completely. In the main, the ordinary law applies (unless stated otherwise) but additional rules are enacted to govern such transactions and, so far as is possible, protect the interests of the weaker party.

It is a complex area, constantly developing, and the student is advised to read a text book on the topic for much more detail than the 'Key points', which follow, can provide.

## 18.2 Key points

It is important that the student understands the following:

a) *Sale of Goods Act 1979 (as amended by the Sale and Supply of Goods Act 1994)*

The general rules of contract apply to contracts for sale of goods and there is no specific form of contract required (s4).

i) For definitions and terminology see the provisions of the Act itself and also read associated case law. For example, the case of *R & B Customs Brokers Ltd* v *United Dominions Trust Ltd, Saunders Abbot (Third Party)* (1988) deals with the definition of the terms 'consumer' and 'dealing as a consumer'.

ii) The Act makes provision for a number of contingencies including:

- If, in the case of specific goods, the goods have without the knowledge of the parties perished, the contract is void (s6). If the goods subsequently perish, the contract is void if risk has not yet passed to the buyer (s7). If risk has passed, the buyer bears the loss.
- Risk passes with the property except where otherwise agreed, or delivery has been delayed by the fault of one party, in which case the goods are at the risk of the party at fault (s20).
- The price must be wholly or partly money, can be fixed by a third party (s9) or in the course of dealing. If there is no provision, it must be reasonable (s8).
- Time of payment is not of the essence unless otherwise agreed (s10).

iii) In addition to such express terms of the contract the Act *implies* certain terms into the contract of sale.

Such implied terms may be either conditions or warranties.

The implied terms include:

s12 : as to title;

s13 : as to sale by description;

s14 : as to satisfactory quality of goods and as to fitness for purpose;

s15 : as to sales by sample.

Normally the implied terms may be varied, either by express wish of the parties, or by trade usage, but s12 can never be varied or negatived and ss13–15 cannot be excluded or restricted in any consumer sale. Other instances of exclusion or variation are subject to the 'reasonableness' test

iv) Sections 17 and 18 cover the question of *passing of property*. (Note that s16 decrees that passing of property in unascertained goods cannot be until the goods are ascertained.) In particular s18 formulates a series of rules under which property is deemed to pass.

v) The general rule as to *transfer of title* is *nemo dat quod non habet* – no one can transfer title to goods, save the true owner or his authorised agent. For a recent examination by the House of Lords of the *nemo dat* rule (and in particular, as applied to an innocent buyer in possession of stolen goods) see *National Employers Mutual General Insurance Association Ltd* v *Jones* (1988). Exceptions to the *nemo dat* rule include:

- estoppel;
- sale by factor;
- sale under a common law or statutory power;

211

- sale under a voidable title;
- sale by a buyer or seller in possession;
- sale by hirer of motor vehicles.

vi) The basic duties imposed by the contract are *delivery* of possession of the goods by the seller and *acceptance* of and payment for the goods by the buyer (s27). Unless otherwise agreed, delivery and payment are concurrent conditions (s28). Whether the buyer is to collect the goods, or the seller to send them is determined by the terms of the contract between them (s29).

vii) In the event of *non-payment a seller has remedies* against the buyer which include:

- a lien against the goods of the buyer, if the seller is still in possession;
- a right of stoppage in transit;
- a right to withhold delivery;
- a right of resale.

All the above are remedies against the goods themselves and are governed by strict conditions in the way they operate. Additionally an unpaid seller may have the right to

- an action for the price, or
- an action for damages for non-acceptance

viii) A *buyer may have a number of remedies* in the breach of contract by the seller. They include:

- remedy for damages for non-delivery;
- specific performance;
- action for breach of warranty.

b) *Consumer Credit Act 1974*

This Act governs contracts of the type known as hire purchase, credit sale or conditional sale agreements; provided they constitute 'consumer credit agreements'. For the purpose of the Act, therefore, at least one of the parties must be an individual consumer and a limit of £5,000 is placed on transactions.

For terminology and definitions, the student should read, in detail, the relevant sections of the Act.

By virtue of the Supply of Goods (Implied Terms) Act 1973, much the same terms are incorporated into contracts covered by the CCA as are implied in sale of goods contracts (see ante).

c) *The Supply of Goods and Services Act 1982*

This statute rectified the main remaining gap in the law which had meant that up until its enactment the supply of services and some transfers of goods were covered only by common law. As with the Sale of Goods Act 1979 ((a) above) this Act was recently amended by the Sale and Supply of Goods Act 1994.

The Act is divided into two major parts: Part I is concerned with the supply of goods for transfer of property in goods. Part II concerns the supply of services.

For all relevant terminology and definitions see the Act itself.

Again, as with the previous Acts there are implied into contracts affected conditions or warranties concerning (as in SGA) title, correspondence with description, merchantable quality and fitness for purpose.

As noted at the commencement of this chapter there is neither time nor space to deal with this area of law in anything other than the most superficial manner. The student is reminded that he should consult a text-book for further detail, as well as reading through the Acts themselves.

## 18.3  Analysis of questions

One or two problem questions concern contracts that are contracts for sale of goods, or consumer credit agreements or whatever, but this usually requires little more than a brief identifying sentence at some point in the answer. Only two questions, Question 3 of the 1984 London University paper and Question 3 of the 1991 paper have specifically referred to the Sale of Goods Act in any detail. Those questions are two of the three quoted below. The other question is not from an Elements of the Law of Contract paper, but from one of the *Commercial Law* papers set by London University. It is very general in its approach and could quite easily be a suitable question on a general law of contract paper; the more so because it requires some knowledge on the student's part of the ordinary common law of damages. To remind himself of the salient points on the latter, the student should refer back to Chapter 14.

## 18.4  Questions

QUESTION ONE

Bill is a wealthy businessman whose hobby is breeding cattle. Last year he bought some animal feedstuff from Archers Ltd. The feedstuff proved to be defective and most of Bill's cattle became ill and died two months after eating it. The contract of sale provided that:

a)  the purchaser must inform the seller of any defects in the product within one week of purchase, and

b)  any liability for defective products was restricted to the contract price.

Advise Bill. How would your advice differ, if at all, if the purchaser had been a farming company?

University of London LLB Examination
(for External Students) Elements of the Law of Contract June 1984 Q3

*Skeleton Solution*

• Sale of goods contract – SGA 1979, amended 1994 – implied terms ss13 and 14.
• Effect of exclusion clause – UCTA 1977
• Bill 'dealing as a consumer'?
• Effect of the alternative if purchaser a farming company – no longer a consumer.
• Reasonableness test as applied to exclusion clauses.
• Relevant case law.

*Suggested Solution*

One must advise Bill whether he has a claim against Archers Ltd for the loss of cattle which died after eating the defective feedstuff. In so doing one must consider the legal effect of provisions a) and b) in the contract of sale and whether either or both constitute obstacles to Bill prosecuting his claim against Archers.

The contract between Bill and Archers was one for the sale of goods into which certain terms would be implied by the Sale of Goods Act 1979, as amended by the Sale and Supply of Goods Act 1994. In particular, on the assumption (which is almost certainly the case) the following conditions would be implied:

i) That the feedstuff was of satisfactory quality, s14(2) and

ii) As the purpose for which the feedstuff was required must have been known to Archers, that it was reasonably fit for feeding to animals, s14(3).

On the facts it is clear that in supplying defective feedstuff Archers were in breach of both of these conditions, and it is therefore not necessary additionally to consider whether the contract was a sale of goods by description giving rise to the implied condition under s13(1) that the goods will correspond with the description. It is possible for goods to be quantitatively so defective that the condition implied by s13(1) will be broken also, but because liability under s14(2) and (3) is so clear, this avenue need not be explored further.

Prima facie, therefore, Bill has a claim for damages for breach of contract against Archers. Next one must consider the effect of provisions (a) and (b) on that claim with particular regard to the Unfair Contract Terms Act 1977.

The 1977 Act is (generally speaking) concerned to control provisions in contracts which exclude or restrict liability for breach; it is submitted that both (a) and (b) fall within its ambit.

Provision (b) is straightforward, it limits liability to a particular sum and provisions excluding or restricting liability for breach of (inter alia) s14 of the 1979 Act are dealt with by s6 of the 1977 Act. Provision a) is covered by s13(1) of the 1977 Act which confers an extended meaning on the term 'exemption clause' so as to include clauses 'making the liability or its enforcement subject to restrictive or onerous conditions' which would include, as here, clauses laying down time limits within which claims must be made.

It is stated that Bill breeds cattle as a hobby; on the other hand it is surmised that Archers sold the feedstuff to him in the course of their business. This throws up the question whether Bill can be said to have been 'dealing as consumer', because if he was, s6(2) and s13(1) of the 1977 Act will render both provisions (a) and (b) totally ineffective. If, however, he was not dealing as consumer, both provisions would be subject only to the test of reasonableness prescribed in s11(1) and amplified in Sch 2 of the 1977 Act, by virtue of s6(3) and s13(1) thereof.

'Dealing as consumer' is defined in s12(1) of the 1977 Act. In the present case there are three requirements which must be satisfied:

a) That Bill neither made nor held himself out as making the contract in the course of a business;

b)   That Archers did make the contract in the course of a business; and

c)   The goods were of a type ordinarily supplied for private use or consumption.

Of these, (a) and (b) are clearly satisfied; (c) is, however, more problematical. There is much scope for argument whether animal feedstuffs is 'ordinarily supplied for private use or consumption', and the answer will depend upon whether the courts interpret that phrase in s12(1)(c) of the 1977 Act as meaning 'commonly supplied' or 'in the majority of cases supplied'. It is submitted that the former, more generous construction should be adopted, so as to extend rather than to narrow the application of the 1977 Act; if the courts adopt this construction, then both provisions (a) and (b) in the contract of sale are rendered totally ineffective by ss6(2) and 13(1) of the 1977 Act and Bill can sue Archers for breach of contract.

The alternative situation postulated, of the purchaser being not Bill but a farming company, can be conveniently considered along with the possibility that the courts would narrowly construe s12(1)(c) and hold that animal feedstuffs is not 'ordinarily supplied for private use or consumption'. In both cases, neither Bill nor the farming company would be 'dealing as consumer' and the applicable section would be s6(3) of 1977 Act.

Section 6(3) allows the exclusion or restriction of liability for breach of (inter alia) s14(2) and (3) 'only insofar as the term satisfies the requirement of reasonableness', thus one must consider whether provisions a) and b) in the contract of sale satisfy the reasonableness test laid down by the 1977 Act. This is laid down in s11(1) of the Act and is 'that the term shall have been a fair and reasonable one to be included having regard to the circumstances which were, or ought reasonably to have been, known to or in the contemplation of the parties when the contract was made, ie reasonableness is to be judged at the time the contract was entered into, not at the date of the breach. Certain guidelines applicable to s6 are laid down in Sch 2 to the Act (s11(2)) and, further, s11(4) provide that where liability is limited to a specified sum – as with provision (b) – the court must have regard to the resources which the party in breach could expect to be available to him to meet the liability and how far it was open to him to cover himself by insurance.

Taking provision (a) first, it is submitted that this provision is unreasonable because the stipulated period is too short. Owners of animals buy feedstuffs sufficient to last them for periods of well in excess of one week and, as here, it may take some time after the animals have consumed the feedstuff for the problem to come to light, a factor specifically referred to in Sch 2(d) of the 1977 Act. One might even go so far as to say that more often than not one week will be insufficient for the defect to be discovered and therefore to hold provision a) applicable will be to impose a virtually total exclusion of liability: a) is therefore unreasonable under s13(1).

Provision (b) is less easily dealt with. It is a limitation of liability rather than a complete exclusion which is certainly a point in its favour: limitation clauses of this nature have been both upheld (*Green* v *Cade Bros* (1978)) and struck down (*George Mitchell* v *Finney Lock Seeds* (1983)) on their particular facts under the old s55(4) of the Sale of Goods Act 1893. In order categorically to assert or deny the reasonableness of (b), further information would be required. In particular one would need to know whether the purchaser knew of the provision (Sch 2(c) of the 1977 Act), whether it is a provision agreed upon in the trade and normally used by buyers and sellers (as in *Green* v *Cade Bros* (1978)) and whether Archers could have protected themselves by insurance without this expense materially affecting the prices they charge (as in *George Mitchell* v *Finney Lock Seeds* (1983)), and of course one bears in mind Lord Diplock's strictures in *Photo Production* v *Securicor* (1980) that commercial organisations should be free to apportion risks as between themselves without interference from the courts. Without knowing these additional facts no final conclusion can be reached, but is it tentatively suggested:

i)   That as against a farming company, it is well arguable that the requirement of reasonableness is satisfied, both parties being commercial organisations;

ii)  that if as against Bill he is not regarded as dealing as consumer due to the court adopting a narrow construction of s12(1)(c), then it is perhaps more likely that the provision would be held to be unreasonable because Bill could be regarded as being a little unfortunate at losing the complete protection of s6(2) due to the (perhaps unintended) effect of s12(1)(c).

QUESTION TWO

'The governing purpose of damages is to put the party whose rights have been violated in the same position, so far as money can do so, as if his rights had been observed.'

To what extent is this object fulfilled by the rules for assessing damages for failure to perform a contract for the sale of goods?

University of London LLB Examination<br>(for External Students) Commercial Law June 1987 Q3

*Skeleton Solution*

• Specifically refers to a contract for sale of goods – reference to statutory rules.
• SGA 1979 preserves two limbs of *Hadley* v *Baxendale* (1854).
• Statutory rights of buyer and seller.
• Any limitations on statutory damages that do not exist in common law, eg SGA does not provide for reliance loss.
• Conclusion in answer to question posed initially.

*Suggested Solution*

The essential obligations of the parties to a contract for the sale of goods are to deliver goods which comply with the contract so far as quantity and quality are concerned (seller) and to accept and pay for them (buyer). The Sale of Goods Act 1979, as amended by the Sale and Supply of Goods Act 1994, cannot, and does not try to, lay down rules for the assessment of damages which cover every possible breach by either party because the contract may contain all sorts of additional terms which are not necessary for the formation of a sale of goods contract but are included by agreement of the parties. The Act, accordingly, only sets out rules of assessment for breaches by the seller of his duty to make delivery of quantitively and qualitatively correct goods and by the buyer of his duty to accept them and pay timeously.

The position of the seller suing the buyer for the price is the simplest of the statutory remedies to explain and will be dealt with first. Once the seller has made proper delivery of the correct goods he is entitled to receive the agreed price. Section 49(1) reflects this and gives him the statutory remedy of 'an action for the price'. The action in such cases is not really for damages, although it is often said to be such a claim, but is for the debt which the buyer owes the seller once the latter has made delivery. Whether one calls the seller's claim one for damages or for a debt makes little difference, because s49 makes clear that he is entitled to the agreed price and not the actual market value of the goods which may, of course, be different. This reflects exactly the quotation in the question, because if the contract had been performed properly then the seller would have received the agreed price and where it is not performed properly he is entitled to sue for the agreed price. The only loss which the seller may suffer arises where the buyer pays the agreed price late, but before the seller has instituted legal proceedings for its recovery. In such cases the seller is not entitled to interest to compensate him for having been kept out of his money, and so must incur that loss (*President of India* v *La Pintada Compania Navigacion SA* (1984)). This is a matter which may, in time, be remedied by statute, but is not covered by the existing provisions of the 1979 Act.

As regards the actions of the seller against the buyer for wrongful failure to accept, the remedy at common law would be for damages to cover the loss, if any, incurred by the seller in having to re-sell the goods elsewhere. In principle the seller is entitled under the contract to have the goods accepted and to receive the agreed contract price for them (s28 Sale of Goods Act 1979); therefore any seller who does not realise that figure on resale should be entitled to damages. Section 50 reflects this position. The common law distinction between losses naturally occurring (1st rule in *Hadley* v *Baxendale* (1854)) and losses peculiar to the seller (2nd rule in *Hadley* v *Baxendale* (1854)) is preserved by the Act and it is in s50(3) that the 1st rule is stated for the purposes of an action against the buyer for non-acceptance. Section 50(3) in fact tries to incorporate two different common law principles.

Firstly it attempts to give the seller a sum of money as damages which properly compensates him for the loss suffered and secondly it imposes on him a duty to mitigate his loss or bear the consequences of not doing so. If the buyer refuses to accept the goods then the seller will find that instead of receiving the contract price all he has are the goods. It follows that he has suffered a loss only where the goods are worth less than the contract price. The so-called duty to mitigate operates to prevent someone from recovering damages for losses which he could reasonably have avoided (*Pazyu Ltd* v *Saunders* (1919)). In order to avoid any increase in losses the seller should sell the goods as soon as he reasonably can to someone else. Where there is a market for the goods, he has no excuse for not going into the market and re-selling. Therefore s50(3) provides that the seller can recover the difference between the contract price and the available market price at the date when the buyer should have accepted the goods. If, in fact, he does not take any steps to sell them then he cannot complain about mounting losses because he is the author of his own misfortune.

The courts have had to allow a little flexibility for the seller because he may not be able to go into the market the same day that the buyer fails to accept, and provided his delay is reasonable he will be entitled to take a market price as at the date when he in fact re-sells (*Johnson* v *Agnew* (1980)).

The Act works in a similar way where it is the seller who is in breach. Section 51 allows the buyer to recover damages where the seller fails to deliver. The buyer's position is that he has not received the goods he should have received, so he can get damages to compensate him for any extra he has to spend in the market in buying alternative goods. If he fails to go into the market quickly then he cannot get any additional damages if the market price rises, because he should mitigate by buying alternative goods as soon as is reasonably possible.

If the breach by the seller is not total non-delivery but delivery of defective goods then the buyer has a choice in many cases. If the breach by the seller is of a condition, as it will be when the goods are unsatisfactory (s14(2) Sale of Goods Act 1979), the buyer may reject them and claim damages as for total non-delivery, or accept them. If he accepts them then he is entitled to damages to cover the extent to which the value of the goods is reduced by reason of the defect. In many cases the proper sum of damages is the cost of repair, because once the goods have been repaired they will be as good as they should have been originally and the buyer's only loss is the cost of repair. The Act does not specifically provide for the seller to pay the cost of repair, but the courts can and do award this as the proper measure of damages (*Minster Trust Ltd* v *Traps Tractors Ltd* (1954)). The rules in the Act are only prima facie rules and will not apply in many cases where the actual loss suffered is greater or less than that provided for by the Act.

The Act also allows a recovery of damages which are peculiar to the parties, provided the common law requirements for such claims are satisfied (s54 Sale of Goods Act 1979). Such claims for damages (under the 2nd rule in *Hadley* v *Baxendale* (1854)) are not affected at all by the Act which merely incorporates the common law into sale cases.

One thing the Act does not provide for is reliance loss. There may be cases where one or other party expends money in reliance on the contract being performed and loses that expenditure when performance fails. For example, a company buying machinery may spend money altering its factory to accommodate that machinery. If alternative machinery of the same type can be bought in the market then the expenditure will not be wasted because that other machinery can be fitted into the altered factory. But if there is no alternative supply then the expenditure would be wasted. Such cases do not fall within s51 because there is no available market, so the common law must be relied on. This does not mean that the buyer can never recover for his loss, but it does mean that the action is not brought under the Act but under the common law.

In general, therefore, the Act does provide for damages to be paid to put the innocent party into the same position he would have been in if the contract had been performed properly, but because it cannot cover all possibilities the common law will need to be relied on in many cases.

QUESTION THREE

P who carried on business at Brighton sold a 1969 MG sports car to Q for £5,000. It had been advertised as 'Fully restored'. Q was driving from P's garage to Q's home in Newcastle when eight miles from his home the steering failed and Q crashed into the window of R's shop. The car was a write-off and Q was injured. The sale agreement contained the following clauses:

'31. It is understood that any statement which is not part of this written agreement is not to be treated as having induced the contract.

32. It is agreed that the vehicle is bought after a thorough examination by the buyer. The vehicle is bought as seen and the seller is not liable for any patent or latent defects.

33. It is agreed that the buyer has not relied on the seller's skill and judgement.

34. In the event of breach the buyer shall have no right to reject the goods or repudiate the contract.

35. It is understood that any damages payable under this contract to the buyer or any other person claiming as a result of the sale to the buyer shall be limited to £500.'

Q is demanding compensation from P.

Advise P.

University of London LLB Examination
(for External Students) Elements of the Law of Contract June 1991 Q3

*Skeleton Solution*

• Actionable misrepresentation?
• 'Fully restored' a contractual term?
• Sale of Goods Act 1979.
• Exclusion clauses.
• UCTA 1977.
• Remedies.

*Suggested Solution*

The car has been advertised as 'Fully restored'. The initial point for decision is whether this statement can be regarded as a contractual term. The question is one of the intention of the parties: *Heilbut, Symons & Co* v *Buckleton* (1913). It could be argued that, because P carries on business (presumably as a car dealer), he has special knowledge, and this would permit the conclusion that the statement was intended to be a contractual term: *Dick Bentley Productions Ltd* v *Harold Smith (Motors) Ltd* (1965); *Esso Petroleum Co Ltd* v *Mardon* (1976). It is submitted, however, that the statement is not sufficiently precise to qualify as a contractual term. Moreover the subsequent reduction of the contract to writing would be a further indication that the statement was not intended to be a term: *Routledge* v *McKay* (1954).

A statement, though not a term, might amount to a representation. In order for it to be a representation it must: (i) be a statement of fact; (ii) be addressed to the party concerned; and (iii) have induced that party to enter into the contract. It is necessary to apply these requirements to the present facts.

Though it has been suggested that the statement is too imprecise to be categorised as a contractual term it must have factual content. 'Fully restored' must mean 'restored to working order' to enable the car to be driven more than a few hundred miles without the steering failing. Thus the first requirement is satisfied. It would also appear that the advertisement was addressed to all potential purchasers, including Q. It can also be assumed that it induced Q to enter into the contract. It should be noted, in this context, that the representation need not be the sole inducing factor; it is sufficient that it played a real and substantial part in inducing Q to purchase the car: *JEB Fasteners Ltd* v *Marks Bloom & Co* (1983). It would also appear that the statement would have induced a reasonable man to contract, therefore the onus of proving that it did not induce Q would fall on P: *Museprime Properties Ltd* v *Adhill Properties Ltd* (1990).

The advertisement therefore amounts to an actionable misrepresentation. However, clause 31 purports to have the effect of excluding liability for any statement inducing the contract. The effectiveness of this exclusion clause must now be considered. It is unnecessary to discuss questions of incorporation or construction of the clause, the sole issue is its validity under the statute. Section 3 of the Misrepresentation Act 1967 as amended by s8 Unfair Contract Terms Act 1977 provides, in effect, that a clause which excludes or restricts liability for misrepresentation, or excludes or restricts any available remedy by reason of such misrepresentation, shall be of no effect unless it satisfies the requirement of reasonableness under s11(1) UCTA.

Section 11(1) provides that in order to determine whether the requirement of reasonableness is satisfied regard is to be had to the circumstances which were, or ought reasonably have been, known to the parties when the contract was made. There is a little case authority on the application of s11(1) to s3 Misrepresentation Act, though a clause excluding liability for misrepresentation has been declared wholly ineffective in *Walker* v *Boyle* (1982) (cf *Howard Marine & Dredging Co Ltd* v *A Ogden & Sons (Excavations) Ltd* (1978)). As the contract was between a business and a consumer, and involved (apparently) a standard form of business, the court would take into account the inequality of bargaining strength between the parties and their respective resources: Schedule 2 UCTA as read with s11(4); *Smith* v *Eric S Bush* (1990). A consideration of these factors suggests that the clause would not meet the reasonableness test and would be held wholly ineffective.

Q is claiming compensation from P (not rescission, to which he may also be entitled). Under s2(1) Misrepresentation Act P would be liable in damages to Q unless he (P) proves that he believed in the truth of the representation up until the time the contract was made, and that he had reasonable grounds for doing so. It does not appear that, as a dealer in cars, he could successfully discharge this onus of proof. The Court of Appeal has recently held in *Royscot Trust Ltd* v *Rogerson* (1991) that the measure of damages under s2(1) is the same as that for deceit, with the result that the innocent party is entitled to recover any loss which flowed from the misrepresentation, even if the loss could not have been foreseen. It would follow, it is submitted, that Q would be entitled to be compensated for his personal injury, the loss of the car and for the damages to which he may be liable to R. (The effect, in this connection, of clause 35 of the sale agreement is considered below.)

The failure of the steering must, it seems, be a breach of the implied condition of the car's satisfactory quality provided for by s14(2) Sale of Goods Act 1979, as amended by the Sale and Supply of Goods Act 1994. This subsection can be invoked: P sold the car in the course of business; the exceptions to the implied condition do not apply; the car does not accord with the criteria of satisfactory quality set out in s14(2A).

Clause 32 of the sale agreement purports to exclude liability for breach of s14(2). But s6(2) UCTA provides that as against a person dealing as a consumer, liability for breach of the obligations arising from (inter alia) s14 SOGA cannot be excluded or restricted by reference to any contract term. Q did not make the contract in the course of business; P did make the contract in the course of business, and the goods passing under the contract are of a type ordinarily supplied for private use. Accordingly Q dealt as a consumer as provided for by s12 UCTA. It follows that clause 32 is wholly ineffective and P is liable for the damages flowing from his breach of contract. It would also appear that all the loss which Q has sustained is within the reasonable contemplation of the parties, and would therefore be recoverable within the rule of *Hadley* v *Baxendale* (1854) as amplified by *Victoria Laundry (Windsor) Ltd* v *Newman Industries Ltd* (1949) and *The Heron II* (1969).

Clause 33 purports to exclude liability arising from s14(3) SOGA. For the reasons set out above it is also wholly ineffective.

Clause 34 restricts the remedies available to the buyer. This is rendered ineffective by s13(1)(a) UCTA.

Clause 35 appears ambiguous. It is not clear whether it refers only to the terms of the contract or whether it can be interpreted as also covering representations. The application of the contra proferentem rule would indicate the former, and for the reasons previously argued would be wholly ineffective. If it does cover representations then it must satisfy the reasonableness requirement under UCTA to which reference has been made above. Clause 35 is a limitation clause and it is suggested in *Ailsa Craig Fishing Co Ltd* v *Malvern Fishing Co* (1983) that in a limitation clause the contra proferentem rule would be less rigorously applied and that the court might be less prone to declare a clause unreasonable if it merely limits damages, but does not totally exclude liability. There is the possibility, therefore, that the clause might be valid with regard to a claim based on misrepresentation, but this is of academic interest to Q who has clear contractual claims.

Two further points must be noted. It is not clear from the facts presented whether or not there has been negligence on P's part with regard to the failure of the steering. As far as Q's personal injury is concerned s2(1) UCTA would render an exclusion of liability for that injury resulting from negligence totally ineffective. The second point is that clause 35 purports to extend the operation of the clause to third parties. The rule as to privity of contract would not permit this.

# 19 ASSIGNMENT

19.1 Introduction

19.2 Key points

19.3 Analysis of questions

19.4 Question

## 19.1 Introduction

This is an area on the very fringes of contract law, indeed some would argue that it might more properly be placed within the ambit of the law of property.

It has already been noted in Chapter 10, in the context of the doctrine of privity that, as a general rule of common law a contract between two people cannot confer obligations on a third party. However it is possible for one of the parties to a contract to transfer the benefits of the contract to another person, by a process known as assignment.

For example if A agrees with B to sell a car for £5,000, A may assign his rights under the contract to X. Once the assignment has been completed X will have the right to receive the £5,000 from B, and may sue B for breach if he refuses to pay.

The contractual right thus assigned is known as a 'chose in action'. Such rights are a group of personal rights of property which may only be protected by an action in law, not by taking physical possession of them. Choses in action are intangible and have no physical substance. They may be either legal or equitable, depending on the method used to create them.

a) Legal choses in action include debts and contractual rights, as well as insurance rights and patents copyrights and bills of lading.

b) Equitable choses in action are a vaguer category and include rights under a trust and inheritances.

Historically there have always been three distinct modes of assignment and the actual method will dictate the rights and duties developing under assignment. Most assignments are voluntary, but it will be seen that there are sometimes circumstances where, by operation of law, assignment occurs automatically.

## 19.2 Key points

It is important that the student understand the following:

a) *Methods of assignment*

It is most convenient to examine this topic in three separate categories:

i)  Common law

Though common law recognised the right to transfer choses in possession (things that could be physically seized) it did not give similar recognition to the right to transfer choses in action.

Thus, at common law assignment of contractual rights was not possible. There were a number of exceptions to this rule, notably negotiable instruments (see post) and also a number of alternatives to assignment such as power of attorney, or novation.

ii) Equity

As often happens, the gap left by common law's failure to recognise assignment of choses in action was filled by equity. Equity did recognise such assignments. Since equity looks to intent rather than form, so long as there was an obvious and definite intention to assign, equity did not require formal methods. There was one exception to this rule – assignments of equitable interests such as rights under trusts or legacies had to be in writing. Equitable assignments may fall into one of two categories:

- if the assignor transfers the total interest – the assignment is absolute;
- if the assignor transfers a part only of his interest, or transfers conditionally or transfers by way of a charge; then these are all non-absolute assignments.

Unless the assignment is complete and perfect it is necessary to give consideration for the assignment to be binding. Gifts are, in the normal way unenforceable, unless complete or in the form of a deed and an assignment will be regarded by the courts as a gift. Like any other contract therefore, if the assignee has provided consideration, the contract will be binding.

An assignee takes 'subject to equities'. This means that he is subject to the same limitations, claims or defences as would have been available against the original assignor.

iii) Statute law

Many of the old conflicts between equity and common law were removed with the enactment of the Judicature Act 1873. A new general method of assignments was created, later incorporated into the Law of Property Act 1925. This means that to be regarded as effective under statutory law an assignment must:

- be absolute;
- be written;
- written notice of it must be given to the debtor.

If these requirements are not met with the assignment will be considered equitable.

b) *Restrictions on assignment*

The two main reasons for refusing to recognise certain types of assignment are:

i) That they offend against public policy

Certain statutes prohibit assignment, eg Social Security Act 1975.

Thus a wife cannot assign maintenance or other payments ordered by a court in matrimonial proceedings. In a number of cases common law makes certain sorts of payment non-transferable.

ii) That the assignment will prejudice the rights of the debtor

In most cases it makes little difference to the debtor whether he repays his debt to the original creditor or an assignee. Certain types of contract are however regarded as 'personal' to the debtor. For example to assign a right to have work done, will prejudice the other party's freedom to choose for whom he wants to work.

Also, although maintenance and champerty are no longer crimes, assignment of certain 'bare' rights in contract will be regarded as contrary to public policy. It is not permitted to assign the right to sue for a breach of contract. This was affirmed in *Trendtex Trading Corporation* v *Credit Suisse* (1982).

c) *Assignment by operation of law*

In certain cases assignment will be involuntary, occurring automatically on the happening of certain events.

These include:

i) assignment on death. As a general rule all contractual rights and duties are assigned to the personal representative of the deceased person's estate. These personal representatives may sue or be sued on any contract to which the deceased was a party, save for personal contracts.

ii) assignment on bankruptcy. A debtor who is adjudged bankrupt will have his property vested in the trustee in bankruptcy. The function of such a trustee is to effect a fair distribution of the debtor's assets between creditors.

d) *Negotiable instruments*

Most of the forms of assignment noted to date have been voluntary. The actual procedure for assignment can be slow and time consuming and would not be practicable if there are to be a series of rapid transfers of a particular chose in action.

The law relating to negotiable instruments evolved especially for this reason, via the old 'Law Merchant' and was subsequently assimilated into common law and equitable law on assignments.

Probably the commonest forms of negotiable instrument are the bill of exchange and the cheque; though there are others. Such negotiable instruments possess qualities not found in other choses in action that are assigned in a more orthodox fashion. In particular transfer of ownership vests in the current holder in the simplest ways; either by endorsement and delivery or by mere delivery, thereby avoiding the cumbersome procedure of traditional assignment.

The student is advised to consult a text book on the subject for more detailed information.

## 19.3 Analysis of questions

This is very much a 'twilight area' of contract law. Few examiners would seek to pose a question on the topic, because few would consider it a legitimate part of a contract course. Certainly, there have been no questions relating to assignment in London University's past papers.

The question quoted below is the sort of question that might be seen, were a question on assignment and choses in action ever to be examined.

## 19.4 Question

Discuss the limitations on assignment.

Written by Editor

*Skeleton Solution*

• Assignment, development, history and definition.
• Formalities for valid assignment.
• Subject to equities.
• Non-assignable rights.

*Suggested Solution*

An assignment is a means by which one party transfers the benefit of a contract to which he is a party to a third person. Thus if A owes B £10,000 under contract A, B may assign to X his rights under the contract and X will possess the right, as assignee to enforce the debt as if he were B.

Assignments are part of a group of rights in law known as choses in action; intangible rights which may be enforced only by suing through the courts.

Common law never recognised assignment, though there were the inevitable means of circumventing this principle such as setting up a power of attorney or novation.

Equity stepped into the breach, with the growth of a number of 'equitable assignments.'

The Judicature Acts 1873–75 with their fusion of common law and equity meant that equitable assignments became enforceable in all courts. Even though the Judicature Act 1873 established a new form of statutory assignment, equitable assignments still retained some degree of importance, since an imperfectly executed assignment (according to the statutory rules) may still be effective in equity (*W Brandt's Sons & Co v Dunlop Rubber Ltd* (1905)).

The statutory provisions, now incorporated into s13(b) of Law of Property Act 1925, make no complex rules as to form or consideration, but there are three basic requirements. The assignment must:

i)  be absolute;

ii) be written;

iii) be notified to the debtor.

Failure to comply with these requirements will result as has been noted in the assignment being imperfect and being regarded as an equitable assignment.

An assignment of part of a debt is not absolute (*Forster* v *Baker* (1910)) nor is assignment by way of a charge, nor is conditional assignment (*Durham Bros* v *Robertson* (1898)).

Although s13(b) LPA requires express notice to be given to the debtor, this need not emanate from the assignor. Notice will be valid, if it comes via a third party, provided it reaches the debtor before the assignee commences any action on the debt (*Holt* v *Heatherfield Trust Ltd* (1942)).

An assignment which fails to satisfy the statute may still take effect as an equitable assignment and to some extent the requirements for validity are rather different. Equity, for example, is more concerned with ascertaining a definite intention on the part of the assignor.

One of the main problems is whether consideration is required to be furnished by the assignee, to make an equitable assignment valid.

Certainly assignments of future property require consideration (*Tailby* v *Official Receiver* (1888)). Similarly an express agreement to make an assignment in the future; then it will only be valid when there is consideration (*Re McArdle* (1951)). Where there is no 'future element' in the assignment, however, the position is less clear.

An assignee takes the chose in action 'subject to equities', that is, he has the same rights only as the assignor, he cannot recover more from the debtor than the assignor could. See *Young* v *Kitchen* (1878), but also *Stoddart* v *Union Trust Ltd* (1912) when it was argued that the debtor could not set off a claim for damages for the assignor's fraud against the assignee on the ground that the fraud was personal to the assignor.

Where the same right is assigned several times, no problem will arise if the chose in action is sufficient to satisfy several different assignees' claims. If the chose is not sufficient, however, there will have to be a system of priorities; the rule is that priority is accorded a rate based on time of giving notice to the debtor. Thus it is possible for an assignment first in time to have to take second place to an assignment which was notified to the debtor earlier (*Dearle* v *Hall* (1823)).

Some rights may not be assigned at all. Some assignments are invalid for reasons of public policy (*Re Robinson* (1884)). Some rights may not be assigned because the contract from which they arise is a personal one, or is founded on the particular attributes of one of the parties (*Peters* v *General Accident & Life Assurance Corp* (1937)). Sometimes the contract which gives use to the right, itself contains an express provision against assignment (*United Dominions Trust* v *Parkway Motors* (1955) and *Helstan Securities* v *Hertfordshire CC* (1978)).

While champerty and maintenance have not been crimes since 1967, the contractual rule that a bare right of action may not be assigned has survived. An assignment will not, however, be considered to be of a bare right, if the assignee has a bona fide right to enforce the interest in question (*Trendtex Trading Corp* v *Credit Suisse* (1982), *Ellis* v *Torrington* (1920)).

Finally it should be noted that while assignment of a benefit under a contract is possible, subject to limitations as discussed; assignment of a burden will be with minimal exceptions, invalid.

# 20 UNIVERSITY OF LONDON LLB (EXTERNAL) 1994 QUESTIONS AND SUGGESTED SOLUTIONS

UNIVERSITY OF LONDON
LLB EXAMINATIONS 1994
for External Students
INTERMEDIATE EXAMINATION (scheme a) and
first and second year examinations (scheme b)

## ELEMENTS OF THE LAW OF CONTRACT

Friday, 17 June: 10.00 am to 1.00 pm

Answer *FOUR* of the following SEVEN questions

1   A wrote to B stating, 'I hear you have a Morris Mini 1969 special model for sale. I would be interested in buying it for £1,200 if it is in good condition.' B wrote to A, 'I agree to sell the car to you but there are still a few things which need doing to it before it is fully restored.' However the letter was lost in the post. A wrote a week later stating, 'As I have not heard from you I assume that the price was not enough. Will you accept £2,000?' B replied by telephone – leaving a message on A's answerphone stating 'I accept the amended offer'. Unfortunately, A was away and three weeks later returned to hear the message. Meanwhile B having heard nothing sold the car to C for £1,500.

   Advise A.

2   'It is high time that English law dropped the pretence of finding valuable consideration in a trifling act such as the withdrawal of an empty threat; the courts should look for other ways of distinguishing between those promises which ought to be enforced and those which ought not.'

   Discuss.

3   G, aged 16 years, was left an orphan by a car crash which killed his parents. He took an evening job as a delivery boy at his local supermarket to supplement his income. He was owed sixteen weeks' wages amounting to £800 but the supermarket failed to pay. He arranged with Dr Manieri to have weekly piano lessons for six months at £50 per lesson. G was determined to complete his studies as he envisaged becoming a professional piano player when he completed his education. After two lessons G decided that he did not want any more lessons and wrote to Dr Manieri to this effect. He arranged with his bank manager to borrow £15,000 till his parents' estates had been settled. He was to repay this loan at a rate of £500 per month. After two months he failed to keep up his payments. He had spent £5,000 on a piano. Also, he owed a bookmaker £300. When the estates of his parents were calculated it was found that as a result of debts there was no inheritance for G.

   Advise G.

4   H saw a 1936 Flying Standard car for sale on a Lom's Garage forecourt for
£4,000. He stopped and examined it thoroughly before taking it out for a test
drive. The sales manager stated that the car, 'was restored but not in concourse
condition. You will have to buy it as found.' H agreed to take the car and drove
it from the garage having arranged to buy it from Fortin Finance Co Ltd to
whom Lom's Garage was going to sell it. H was to make monthly instalments of
£200 per month for two years. Three months after he agreed to buy the car the
brakes failed and H ran into a car driven by J. Both were seriously injured.

The agreement between H and Fortin Finance Co Ltd stated,

'44 It is understood that any statements made by the supplier have no contractual
effect between us and the purchaser from us.

45 Fortin Finance Co Ltd accepts no responsibility for the condition of the vehicle
and shall not be liable for any consequential losses resulting from the condition,
use or safety of the vehicle.

46 H agrees to indemnify Fortin Finance Co Ltd for any damages which are or
may become payable under this contract in the event of any judgment that they
are in breach of contract or any other legal duty.'

Advise H.

5   M, pretending that he was Lord Nobb, went to O's antique shop and agreed to
buy four Welsh Gaudy plates worth £400. He offered to pay by cheque for the
plates but O refused to accept a cheque unless it was supported by a banker's
card. Although M had Lord Nobb's cheque book (which he had stolen) he did not
have the bank card. M showed O his membership card of the Welsh Plate
Collectors Club which contained M's photograph and the name of Lord Nobb.
O went to check that Lord Nobb existed in Who's Who and the telephone
directory. O phoned Lord Nobb's telephone number but received no reply. O
allowed M to take the plates in return for a cheque. Two days later the cheque
was dishonoured and O contacted the Welsh Plate Collectors Club to explain what
had happened and told the police. A day later M sold the plate to Q, who was
unaware of the previous dealings, for £500.

Advise O.

6   'The commercial reality is that contracts *are* made for the benefit of third parties
and the law finds ways of enforcing them; for better or for worse, burdens do
not pass.'

Discuss.

7   a) 'The parties decide what is to be a condition of the contract. The law defines
the consequences of that decision.'

Discuss.

b) In March X engaged Miss Y for 3 years as his research assistant at a salary
of £25,000 under a written agreement which included the following clauses:

'6 The research assistant will dress smartly at all times. It is understood that
trousers are not an acceptable form of dress under any circumstances.

7 The research assistant will work whatever hours are necessary to complete the assignments given to her.'

On 1 June X asked Y to produce certain statistics for a meeting with an important client at 9 am on 2 June. In spite of staying in the office until midnight, Y was not able to complete the statistics on 1 June. She returned to the office at 7 am on 2 June but had still not quite finished the work when X arrived at 8.30.

X was angry. He then noticed that Y was wearing trousers and told her, in front of several colleagues, that her contract was terminated. Y was extremely upset and humiliated: she is now receiving medical treatment for depression.

Advise Y.

QUESTION ONE

A wrote to B stating, 'I hear you have a Morris Mini 1969 special model for sale. I would be interested in buying it for £1,200 if it is in good condition.' B wrote to A, 'I agree to sell the car to you but there are still a few things which need doing to it before it is fully restored.' However the letter was lost in the post. A wrote a week later stating, 'As I have not heard from you I assume that the price was not enough. Will you accept £2,000?' B replied by telephone – leaving a message on A's answerphone stating 'I accept the amended offer'. Unfortunately, A was away and three weeks later returned to hear the message. Meanwhile B having heard nothing sold the car to C for £1,500.

Advise A.

University of London LLB Examination
(for External Students) Elements of the Law of Contract June 1994 Q1

*General Comment*

This is a straightforward question on offer and acceptance. It involves discussion of an invitation to treat as distinct from an offer and the communication of the offer and the acceptance.

*Skeleton Solution*

• A's initial letter – whether an offer or an invitation to treat.

• B's reply – whether it constitutes an acceptance or a fresh offer – the question of communication.

• A's further letter – whether this constitutes an offer.

• B's telephone message; was there communication of acceptance.

*Suggested Solution*

The initial point that falls for discussion is whether A's first letter to B can be considered to be an offer or is merely an invitation to treat. An offer is defined by Treitel (*Law of Contract*, 8th ed, p8) as an 'expression of willingness to contract on certain terms, made with the intention that it shall become binding as soon as it is accepted by the person to whom it is addressed.' The wording of the letter suggests that it does not constitute an offer in this sense, it does not evidence the intention 'that it shall become binding', but does no more than express an interest in buying the car and, moreover, A wishes to be assured that the car is in good condition. On this analysis the letter is an invitation to treat. The decisions in *Harvey* v *Facey* (1893) and *Gibson* v *Manchester City Council* (1979) would, it is submitted, support this view.

However, it is not always easy to distinguish an offer from an invitation to treat, the wording is not necessarily conclusive. B appears to have regarded A's letter as an offer. It appears also, from A's second letter, that he regarded his first letter as making an offer. I must consider the possibility, therefore, that A was making an offer which was conditional on the car being in good condition.

On this assumption I must examine whether B has accepted the offer. At first sight the wording of B's letter appears to be ambiguous; it is by no means certain that B is unequivocally accepting the terms of the offer. However, B does not introduce any new terms into his letter and it is, therefore, possible to construe it as an acceptance. If it is an acceptance, the next question is whether the acceptance has been communicated.

The postal rule, established in *Adams* v *Lindsell* (1818), is that in the case of postal communications, the acceptance is deemed to be communicated as soon as the letter of acceptance is posted. The postal rule will apply whenever use of the post is, or is deemed to be, contemplated by the parties, and the presumption that it is so contemplated will arise when the offeror makes his offer by post: *Henthorn* v *Fraser* (1892). Here A has made the offer (on the assumption that it is an offer) by post. B's letter is lost in the post, but nevertheless, where the postal rule applies, the contract is concluded when the letter is posted and the contract cannot be 'unmade' because of a casualty in the post: *Household Fire and Carriage Accident Insurance Co* v *Grant* (1879).

On the above assumptions, therefore, it is possible to argue that a contract has been concluded for the sale of the car at £1,200. But it is at least doubtful as to whether there has been offer and acceptance and whether the postal rule will apply. The postal rule is not an inflexible one. In *Holwell Securities Ltd* v *Hughes* (1974) Lawton LJ expressed the view that the rule 'probably does not operate if its application would produce manifest inconvenience and absurdity'. The subsequent conduct of the parties, involving apparently a fresh offer and acceptance, would, it is submitted, produce 'inconvenience and absurdity' in applying the postal rule.

Consequently I am proceeding on the basis that no contract had been concluded at this stage.

A, in his second letter, makes a further offer to buy the car at £2,000. Although the letter is couched in the form of a query it does, in my view, clearly express the willingness to be bound at the new price. If that is so, I have to consider whether the fresh offer has been accepted.

B purported to accept the fresh offer. But the question is – has this acceptance been effectively communicated? In the case of instantaneous communications the contract is only concluded when the acceptance has been actually received: *Entores* v *Miles Far East Corporation* (1955). There is no direct authority in English law on the use of answerphones, but it appears from the authority of *Entores* and *Brinkibon Ltd* v *Stahag Stahl* (1983) that B's acceptance is communicated not when he leaves the message on the machine, but only when it is heard by A.

When A returns and hears the message the acceptance is, therefore, then communicated, and the contract would be concluded at that point. However, it appears that at that stage B had already sold the car to a third party.

A must be advised that he has no clear-cut cause of action. For the reasons set out above I have concluded that the formation of a contract at the initial price of £1,200 cannot be supported. Whilst there may well be a concluded contract for the sale of the car at £2,000 – there is no suggestion that B effectively withdrew his acceptance – A has no satisfactory remedy. An order for specific performance would not be available to him. A court will not make such an order where compliance with it is impossible: *Castle* v *Wilkinson* (1870). A remedy in damages would be available to A, but on the information given one cannot say whether this would be worth pursuing.

QUESTION TWO

'It is high time that English law dropped the pretence of finding valuable consideration in a trifling act such as the withdrawal of an empty threat; the courts should look for other ways of distinguishing between those promises which ought to be enforced and those which ought not.'

Discuss.

University of London LLB Examination
(for External Students) Elements of the Law of Contract June 1994 Q2

*General Comment*

Candidates should not have been tempted by this question simply to write all they knew about the doctrine of consideration. Having defined the doctrine, emphasis should have been placed on examples of the 'trifling act' that have been held to constitute valuable consideration, followed by a discussion of the purpose of the doctrine and a discussion of alternative methods of achieving this purpose.

*Skeleton Solution*

• Definitions of 'consideration'.
• Case examples of trivial acts which have been held to constitute valuable consideration: the principle that consideration need not be adequate.
• The purpose of the doctrine.
• Is there an alternative to the doctrine?

*Suggested Solution*

In English law a promise is not enforceable unless it is made in a deed or supported by 'consideration'. The basic feature of the doctrine of consideration is that for a promise to have contractual effect there must be 'something of value in the eye of the law' given in return for the promise: *Thomas* v *Thomas* (1842). This 'something of value' can take the form of a counter promise, an act or a forbearance.

The much quoted definition of consideration is that given by Lush J in *Currie* v *Misa* (1875):

'a valuable consideration in the sense of the law may consist either in some right, interest, profit or benefit accruing to the one party, or some forbearance, detriment, loss or responsibility given, suffered or undertaken by the other'.

This definition has been subject to some criticism. In *Cheshire, Fifoot and Fursmston's Law of Contract* (12th ed, p72) the learned authors observe that, where the parties have exchanged promises, it is difficult to see at what stage either party has conferred a benefit or suffered a detriment; moreover 'benefit' and 'detriment' are often understood in a highly technical sense. They prefer the definition of consideration given by Sir Frederick Pollock (*Pollock on Contracts*, 13th ed, p72):

'An act or forbearance of one party, or the promise thereof, is the price for which the promise of the other is bought, and the promise thus given for value is enforceable.'

This definition was adopted by the House of Lords in *Dunlop Pneumatic Tyre Co Ltd* v *Selfridge & Co Ltd* (1915).

It is clear that English law does find 'valuable consideration in a trifling act'. This results from the application of the maxim that consideration must be sufficient but need to be adequate. In *Chappell & Co Ltd* v *Nestle & Co Ltd* (1960) chocolate wrappings were held to be part of the purchase consideration. An example of 'the withdrawal of an empty threat' being held to constitute valuable consideration is the case of *Callisher* v *Bischoffsheim* (1870) where a promise to abandon a claim that was bad in law was held to be valuable consideration; see also *Cook* v *Wright* (1861). In *Haigh* v *Brooks* (1839) a promise to give up a guarantee was held to be binding although the validity of the guarantee was doubtful. There are, however, limits to finding valuable consideration in acts of forbearance. A promise not to bore his father with complaints was held not to be good consideration: *White* v *Bluett* (1853). Nor was it good consideration to refrain from a course of conduct which it was never intended to pursue: *Arrale* v *Costain Civil Engineering Ltd* (1976).

This discussion would not be complete without reference to developments in which the courts have found valuable consideration in the performance or the promise to perform an existing duty. It is now clearly established that the performance of an existing duty to a third party is good consideration: *New Zealand Shipping Co Ltd* v *A M Satterthwaite & Co Ltd, The Eurymedon* (1975); *Pao On* v *Lau Yiu Long* (1980).

Furthermore, the performance of an existing contractual duty to the promisor may well be good consideration where the promisee confers a *factual* benefit on the promisor: *Williams* v *Roffey Bros & Nicholls (Contractors) Ltd* (1990). In this case the Court of Appeal modified the old decision in *Stilk* v *Myrick* (1809) where the court appeared to have found that the conferment of a legal benefit was required to constitute valuable consideration.

The practice of finding valuable consideration in trifling acts does lend some credence to the view expressed in the question before me. It remains to consider the purpose of the doctrine of consideration and to examine whether that purpose could be achieved by some other method.

Clearly not all promises can be held to be legally enforceable. In Atiyah's view (*Essays on Contract* , p241) 'consideration means the reason for the enforcement of a promise, or, even more broadly, a reason for the recognition of an obligation'. To talk of the abolition of the doctrine of consideration is, Atiyah states, 'nonsensical'. Abolition of the doctrine would require the courts to begin all over again the task of deciding what promises are to be enforceable. The only alternative that presents itself is, as Atiyah suggests, a requirement to find the intention to create legal relations. But, it is submitted, there are no grounds for believing that this would be a more satisfactory alternative. It is, perhaps, only necessary to mention the difficulties faced by the Court of Appeal in *Gould* v *Gould* (1970) and *Jones* v *Padavatton* (1969) in applying the test of an intention to create legal relations. It is difficult to quarrel with Atiyah's view that the application of this test would create uncertainty as to what promises would be enforceable.

QUESTION THREE

G, aged 16 years, was left an orphan by a car crash which killed his parents. He took an evening job as a delivery boy at his local supermarket to supplement his income. He was owed sixteen weeks' wages amounting to £800 but the supermarket failed to pay. He arranged with Dr Manieri to have weekly piano lessons for six months at £50 per lesson. G was determined to complete his studies as he envisaged becoming a professional piano player when he completed his education. After two lessons G decided that he did not want any more lessons and wrote to Dr Manieri to this effect. He arranged with his bank manager to borrow £15,000 till his parents' estates had been settled. He was to repay this loan at a rate of £500 per month. After two months he failed to keep up his payments. He had spent £5,000 on a piano. Also, he owed a bookmaker £300. When the estates of his parents were calculated it was found that as a result of debts there was no inheritance for G.

Advise G.

University of London LLB Examination
(for External Students) Elements of the Law of Contract June 1994 Q3

*General Comment*

This question is on the contractual capacity of minors. It should have presented little difficulty.

*Skeleton Solution*

- General statement of the law as to the capacity of minors in contract.
- The contract with the supermarket – their liability.
- The service contract with Dr Manieri – the question of G's liability.
- The loan from the bank – whether a minor can be held liable for a loan; the expenditure of portion of the loan on a piano; whether the piano is a necessary good; whether the bank has any other remedy.
- The debt to the bookmaker.

*Suggested Solution*

G, being aged 16 years, is a minor in law: the age of majority is 18 years (s1 Family Law Reform Act 1969).

The purpose of the law with regard to minors' contracts is to prevent minors from incurring liability for imprudent bargains because of their inexperience, but also to avoid causing hardship to adults who deal with minors in good faith. Certain contracts are binding on minors; contracts for necessary goods and services; and contracts of service, if for the benefit of the minor as a whole. Certain contracts are voidable at the instance of the minor – but these are not relevant to this problem. Even if a minor is not bound by a contract, the other party may be bound and the contract may have other effects.

*The contract with the supermarket*

G entered into a service contract with the supermarket. It is not necessary to discuss whether or not G was bound by that contract; in either event the supermarket is bound. Where a contract is not binding on the minor, but is binding on the other party, the minor's remedies are limited in that he cannot claim specific performance: *Flight* v *Boland* (1828). G's claim is, however, for the payment of an agreed sum; whilst it is a claim for the specific performance of the supermarket's obligation to pay the agreed wages, as it is simply a claim for money it is not subject to the restrictions which equity imposes on the enforcement of specific performance. Accordingly, G can claim the £800 owing to him.

## The contract with Dr Manieri

Minors are bound by contracts for necessaries. Necessaries consist of necessary goods and necessary services; such services include education of either a liberal or a vocational nature: *Chapple* v *Cooper* (1844). Necessaries are defined – in relation to goods – as 'such articles as are fit to maintain the particular person in the state, station and degree ... in which he is': *Peters* v *Fleming* (1840). According to Treitel (*Law of Contract*, 8th ed, p483) any service can be necessary if it satisfies the test in relation to necesary goods.

As G is intent on becoming a professional piano player it would appear that the piano lessons do fall within the category of necessary services. The question is, however, whether G is bound by an executory contract for these services. It is still a matter for dispute whether a minor is bound by an executory contract for necessary goods: see the differing views of Fletcher Moulton LJ and Buckley LJ in *Nash* v *Inman* (1908). The definition of necessary goods in s3(3) Sale of Goods Act 1979 suggests that goods can only be necessaries when they have been actually delivered; a minor would not be bound by an executory contract for such goods. On the authority of *Roberts* v *Gray* (1913), however, it is submitted that so far as necessary services are concerned a minor is bound by the contract for such services even though it is partly executory. G can, therefore, be held liable in damages to Dr Manieri.

## The loan from the bank

A minor cannot be made liable on a loan, nor can he be made liable on a loan advanced to enable him to purchase necessaries: *Darby* v *Boucher* (1694). Where the minor has actually used a portion of the loan to discharge his liability for necessaries supplied to him, the lender can in equity recover that portion of the loan used for that purpose: *Marlow* v *Pitfield* (1719); *Re National Permanent Benefit Building Society* (1869). It appears that G has purchased, and paid for, a piano for the sum of £5,000 from the proceeds of the loan. Was the piano a necessary? This question is not without difficulty.

In s3(3) Sale of Goods Act 1979 necessaries are defined as 'goods suitable to the condition in life of the minor ... and to his actual requirements at the time of sale and delivery.' In view of his ambition to become a professional piano player, a piano might well be regarded as a necessary. What is questionable is whether an apparently expensive instrument, one costing £5,000, could be suitable to G's 'condition in life' and to 'his actual requirements at the time of sale and delivery'. At the time G obtained the loan from the bank, and presumably when he purchased the piano, G apparently believed that he was to receive a substantial inheritance – a belief that proved to be ill-founded. If the piano could be considered a necessary then the bank could recover the £5,000 expended on it. But I am inclined to the view that, even if at the time of purchase G was potentially wealthy, a piano costing £5,000 was not suitable to the condition in life of a minor then having to supplement his income by working as a delivery boy: nor, at the commencement of his piano studies, was it suitable to his actual requirements.

There is the possible suggestion in the question that G may have misrepresented the position with regard to his parents' estate to the bank – perhaps fraudulently. Even if this were so the bank would not be able to sue G in tort for recovery of the loan made to him. To allow the bank to do so would be an indirect method of enforcing the invalid contract: *R Leslie Ltd* v *Sheill* (1914).

My conclusion is that the bank can neither recover the loan, nor can it recover the £5,000 as expenditure made on a necessary. G is advised, however, that the bank is not without a remedy. Under s3(1) Minors' Contracts Act 1987 the court 'may, if it is just and equitable to do so, require (G) to transfer to the (bank) any property acquired by (G) under the contract, or any property representing it.' By virtue of this provision the bank may be able to obtain an order for the transfer of the piano to them.

It remains to note that, although G is not bound by the contract of loan, he cannot recover any payments he has made to the bank: *Corpe* v *Overton* (1833).

*The debt to the bookmaker*

There is no question of G being held liable for this debt.

QUESTION FOUR

H saw a 1936 Flying Standard car for sale on a Lom's Garage forecourt for £4,000. He stopped and examined it thoroughly before taking it out for a test drive. The sales manager stated that the car, 'was restored but not in concourse condition. You will have to buy it as found.' H agreed to take the car and drove it from the garage having arranged to buy it from Fortin Finance Co Ltd to whom Lom's Garage was going to sell it. H was to make monthly instalments of £200 per month for two years. Three months after he agreed to buy the car the brakes failed and H ran into a car driven by J. Both were seriously injured.

The agreement between H and Fortin Finance Co Ltd stated,

'44 It is understood that any statements made by the supplier have no contractual effect between us and the purchaser from us.

45 Fortin Finance Co Ltd accepts no responsibility for the condition of the vehicle and shall not be liable for any consequential losses resulting from the condition, use or safety of the vehicle.

46 H agrees to indemnify Fortin Finance Co Ltd for any damages which are or may become payable under this contract in the event of any judgment that they are in breach of contract or any other legal duty.'

Advise H.

University of London LLB Examination
(for External Students) Elements of the Law of Contract June 1994 Q4

## General Comment

A complete answer to this question would have to consider the possible implications of the Consumer Credit Act 1974. But as this act does not form part of the Intermediate syllabus, it is not examined in detail in this suggested solution, which is largely confined to the contract between H and Fortin Finance Co and the effect of the exclusion clauses in that contract. Attention must also be devoted, however, to the possibility of a collateral contract between H and Lom's Garage.

## Skeleton Solution

- Were Fortin Finance in breach of contract? – the nature of the breach, s14(2) Sale of Goods Act 1979, as amended 1994, and the statement by the service manager of Lom's Garage.
- The effect of the exclusion clauses – the common law, incorporation and construction.
- The validity of the exclusion clauses under the Unfair Contract Terms Act 1977.
- The possibility of liability of Lom's Garage under a collateral contract.

## Suggested Solution

It is firstly necessary to determine what, if any, is the breach of contract as between Fortin Finance and H.

The contract between H and Fortin Finance is one of sale of goods (it is, apparently, a credit sale, and not a hire-purchase agreement) and one must examine whether there has been a breach of the implied condition in s14(2) Sale of Goods Act 1979, as amended by the Sale and Supply of Goods Act 1994. This subsection provides that:

'Where the seller sells goods in the course of business, there is an implied condition that the goods supplied are of satisfactory quality, except that there is no such condition –

(a) as regards defects specifically drawn to the buyer's attention before the contract is made; or

(b) if the buyer examines the goods before the contract is made, as regards any matter making the goods unsatisfactory, which that examination ought to reveal.'

Fortin Finance clearly sell in the course of a business. It does not appear that any defects were specifically drawn to H's attention, so that proviso (a) does not apply. I am informed that H examined the car thoroughly before taking it out for a test drive, which suggests that proviso (b) may be relevant. However, one can assume that H's examination would not have revealed a defect in the brakes. I am, therefore, proceeding on the assumption that s14(2) applies. That being so, was there a breach of the subsection? Was the car of 'satisfactory quality'?

Under s14(2A) of the Act goods are of 'satisfactory quality' –

'if they meet the standard that a reasonable person would regard as satisfactory, taking account of any description of the goods, the price (if relevant) and all other relevant circumstances.'

237

The car in question is a second-hand 1936 model. A second-hand car 'is merchantable if it is in usable condition, even if it is not perfect ...' per Lord Denning MR in *Bartlett* v *Sydney Marcus* (1965); but a car which is unsafe to drive is clearly unsatisfactory: *Lee* v *York Coach and Marine* (1977). A car whose brakes fail is patently unsafe to drive.

The definition of 'unsatisfactory' in s14(2A) requires that regard be had to the price – £4,000 is a not an inconsiderable price. The definition also requires reference to 'all other relevant circumstances'. In this context one must examine the statement of the sales manager of Lom's Garage. He said that the car was not in *concours* (the word is misspelt in the question) condition. This means that the car was not in superb condition, fit for exhibition. He added that H would 'have to buy it as found.' But he also said that the car was 'restored'. This can only mean that it was restored so as to be able to function safely as a car. Fortin Finance are, it is submitted, liable for this statement. It is safe to assume that Lom's Garage was acting as agent for Fortin Finance. (There might be deemed to be this agency relationship by s56(2) Consumer Credit Act 1974.)

I conclude, therefore, that Fortin Finance are liable for the breach of the implied condition as to satisfactory quality. What now falls for discussion is the effect of the exclusion clauses on this liability.

The clauses are stated to be incorporated in the contract. This does not have to be further discussed. Nor is it necessary to discuss whether, as a matter of construction, the clauses cover the breach and are otherwise effective at common law. This is clearly so. What requires examination is the validity of the clauses under the Unfair Contract Terms Act 1977 (UCTA). I shall examine each clause in turn.

*Clause 44*

This clause purports to exclude liability for the statement made by the sales manager of Lom's Garage that the car was restored. If this statement was a misrepresentation, then the provisions of s3 Misrepresentation Act 1967 (as amended by s8 UCTA) would make this clause subject to the requirement of reasonableness. If the statement was a contractual term then, paradoxically, s3 would not apply (see *Cheshire, Fifoot and Furmston's Law of Contract*, 12th ed, p195). But I would argue that Fortin Finance are in breach of the implied condition as to merchantibility even in the absence of this statement. In any event Clause 44 of the agreement might be rendered void by s56(3) Consumer Credit Act 1974, so I do not propose to consider it further.

*Clause 45*

H was 'dealing as a consumer' within the provisions of s12 UCTA. Accordingly s6(2) of UCTA applies. This renders the clause totally void.

*Clause 46*

This clause falls within s4 UCTA which makes such an indemnity clause subject to the requirement of reasonableness as set out in s11. In *Smith* v *Eric S Bush* (1989) Lord Griffiths refers to factors which should always be taken into account in determining whether a clause satisfies the requirement. Among the factors he mentions are the bargaining strength of the parties and their respective financial resources. It can be assumed that H was confronted with a standard form contract with little or no opportunity of negotiating its terms. The parties were, consequently, of unequal bargaining strength. It seems to me also, that it is indisputable that Fortin Finance have the greater financial resources, including the greater facility to cover themselves by insurance.

I conclude, therefore, that Fortin Finance are liable to H for the loss he has suffered and cannot rely on the indemnity clause in the event of J, the other driver, pursuing a claim against them.

It remains to consider whether Lon's Garage have incurred liability to H at common law. (By statute, under s75(1) Consumer Credit Act 1974 Fortin Finance and Lom's Garage might have incurred joint and several liability.)

At common law it appears that Lom's Garage would be liable on a collateral contract for the statement of the sales manager that the car had been restored on the principle in *Shanklin Pier Ltd* v *Detel Products Ltd* (1951). This principle was applied in *Andrews* v *Hopkinson* (1957), a case particularly relevant to the situation under discussion.

QUESTION FIVE

M, pretending that he was Lord Nobb, went to O's antique shop and agreed to buy four Welsh Gaudy plates worth £400. He offered to pay by cheque for the plates but O refused to accept a cheque unless it was supported by a banker's card. Although M had Lord Nobb's cheque book (which he had stolen) he did not have the bank card. M showed O his membership card of the Welsh Plate Collectors Club which contained M's photograph and the name of Lord Nobb. O went to check that Lord Nobb existed in Who's Who and the telephone directory. O phoned Lord Nobb's telephone number but received no reply. O allowed M to take the plates in return for a cheque. Two days later the cheque was dishonoured and O contacted the Welsh Plate Collectors Club to explain what had happened and told the police. A day later M sold the plate to Q, who was unaware of the previous dealings, for £500.

Advise O.

University of London LLB Examination
(for External Students) Elements of the Law of Contract June 1994 Q5

*General Comment*

This is self-evidently a question on unilateral mistake as to identity. No further comment is required.

*Skeleton Solution*

• The effect of operative unilateral mistake at common law.
• The distinction between void and voidable contracts; the effect of the distinction for O.
• An examination of mistake as to identity in the light of the decided cases.
• O's right to rescind the contract with M – whether O has rescinded the contract with M before the intervention of rights by the third party, Q.

*Suggested Solution*

In *Bell* v *Lever Brothers Ltd* (1932) Lord Atkin said that –

'If mistake operates at all it operates so as to negative consent or in some cases to nullify consent ... Thus a mistaken belief by A that he is contracting with B, whereas he is contracting with C, will negative consent where it is clear that the intention of A was to contract only with C.'

Where mistake is operative at common law, the effect is to render the contract void. In situations such as the present the original owner of the goods may well have the right to set aside the contract with the imposter – the contract is voidable. But the right to set it aside may be lost if third party rights have intervened. The owner will seek to establish that the contract was void, in order to be able to recover the goods from the third party.

It will be seen that the situations in which mistake as to identity render the contract void are comparatively rare, particularly when the parties are inter praesentes. Lord Atkin, in the passage cited above, suggested that the mistake would not be operative unless the intention was to contract only with a particular person. A similar approach was adopted in the recent case of *Citibank NA* v *Brown Shipley & Co* (1991), where Waller J said that, for the mistake to render the contract void, the identity of the person (with whom it was believed the contract was being made) must be of 'crucial importance'.

I propose to attempt an analysis of the cases in the light of these judicial statements. It would, perhaps, be useful firstly to examine those cases in which the mistake as to identity was held to be operative and to render the contract void. In the early case of *Boulton* v *Jones* (1857) the defendant intended to contract with a certain Brocklehurst, there was apparently good reason for his offer being intended only for that particular person. The decision that there was no contract with the plaintiff can be explained on the principle that an offer made to one person cannot be accepted by another. A similar explanation can be made of the decision in *Cundy* v *Lindsay* (1878) – see the observations of Lord Denning MR in the Court of Appeal in *Gallie* v *Lee* (1969). It must be emphasised that in neither *Boulton* v *Jones* nor *Cundy* v *Lindsay* were the parties inter praesentes. *Hardman* v *Booth* (1863) and *Lake* v *Simmons* (1927) are cases in which the contracts were held to be void because the intention was to contract only with a particular person, the issue of identity was crucial.

The authorities which appear to be decisive to the present problem are *Phillips* v *Brooks* (1919) and the Court of Appeal decision in *Lewis* v *Averay* (1972). In the former case a jeweller was persuaded to part with goods on credit because he had been led to believe that the person before him was some other, reputable, person. In the latter case, the facts of which are closely similar to those before me, the owner of a car was induced to part with possession of it in exchange for a cheque, in the belief that the imposter was a well-known screen and television personality. Here too the imposter showed a card and photograph in order to lend credence to his deception. In both of these cases the contract was valid in law, so that third parties who had acquired the goods in good faith and for value obtained good title.

A case which is difficult to reconcile with the above two authorities is that of *Ingram* v *Little* (1961), where on facts not dissimilar to those in Lewis v Averay a Court of

Appeal by a majority, Devlin LJ dissenting, held that the contract was void, so that the third party did not acquire rights to the goods in question. In my view the decision in *Lewis* v *Averay* should prevail. In that case Lord Denning MR stated the principle of law as follows:

'When a dealing is had between a seller ... and a person who is actually there present before him, then the presumption in law is that there is a contract, even though there is a fraudulent impersonation by the buyer representing himself as a different man than he is. There is a contract made with the very person there, who is present in person.'

Applying that principle to the present problem leads me to conclude that there was a contract between O and M.

O does, of course, have a cause of action against M for fraudulent misrepresentation, entitling him to damages against the imposter for fraud and to the equitable remedy of rescission of the contract. The right to rescind a contract for misrepresentation is barred, however, if an innocent third party has acquired the goods for value before the contract has been effectively rescinded. Q, the third party, did acquire the goods for value and in good faith. In order to be able to pursue an action against Q, for the recovery of the goods or damages for conversion, O must establish that he effectively rescinded the contract before Q's acquisition of the goods. Normally notice of rescission would have to be communicated to M. If O could not find M, or communicate with him, then he would be held to have exercised his right of rescission if he immediately took all possible steps to recover the goods: *Car and Universal Finance Co Ltd* v *Caldwell* (1965). This O appears to have done by informing the Welsh Plate Collectors Club and contacting the police when he discovered the fraud: and he took these steps before the acquisition by Q. On the assumption that O could not find M, or communicate with him, and that therefore O effectively rescinded the contract, he would have a cause of action against Q.

QUESTION SIX

'The commercial reality is that contracts are made for the benefit of third parties and the law finds ways of enforcing them; for better or for worse, burdens do not pass.'

Discuss.

University of London LLB Examination
(for External Students) Elements of the Law of Contract June 1994 Q6

*General Comment*

This question is on the doctrine of privity of contract. The two aspects of the doctrine have to be considered: the conferring of benefits in a contract on a person who was not party to the contract; and the imposition of burdens on a such third party.

*Skeleton Solution*

• Statement of the doctrine.
• Enforcement by the third party.

• Remedies of the promisee.
• Benefit of exclusion clauses.
• Evasion of and exceptions to the doctrine.
• Imposing burdens on third parties.

*Suggested Solution*

The principle of law in relation to third party rights under a contract was expressed by Viscount Haldane LC in *Dunlop Pneumatic Tyre Co Ltd* v *Selfridge & Co Ltd* (1915) as follows:

'... in the law of England certain principles are fundamental. One is that only a person who is a party to a contract can sue on it. Our law knows nothing of a *jus quaesitum tertio* arising by way of contract.'

This principle derives from the decision in *Tweddle* v *Atkinson* (1861) and was re-affirmed by the House of Lords in *Beswick* v *Beswick* (1968), where their Lordships rejected the argument that the common law had been radically altered by s56(1) Law of Property Act 1925 – an argument which had found favour in the Court of Appeal.

Whilst it is the general rule that the third party cannot enforce the promise in the contract, a remedy may be available to the promisee: in *Beswick* v *Beswick* the promisee was able to obtain an order for specific performance.

This is an uncertain remedy, specific performance being an equitable, discretionary remedy, may not always be available.

A remedy in damages may also not be available to the promisee. The promisee would be entitled to sue for his own loss, but in many circumstances he would not have suffered any loss. It seems clear that the promisee cannot sue for the third party's loss. In *Jackson* v *Horizon Holidays Ltd* (1975) Lord Denning MR had held that he could do so, but this view was rejected by the House of Lords in *Woodar Investment Development Ltd* v *Wimpey Construction UK Ltd* (1980). The rule that the promisee can recover only for his own loss and not that of the third party was regarded by Dillon J in *Forster* v *Silvermere Golf and Equestrian Centre* (1981) as 'a blot on our law and most unjust'.

Where A promises B, for consideration, not to sue C, although this would not provide a defence to C, it may be possible for B to prevent A from doing so, where B has a sufficient interest in the enforcement of the promise: *Gore* v *Van Der Lann* (1967); *Snelling* v *Snelling Ltd* (1973).

A third party cannot generally rely on the benefit of an exclusion clause in a contract: *Scruttons Ltd* v *Midland Silicones Ltd* (1962). However, in that case Lord Reid set out certain conditions which might enable him to do so. These were (i) that the third party was intended to be benefited by the provisions of the exclusion clause; (ii) that the promisee made it clear that in addition to acting on his own behalf, he was also acting as agent for the third party; (iii) that he had authority to do so; and (iv) that any difficulty about consideration moving from the third party was overcome. These conditions were held to be satisfied in *New Zealand Shipping Co Ltd* v *A M Satterthwaite & Co Ltd, The Eurymedon* (1975) and *Port Jackson Stevedoring Pty Ltd* v *Salmond & Spraggon Pty Ltd, The New York Star* (1980).

In *Norwich City Council* v *Harvey* (1989) the contract between the plaintiff and the contractors provided that the risk of loss or damage by fire should be borne by the plaintiff. The sub-contractors, who were not privy to that contract, set fire to the building. Though they would have been in breach of duty to the plaintiff, the provisions of the main contract, in the circumstances of the case, negatived that duty. Thus the third party could invoke those provisions as a defence to the claim against him.

The trust concept might provide a possibility for the third party to enforce the benefit. If it can be shown that in a contract between A and B, conferring a benefit on C, B was acting as trustee for C, then C can directly enforce A's obligation in equity. However, the trust concept can rarely be successfully invoked: *Vandepitte* v *Preferred Accident Insurance Corp of New York* (1933). In *Re Schebsman* (1994) Lord Greene MR said that, 'it is not legitimate to import into a contract the idea of a trust when the parties have given no indication that such was their intention.'

Whilst, therefore, the law can find ways of enforcing contracts for the benefit of third parties, the doctrine of privity of contract limits the circumstances in which this can be achieved at common law. There are a number of statutory exceptions to the doctrine: s11 Married Woman's Property Act 1882; s14(2) Marine Insurance Act 1906; ss47(1), 56(1) Law of Property Act 1925; s148(4) Road Traffic Act 1972.

With regard to the imposition of burdens on third parties the general principle is that a contract cannot do so. This aspect of the doctrine of privity of contract is less open to controversy; there can be little justification for a party having to submit to obligations in a contract to which he was not a party. The only exceptions to this principle are in the law of property. Covenants in leases are binding not only on the original parties, but also on their successors in title. Covenants restricting the use of land may be binding in equity on subsequent purchasers of the land with notice of the covenant: *Tulk* v *Moxhay* (1848). In *Taddy* v *Sterious* (1904) the court refused to extend this principle to goods. The attempted extension of the principle to contracts for the hire of ships by the Privy Council in *Lord Strathcona Steamship Co* v *Dominion Coal Co* (1926) has been disavowed: *Port Line Ltd* v *Ben Line Steamers Ltd* (1958); *Bendall* v *McWhirter* (1952).

Where there has been interference with contractual rights a cause of action may arise in tort, but not in contract, against the third party guilty of the interference: *Lumley* v *Gye* (1853).

A reform of the law with regard to third party rights has long been advocated. Most recently the Law Commission has provisionally recommended that legislation should be enacted to enable third parties, as well as promisees, to enforce benefits in favour of third parties; subject to the right of the promisor to the same defences as he would have against the promisee. The Commission does not favour a change in the law regarding the imposition of burdens on third parties, save that the promisor should be able to impose conditions on the enjoyment by third parties of any benefit conferred under the contract ('Privity of Contract: Contracts for the Benefit of Third Parties' (Consultation Paper No 121, 1992)).

QUESTION SEVEN

a) 'The parties decide what is to be a condition of the contract. The law defines the consequences of that decision.'

Discuss.

b) In March X engaged Miss Y for 3 years as his research assistant at a salary of £25,000 under a written agreement which included the following clauses:

'6 The research assistant will dress smartly at all times. It is understood that trousers are not an acceptable form of dress under any circumstances.

7 The research assistant will work whatever hours are necessary to complete the assignments given to her.'

On 1 June X asked Y to produce certain statistics for a meeting with an important client at 9 am on 2 June. In spite of staying in the office until midnight, Y was not able to complete the statistics on 1 June. She returned to the office at 7 am on 2 June but had still not quite finished the work when X arrived at 8.30.

X was angry. He then noticed that Y was wearing trousers and told her, in front of several colleagues, that her contract was terminated. Y was extremely upset and humiliated: she is now receiving medical treatment for depression.

Advise Y.

University of London LLB Examination
(for External Students) Elements of the Law of Contract June 1994 Q7

*General Comment*

Part (a) of the question requires discussion of the relative importance of contractual terms; conditions, warranties and innominate terms and the consequences in law of the breach of such terms. Part (b) is a problem in this area of the law; the two clauses of the contract have to be analysed into which of these categories they fall in order to determine the consequences of their breach by Miss Y. Consideration must also be given to the possibility of a breach of contract by X.

*Skeleton Solution*

a) • The definition of 'condition', warranty' and 'innominate term'.

   • The consequences of a breach of condition as distinct from a breach of warranty.

   • When a term becomes a condition.

b) • Analysis of the two clauses, whether either of them can be classified as conditions.

   • Consequences of Miss Y's breach of the clauses.

   • The possible breach of contract by X and its consequences.

*Suggested Solution*

a) A party must perform, or be willing to perform, all his obligations under the contract. But English law has long recognised that not all the obligations are of

244

equal importance. In the Court of Appeal, in *Wallis, Son & Wells* v *Pratt and Haynes* (1910), Fletcher Moulton LJ described some obligations as going to the substance of the contract, so that a failure to perform them would be regarded as a substantial failure to perform the contract at all. Other obligations, though they must be performed, are not so vital that they go to the substance of the contract. Those obligations that go the substance of the contract have been classified as 'conditions', the latter obligations as 'warranties'. Breach of condition entitles the injured party to treat the contract as repudiated, and he can elect to terminate it. For breach of warranty, there is no right to terminate, the injured party's remedy is confined to a claim for damages. There are certain terms which it may be difficult to classify as either a condition or a warranty; breaches of them may be serious or trivial. Such terms, though previously recognised by the courts (compare, for example, the decisions in *Poussard* v *Spiers & Pond* (1876) and *Bettini* v *Gye* (1876)) were first categorised as 'innominate terms' by Diplock LJ in *Hongkong Fir Shipping Co Ltd* v *Kawasaki Kishen Kaisha Ltd* (1962). Whether a breach of such term is treated as a breach of condition or only as a breach of warranty 'depends on the nature, consequences and effect of the breach' – per Lord Scarman in *Bunge Corporation* v *Tradax Export SA* (1981).

When does a term of a contract become a condition? In *Bentsen* v *Taylor, Sons & Co* (1893) Bowen LJ said –

'There is no way of deciding that question except by looking at the contract in the light of the surrounding circumstances, and then making up one's mind whether the intention of the parties, as gathered from the instrument itself, will best be carried out by treating the promise as a warranty sounding only in damages, or as a condition precedent by the failure to perform which the other party is relieved of his liability.'

Thus his Lordship stressed the paramountcy of the intention of the parties. The statement in the question before me that – 'The parties decide what is to be a condition of the contract' is, however, less than complete. Certain terms are, by statutory implication, conditions of the contract: inter alia ss12–15 Sale of Goods Act 1979; ss8–11 Supply of Goods (Implied Terms) Act 1973; ss2–5, 7–10 Supply of Goods and Services Act 1982.

The courts, too, have ruled that certain terms are to be construed as conditions. In mercantile contracts there is binding authority that 'time is of the essence': *The Mihalis Angelos* (1971); *Bunge Corporation* v *Tradax Corporation* (above); *The Naxos* (1990). Here the intention of the parties is imputed rather than actual.

It can be suggested, also, that the courts do not always give effect to the intention of the parties. In *L Schuler AG* v *Wickman Machine Tool Sales Ltd* (1974) one clause in the contract was described as a 'condition'. No other clause was so described. In the light of the circumstances and the contract as a whole the majority of the House of Lords decided that despite employing the term 'condition' it could not have been the intention of the parties that the clause would operate as such. But see the speech of Lord Wilberforce, dissenting.

The consequences of a term being a condition have been set out above.

b) In this problem, in order to determine Y's rights, it is necessary to examine the relevant clauses in the contract. Clearly she has been in breach of both these clauses. Are either of them to be treated as a breach of condition entitling X to terminate the contract? I shall consider each clause in turn.

*Clause 6*

Although the clause provides that 'trouser are not an acceptable form of dress *under any circumstances*', I find it difficult to construe this as a condition. It is a term capable of a range of breaches, from serious to trivial. In my view it is an innominate term, and one must, therefore, look at 'the nature, effect and consequences of the breach'. Adopting the words of Diplock LJ in *Hongkong Fir Shipping* (above), does the breach deprive X of 'substantially the whole benefit which it was the intention of the parties as expressed in the contract that he should obtain'? I do not believe that the breach can be considered as doing so. Consequently it cannot be treated as a breach of condition. X cannot terminate the contract on this ground.

*Clause 7*

This term may well be a condition. It appears to go to the substance of the contract. If it is regarded as an innominate term, the nature of the breach in, apparently, not completing the assignment in time for an important meeting, would entitle X to treat it as a breach of condition. I conclude, though not without some doubt, that X would be entitled to terminate the contract on this ground.

If X is entitled to terminate the contract Y has no redress. As, however, I have expressed some doubt as to whether he is so entitled, I must consider the possibility that the termination was unlawful. In this event X would be in breach of contract, and Y would have an action for wrongful dismissal. She could claim for her pecuniary loss. But she could not claim for the distress and subsequent depression that she suffered: *Bliss v South East Thames Regional Health Authority* (1987).

# APPENDIX I

Questions from University of London LLB (External) Elements of the Law of Contract papers (June 1983–1993). Shown by **year and chapter**.

| 1983 | Question | 6 | Ch 8 |
|------|----------|---|------|
|      |          | 8 | Ch 10 |
|      |          | 7 | Ch 12 |
|      |          | 9 | Ch 9 |
| 1984 | Question | 3 | Ch 18 |
|      |          | 5 | Ch 5 |
|      |          | 6 | Ch 11 |
| 1985 | Question | 2 | Ch 2 |
|      |          | 7 | Ch 10 |
|      |          | 8 | Ch 12 |
| 1986 | Question | 3 | Ch 4 |
|      |          | 6 | Ch 5 |
|      |          | 9 | Ch 7 |
| 1987 | Question | 1 | Ch 1 |
|      |          | 3 | Ch 4 |
|      |          | 8 | Ch 14 |
| 1988 | Question | 1 | Ch 1 |
|      |          | 3 | Ch 6 |
|      |          | 4 | Ch 8 |
|      |          | 5 | Ch 13 |
|      |          | 6 | Ch 7 |
|      |          | 7 | Ch 2 |
| 1989 | Question | 2 | Ch 12 |
|      |          | 4 | Ch 14 |
|      |          | 5 | Ch 8 |

*Note also* **Commercial Law**

# APPENDIX II

Questions from University of London LLB (External) Elements of the Law of Contract papers (June 1983–1994) indicated according to **subject matter and format.**

**KEY**

| | | |
|---|---|---|
| E | = | Essay question |
| P | = | Problem |
| E/P | = | Combined elements of both |

**1983**                               **Question**

| | | |
|---|---|---|
| P | 1 | Offer/acceptance, prescribed mode of acceptance, revocation and related topics |
| P | 2 | Promissory estoppel. The *High Trees* case and afterwards |
| P | 3 | Misrepresentation, exclusion clauses and remedies for breach of contract |
| E | 4 | Breach of contract. Terms and conditions |
| P | 5 | Restraint of trade as between (i) partners and (ii) employer/ee |
| P | 6 | Common mistake and equitable doctrine flowing from *Solle* v *Butcher* |
| P | 7 | Frustration and its effects on a contract |
| E | 8 | Circumvention of the doctrine of privity by the courts |
| E | 9 | Undue influence/ non est factum/ contracts for necessaries |

**1984**

| | | |
|---|---|---|
| P | 1 | Acceptance, postal rules, communication of acceptance, silence as acceptance? |
| E/P | 2 | Consideration, especially past consideration, promissory estoppel |
| P | 3 | Sale of goods contracts, implied terms from SGA 1979, exclusion and limitation clauses, UCTA 1977 |

1984 (continued)

| | | | |
|---|---|---|---|
| P | 4 | Mistake and its effects on contracts. Void or voidable contracts |
| P | 5 | Misrepresentation, its effect on contract, remedies: especially damages |
| E | 6 | Illegal contracts, types of illegality, courts' approach to illegality |
| P | 7 | Frustration – criteria for a frustrated contract/ privity/remedies for breach of contract |
| E/P | 8 | a) Infants' capacity to contract – necessary contracts<br>b) Restraint of trade with particular reference to infants |
| E | 9 | Damages, remoteness, assessment of non-pecuniary losses |

**1985**

| | | | |
|---|---|---|---|
| P | 1 | Invitations to treat, offers, counter offers, postal offer and acceptance |
| P | 2 | Intention to create legal relationships, family agreements, consideration, conditions and terms of a contract |
| P | 3 | Exclusion clauses, incorporation and construction, 1977 UCTA, the 'reasonableness' test |
| P | 4 | Terms of contract, mere representations, misrepresentation, remedies |
| E | 5 | Common mistake, the differing approaches of common law and equity |
| P | 6 | Infants' capacity – contracts for necessaries and other contracts |
| E | 7 | Doctrine of privity of contract, exceptions, possible future reforms |
| E | 8 | Application of the doctrine of frustration – criteria for a frustrated contract |
| P | 9 | Damages, various heads of claim |

**1986**

| | | |
|---|---|---|
| P | 1 | Existence of a concluded contract, invitation to treat, offers, revocation, acceptance, postal rules |
| P | 2 | a) Intention to create legal relationships, sufficient or adequate consideration, exceptions to rule on past consideration |
| | | b) Promissory estoppel |
| P | 3 | Terms and conditions of a contract, their breach |
| E/P | 4 | Mistake as to identity/ attributes, effect of such mistakes |
| E/P | 5 | Damages, remoteness, heads of claim and assessment |
| P | 6 | Misrepresentation, remedies |
| E/P | 7 | Doctrine of frustration, redress in the event of a frustrated contract |
| P | 8 | Exclusion clauses, common law, UCTA 1977 |
| E | 9 | Infants' capacity, contracts for necessaries, other void or voidable contracts, possible reforms |

**1987**

| | | |
|---|---|---|
| P | 1 | Invitations to treat, offers, counter offers, acceptance, postal rules |
| E/P | 2 | a) Consideration, performance of an existing contractual duty |
| | | b) Payment of a smaller sum in full settlement and promissory estoppel |
| E | 3 | Conditions, warranties and innominate terms – a review of judicial attitudes |
| P | 4 | Terms of a contract, their breach. SGA 1979 and implied terms as to quality, remedies |
| E/P | 5 | a) Different forms of mistake |
| | | b) Mistake as to identity |
| P | 6 | Exclusion clauses, incorporation, construction, UCTA 1977, privity of contract |

1987 (continued)

| | | | |
|---|---|---|---|
| | P | 7 | Criteria for frustration, parties' respective rights and liabilities on frustration |
| | E/P | 8 | Damages, remoteness, heads of claim |
| | E | 9 | Contracts in restraint of trade, (i) employer/ee, (ii) sale of a business, (iii) solus petrol agreements |

**1988**

| | | | |
|---|---|---|---|
| | P | 1 | Traditional analysis of offer and acceptance |
| | E | 2 | Criteria for frustration, basis of the doctrine |
| | P | 3 | Exclusion clauses, incorporation, construction, UCTA 1977, the 'reasonableness' test |
| | E | 4 | Types of mistake, their effect on contract, approaches of common law/equity, remedies |
| | P | 5 | Breach of contract, especially repudiatory breach |
| | P | 6 | Contractual capacity of infants, contracts for necessaries, other void/ voidable contracts |
| | P | 7 | Rules relating to consideration, duress, promissory estoppel |

**1989**

| | | | |
|---|---|---|---|
| | P | 1 | Terms or mere representations? Misrepresentation, remedies |
| | P | 2 | Criteria for frustration, respective rights of parties on frustration |
| | P | 3 | Rules relating to offer, revocation, acceptance |
| | E | 4 | Damages, remoteness, heads of claim and assessment |
| | P | 5 | Mistake as to identity, mutual mistake |
| | E | 6 | Restraint of trade, areas where the doctrine operates |
| | P | 7 | Exclusion clauses, UCTA 1977 |

**1990**

| | | | |
|---|---|---|---|
| | P | 1 | Consideration – sufficiency – promissory estoppel |

1990 (continued)

|  | P | 2 | Contractual terms – conditions – warranties – innominate terms |
|---|---|---|---|
|  | E | 3 | Remedies for misrepresentaiton – for breach of contract – relative effectiveness of the two compared |
|  | P | 4 | Offer and acceptance – postal rules – instantaneous communication |
|  | E | 5 | Illegality – possibility of recovery of money or goods |
|  | P | 6 | Privity of contract – damages for distress after breach |
|  | P | 7 | Capacity – minors – contracts for necessaries |

**1991**

|  | P | 1 | Offer and acceptance – invitations to treat – postal rules |
|---|---|---|---|
|  | E | 2 | Economic duress, relationship between duress and commercial pressure |
|  | P | 3 | Misrepresentation, implied conditions, exclusion clauses, remedies |
|  | P | 4 | Illegality – recovery of money or goods |
|  | P | 5 | Mutual mistake – unilateral mistake – mistake as to identity |
|  | E | 6 | Frustration – foreseen or foreseeable events |
|  | P | 7 | Remedies for breach of contract – damages – remoteness |

**1992**

|  | P | 1 | Exclusion clauses; illegality |
|---|---|---|---|
|  | E | 2 | Consideration – doctrine and its abolition |
|  | P | 3 | Offer, acceptance, estoppel |
|  | E | 4 | Misrepresentation – remedies |
|  | P | 5 | Frustration |
|  | E/P | 6 | Doctrine of privity – defects of doctrine |

1992 (continued)

| | P | 7 | Common and unilateral mistake |

**1993**

| | E/P | 1 | Misrepresentation, damages, rescission |
| | E | 2 | Mistake, common law and equity |
| | E/P | 3 | Part performance, quantum meruit Contractual terms |
| | P | 4 | Offer and acceptance |
| | P | 5 | Consideration, breach, frustration |
| | E/P | 6 | Illegality |
| | E | 7 | Promissory estoppel |

**1994**

* Note: all the questions from this paper (together with solutions) are included in Chapter 20.

| | P | 1 | Invitations to treat, offer, acceptance |
| | E | 2 | Consideration, sufficiency, reasons for retention of the doctrine |
| | P | 3 | Contractual capacity of minors |
| | P | 4 | Sale of goods, exclusion clauses, collateral contracts |
| | P | 5 | Unilateral mistakes of identity, remedies |
| | E | 6 | Privity of contract, avoidance, criticisms of the doctrine |
| | E/P | 7 | Conditions, warranties, innominate terms |

# HLT Publications

HLT books are specially planned and written to help you in every stage of your studies. Each of the wide range of textbooks is brought up-to-date annually, and the companion volumes of our Law Series are all designed to work together.

You can buy HLT books from your local bookshop, or in case of difficulty, order direct using this form.

The Law Series covers the following modules:

Administrative Law

Commercial Law

Company Law

Conflict of Laws

Constitutional Law

Contract Law

Criminal Law

Criminology

English Legal System

Equity and Trusts

European Union Law

Evidence

Family Law

Jurisprudence

Land Law

Law of International Trade

Legal Skills and System

Public International Law

Revenue Law

Succession

Tort

## The HLT Law Series:

A comprehensive range of books for your law course, and the legal aspects of business and commercial studies.

Each module is covered by a comprehensive six-part set of books

- ● Textbook
- ● Casebook
- ● Revision Workbook
- ● Suggested Solutions, for:
  - ● 1985-90
  - ● 1991-94
  - ● 1995

| Module | Books required | Cost |
|---|---|---|
| | | |
| | | |
| | | |
| | | |
| | | |
| | | |
| | | |
| To complete your order, please fill in the form overleaf | Postage | |
| | TOTAL | |

Prices (including postage and packing in the UK): Textbooks £19.00; Casebooks £19.00; Revision Workbooks £10.00; Suggested Solutions (1985-90) £9.00, Suggested Solutions (1991-94) £6.00, Suggested Solutions (1995) £3.00.

For Europe, add 15% postage and packing (£20 maximum). For the rest of the world, add 40% for airmail (£35 maximum).

## ORDERING

**By telephone** to 01892 724371, with your credit card to hand

**By fax** to 01892 724206 (giving your credit card details).

**By post** to:

HLT Publications,
The Gatehouse, Ruck Lane, Horsmonden, Tonbridge, Kent TN12 8EA

When ordering by post, please enclose full payment by cheque or banker's draft, or complete the credit card details below.

We aim to dispatch your books within 3 working days of receiving your order.

Name

Address

Postcode

Telephone

Total value of order, including postage: **£**

**I enclose a cheque/banker's draft for the above sum, or**

**charge my** ☐ Access/Mastercard ☐ Visa ☐ American Express

Card number

Expiry date

Signature

Date

# Publications from **The Old Bailey Press**

## Cracknell's Statutes

A full understanding of statute law is vital for any student, and this series presents the original wording of legislation, together with any amendments and substitutions and the sources of these changes.

## Cracknell's Companions

Recognised as invaluable study aids since their introduction in 1961, this series summarises all the most important court decisions and acts, and features a glossary of Latin words, as well as full indexing.

**Please telephone our Order Hotline on 01892 724371, or write to our order department, for full details of these series.**